DEFENSIVE RESTRUCTURING OF THE ARMED FORCES IN SOUTHERN AFRICA

For Helle

Defensive Restructuring of the Armed Forces in Southern Africa

Edited by
GAVIN CAWTHRA
University of the Witwatersrand, South Africa
and
BJØRN MØLLER
Copenhagen Peace Research Institute, Denmark

Routledge
Taylor & Francis Group
LONDON AND NEW YORK

First published 1997 by Ashgate Publishing

Reissued 2018 by Routledge
2 Park Square, Milton Park, Abingdon, Oxon, OX14 4RN
711 Third Avenue, New York, NY I 0017, USA

Routledge is an imprint of the Taylor & Francis Group, an informa business

A Library of Congress record exists under LC control number: 97002977

ISBN 13: 978-1-138-61413-0 (hbk)
ISBN 13: 978-1-138-61416-1 (pbk)
ISBN 13: 978-0-429-46380-8 (ebk)

Contents

Preface

BJØRN MØLLER AND GAVIN CAWTHRA

Most of the contributions to the present work were originally written for a conference on Defensive Restructuring of the Armed Forces in Southern Africa. It was held at Helderfontein near Johannesburg in March 1996, organised by the Global Non-Offensive Defence Network and the Defence Management Programme at the Graduate School of Public and Development Management, University of the Witwatersrand, Johannesburg. The conference was attended by military officers, defence officials and academics from throughout Southern Africa as well as international experts. This was the first time that the issue had been discussed openly and on a multilateral basis in Southern Africa.

For financial support for this conference the editors wish to thank the Ford Foundation and the Danish Ministry of Foreign Affairs. For their practical and technical assistance in the conference as well as with the production of the present work they are also indebted to Mrs. Janne Rotberg, Ms. Rikke Strange and Ms. Cennet Ünver. Above all, however, they are grateful to Mrs. Helle Christiansen Cawthra who has been a tremendous help through all stages of the project.

Johannesburg and Copenhagen
December 1996
Bjørn Møller and Gavin Cawthra

1 Non-Offensive Defence in a Global Perspective

BJØRN MØLLER

This chapter is intended as an introduction to the concept of non-offensive defence (NOD): its underlying philosophy and the basic 'design principles'. Some attention is given to the amendments of the original NOD conceptions that will be required to make them applicable to a Third World setting. The chapter further provides a short historical account of the global debate on defence restructuring followed by an assessment of the present state of this debate. By arguing the relevance of NOD to regions such as the Middle East and East Asia the chapter thus places the South(ern) African debate in perspective.[1] Before proceeding any further it does, however, seem advisable to clear away some conceptual confusion often encountered.

- As a *concept*, NOD refers to a strategy, materialised in a military posture which possesses sufficient defensive strength while lacking offensive capabilities (*vide infra*).
- There are several *terms* for this concept. As a term, 'NOD' thus has many synonyms such as 'defensive defence', 'non-provocative defence', 'non-aggressive defence', 'confidence-building defence' or 'structural inability to attack'. While referring to the same concept, the various terms highlight different aspects thereof (just as the proverbial blind men describing the same elephant, one focusing on its legs, another on the trunk, etc.).
- There are numerous alternative *design principles*, i.e. 'models', such as territorial defence, barrier-type defence, disengagement, etc. (*vide infra*). Even though each 'model designer' (including those represented in the present volume) has his favourite term, this does not mean that these preferred terms refer to particular models. They all refer to the same concept, on the best realisation of which opinions differ.

What is NOD?

While a few authors have recommended non-offensive defence (NOD) for reasons of sheer military efficiency, the reasoning of most NOD advocates is political. They argue that it will serve the national interests of states to pursue policies of 'common security', and that the international system as a whole will become more stable and peaceful if all states do so.[2] Because of the 'security dilemma' it is counterproductive to seek security at an adversary's expense, which will only spur malign interactions such as arms races in peacetime and mobilisation races in periods of crisis.[3]

> • If one state, for instance, builds up its military power to correct a perceived deterioration in the balance of power, this will be perceived (correctly, regardless of intentions) by its adversaries as a growing threat. Hence the latter will be inclined to reciprocate with a rearmament that will only make the former state feel even more insecure. The result may well be a spiralling arms race.
> • In a political crisis mobilisation and other defensive measures may be mistaken for attack preparations, which will give a state's adversaries incentives for preventive war and/or pre-emptive attack, implying a considerable crisis instability.

In its more parsimonious interpretations, the principle of common security entails little more that an acknowledgement that the security of an adversarial dyad has to be viewed as a whole, i.e. that neither side can achieve lasting security at the expense of its respective adversary. The post-Cold War version of this philosophy is better known as 'cooperative security', an approach endorsed (with some delay) by European organisations such as the OSCE and NATO, and which also plays an important role of security political reorientation in Southern Africa (see, the chapter by Gavin Cawthra as well as the appendix). Cooperative security is largely synonymous with common security, only with a slightly greater emphasis on intentional and institutionalised cooperation.[4]

The simple maxim of common security should, of course, also be applied to defence policies where it immediately translates into the concept of NOD: the acknowledgement that security against military attack is not achievable by means of offensive threats which will only be reciprocated, leaving both sides in a worse situation.[5] NOD might best be defined in functional and relative terms that allow for viewing it by degrees, i.e. to conceive of 'NODdiness' as a continuum: *'NOD is a strategy, materialised in a national posture that emphasises defensive at the expense of offensive military options'*.

A shift to NOD will both improve arms race and crisis stability. First of all, 'inadvertent arms races' may be averted: if the weapons deployed only enhance defensive strength without posing threats, one state's build-up of arms will call for no reciprocal steps on the part of its adversaries. States with aggressive intentions may, of course, want to respond to the strengthening of defensive capability by others with a commensurate build-up of their offensive strength, but by doing so they will reveal their intentions. This revelation will, in itself, improve the security of their adversaries who will know for what to prepare. Above all, however, dyads of genuinely defensively oriented states may escape the vicious circle of mutually reinforcing and legitimating arms acquisitions and, hopefully, proceed to actual disarmament.

Second, inadvertent wars will become practically inconceivable, as neither pre-emptive attacks nor preventive wars will make any sense against opponents posing no military threat. Their unmistakably defensive steps (such as a partial mobilisation and/or the manning of front-posts) will not invite pre-emption, even if undertaken in a tense political crisis situation, simply because they cannot possibly be mistaken for attack preparations. To have at their disposal a panoply of strictly defensive measures will also allow states to defend themselves more effectively against premeditated attack than if the 'response menu' only includes measures with an offensive potential that entail the risk of provoking an otherwise perhaps avoidable war. States with strictly defensive postures have no reason to postpone mobilisation.

Ideally, a shift to NOD on the part of two (fairly evenly matched) opponents will produce a highly stable situation of 'mutual defensive superiority', i.e. a stalemate where the defensive strength of either side surpasses the offensive strength of the respective other, implying that neither side has anything to gain from starting a war. Such an attempted stalemate might be described in the following ('pseudo-mathematical') formula, where A and B are two states, and 'O' and 'D' stand for offensive and defensive strength, respectively:[6]

$$D^A > O^B \ \& \ D^B > O^A$$

Seductively simple though this may seem, to operationalise the variables poses several problems: How does one measure defensive and offensive strength? Should tanks or antitank weapons, for instance, be counted as one or the other? Also, to apply the same formula to a multipolar setting immediately raises numerous problems—indeed may be tantamount to squaring the circle: A should be strong enough to defend itself successfully against the combined offensive strength of B, C ... N, yet not (offensively) so strong as to be able to defeat B, even in collaboration with C, D ... N? To take a regional example, it would imply that South Africa should be strong enough to defend itself against the rest of Southern Africa, yet not strong enough to conquer Lesotho?[7]

Besides these pertinent questions, to which I shall return in due course, other questions immediately pose themselves:

- Is it possible to distinguish reliably between 'offensive' and 'defensive'? If so, at which level of analysis?
- Is it possible to reduce offensive strength to a significant extent without thereby critically diminishing the ability to defend oneself?
- If so, are there any universally applicable guidelines for the design of such a defence?

The Offence/Defence Distinction

Many suggestions have been made for how to distinguish between offence and defence, yet most suffer from serious flaws and inconsistencies. The reason may be that a distinction of universal validity has been sought via generalisation rather than abstraction. Also, analysts may have looked for the answer at the wrong level of analysis.

The most common misunderstanding about NOD—to which a few NOD proponents have, admittedly, contributed—is that it entails a ban on 'offensive weapons' in favour of 'defensive weapons'. However, not only is such a distinction meaningless, it may also be harmful, as was the case during the League of Nations' notorious 1932 World Disarmament Conference. On this occasion, states sought to conceal their quest for military supremacy with proposals for banning 'offensive weapons', which tended to be precisely those categories in which their opponents were superior.[8]

As all military experts know, both offensive and defensive operations require a whole panoply of weapons categories. Indeed, the overlap between the two forms of combat is so extensive that the categories of 'offensive (defensive) weapons' —tentatively defined as 'weapons that are only useful to an attacker (defender)' are practically empty, hence not even of academic interest. Tanks may, for instance, be of value to a defender, just as anti-tank weapons are indispensable for an attacker. Not only a defender, but also an attacker may find a use for landmines, etc. Indeed, closer inspection even reveals seemingly defensive military items such as fortifications (the Great Wall of China or the French Maginot Line, for instance) as ambivalent: They may facilitate attack, simply because they free forces for offensive use that would otherwise be required for defensive duties.

This should not be taken to mean that weapons do not matter at all. In a given historical and geographical setting, weapons are not useful or indispensable to quite the same extent to an attacker and a defender. Even though, in a European context *anno* somewhere between 1945 and today, tanks would be of use to both an attacker and a defender, they are only indispensable for the former, whereas the latter will be absolutely dependent on anti-tank weapons, etc. By implication, the offensive capabilities of military formations (e.g. divisions) may differ according to their 'weapons mix'. A light division, which is 'slender' in terms of tanks, is thus less capable of offensive operations than a 'heavy', armoured and mechanised one.

However, a successful attack not merely requires heavy divisions, suitable for breakthrough operations, but also light divisions with a large infantry component, by means of which to 'mop up' bypassed pockets of defending forces, defend conquered ground, etc. Likewise, a defender may well need some heavy armoured forces for forcefully evicting an invader, only fewer of them (and perhaps slightly lighter) than an attacker. Also, a state with strictly defensive national ambitions, but taking international obligations seriously, cannot dispense completely with offensive-capable force components, e.g. for peace enforcement operations under UN auspices (*vide infra*).

A reliable offence/defence distinction can therefore only be made at the level of total military postures, say by an assessment of the distribution of total military strength between predominantly offensive and largely defensive units. This will, e.g. be reflected in different effective ranges (i.e. reach) of the state's military power, i.e. its power projection capability. This is, however, also a function of the logistical system, since states without tank transporters and/or bridging equipment may be effectively immobile, depending on the topography and infrastructure.

Defensiveness is largely a matter of the timing and scale of counter-offensive operations.[9] Here, a very clear line of demarcation may be drawn between offensive and defensive levels of ambition, namely the border: A NOD-type defence needs the ability to forcefully evict an invader (presupposing that the forward defence has been penetrated) and restore the *status quo ante bellum*. However, even though it will serve no purpose to entirely exclude 'hot pursuits' across the border, strictly defensive forces certainly do not need the ability to pursue the invader onto his own territory in order to enforce an unconditional surrender.

The strategic reach of an offensive posture has to be longer than that of a defensive one, simply because an attacker is out to conquer ground while the defender's level of ambition is merely to defend his home territory. However, what should count as 'long' or 'short' depends on the context, if only because distances are relative: Whereas only truly long-range mobility matters between, say, Russia and China (or between South Africa and Angola), countries in 'crowded' regions such as the Middle East or the Korean peninsula may well be concerned about their respective adversaries' ability to traverse much shorter distances. Also, distance is a function of technology and of topography: Island states thus only need to worry about enemies in possession of navies (and/or long range air forces), etc., whereas land-locked states such as Switzerland or Lesotho need not bother too much about naval powers.

Even though these analytical complexities speak against certain simplistic distinctions, they do not warrant complete agnosticism. Not everything is in the eye of the beholder: With regard to a particular region at a particular point in time, 'informed expert opinion' will generally have no trouble with reaching agreement on at least the basic criteria, e.g. with singling out what categories of weapons to reduce in order to make postures less capable of offensive use. Nor do states find it difficult to identify offensive elements in the military postures of their respective opponents. Hence, for instance, the consensus among the states participating in the European CFE (Conventional Armed Forces in Europe) negotiations on a focus on reductions of main battle tanks, armoured personnel carriers, and artillery, subsequently also combat aircraft and helicopters—a focus that may, but need not be appropriate for other regions, e.g. Southern Africa.

Defensive Strength

Even though meaningful analytical distinctions can be drawn between offensive and defensive strategies and postures, it might still be impossible in practice to disentangle the two without detrimental effects on defence efficiency, i.e. without jeopardising national security. If so, many states may be well-advised *not* to adopt NOD as their guideline. Fortunately, as a general rule with allowance for possible exceptions, it is in fact possible to strengthen one's defences while building down offensive capabilities, simply because the defensive form of combat is inherently the strongest, as pointed out by Clausewitz.[10]

- There are capabilities which a 'pure' defender no longer needs, or at least needs much less. Savings on such items may be used for enhancing defensive strength.
- A defender enjoys several 'home ground advantages', i.e. 'force multipliers': Interior lines of communications and supply; the option of creating widely distributed depots; of building various types of fortifications and barriers, and even of a certain landscaping.
- The 'moral' advantages are, likewise, considerable: The defenders will enjoy the support (morally, materially and otherwise) of the population, which may in some cases be personified in militia-type home guard forces. This is, however, no attractive option for countries where civil war is conceivable.
- Against breakthrough operations, prepared defenders, as a rule of thumb, only require one third of the attackers' strength in order to prevail: the well-known 'three-to-one rule'. There is little disagreement about the validity of this assessment (which may even be too conservative), yet considerable controversy about its applicability. It only applies to individual engagements, and neither to entire wars nor campaigns, nor to such battles where the surprise factor does enter into the picture.[11]
- The defender can disperse his forces to a much greater extent than the attacker, thereby becoming less vulnerable to concentrated attacks: the 'no-target principle' that has been central to most NOD proposals.
- Command structures may be partly decentralised, thereby made more robust than the hierarchical ones on which an aggressor must rely.[12] Once again, to which extent this is advisable depends on whether civil war is conceivable, in which case hierarchical structures are a blessing.
- Defenders are able to exercise under more realistic conditions than a prospective attacker, as they know exactly where they will have to fight.
- Even though there are no technological panaceas (a 'defensive super-weapon', for instance), certain trends in the development of modern weapons technologies tend to benefit the defender disproportionately: The revolutionary developments in micro-electronics, for instance, allow for

miniaturisation which, in its turn, may render large weapons platforms superfluous for defensive purposes, whereas they remain indispensable for offensive operations.[13]

The Span of Models

How effective NOD will be depends, of course, on which particular model (or mixture of models) is chosen for implementation. Just as they are not equally defensive, NOD models are also not equally effective,[14] and their suitability is context-dependent. Most proposals fall within the following categories, or are blends thereof:

- Area-covering territorial defence as in the 'spider and web' model of the SAS (Study Group Alternative Security Policy): a combination of a stationary, area-covering defence web and mobile forces ('spiders'), that are integrated with, and thereby made dependent on, the web so as to be very mobile within, but virtually not beyond, the confines of the web. A concrete application of this model to Southern Africa is to be found in the chapters by Conetta, Knight and Unterseher and by Rocklyn Williams.
- 'Stronghold defence', as suggested by members of the SAS group, especially for the Middle East (except Israel) and other regions with low force-to-space ratios and/or long borders. This implies concentrating a state's defence on certain areas that are politically important (typically the approaches to the national capital or other major populations centres) and/or which allow for a cohesive defence.
- Strictly defensive forward defence by means of 'fire barriers', 'killing zones', fortifications and/or fixed obstacles along the border.
- The 'missing link approach', implying deliberate omission of one or several components without which the total force is no longer capable of offensives.
- Disengagement, implying the withdrawal of certain forces (usually the most offensive-capable ones) from the border to rearward locations, combined with a forward defence by strictly defensive means. Disengagement hampers surprise attack and contributes to confidence-building. The depletion zone simply serves as an early warning device, since the deployment of proscribed weapons and forces into the zone will alert the other side to the impending attack and allow him to mobilise and prepare for combat. In such cases where only surprise attack offers a would-be aggressor any chance of prevailing, disengagement will suffice for mutual defensive superiority.
- 'Stepping down' is based on the same logic. It implies a lowering of the general level of readiness. Forces might be cadred (e.g. through a shift to a reserve army system) or otherwise prevented from launching surprise

attacks, say by a separation of munitions from weapons.

However, the advantages resulting from both disengagement and 'stepping down' have to be weighed against the risk of malign interactions in a crisis period. If the forces withdrawn from the forward line are those possessing the greatest offensive capability (as in many proposals), to redeploy them into the zone for defensive purposes in an intense political crisis could easily be misinterpreted as preparations for an attack.

Multidimensional NOD

The land forces must logically form the core of NOD, since the possession of offensive-capable ground forces is a *sine qua non* of genuine offensive capability. Without the ability to invade and occupy an opponent's territory, no state can win wars in the usual sense. To do so requires ground forces (albeit perhaps transported by air or sea), whereas neither navies nor air forces are able to attain victory on their own. If a state (or an alliance) therefore completely lacks ground forces capable of offensive utilisation (i.e. of taking and holding ground), the capabilities of its navy and/or air force are irrelevant according to the NOD criteria.

However, the synergism between the three military 'arms' implies that their total offensive potential exceeds the sum of their constituent parts. The other services may, for instance, serve as 'offensive force multipliers' for the ground forces—as demonstrated by the Israeli victory in the 1967 June War and that of the Coalition during the recent Gulf War. There are thus good reasons for taking the other services into account, at least as far as their contribution to the offensive capabilities of the ground forces is concerned. Both navies and air forces thus have to be, at the very least, compatible with the NOD requirements for the land forces, preferably supportive thereof. (See the chapter by Robert Higgs).

Collective Security

Of course, even the most effective design of a NOD-type defence will not allow all states to successfully defend themselves against every conceivable attack. Some states are simply too small (Lesotho is a good example) and/or their neighbours (e.g. South Africa) too large. Some states have sought an ultimate ('existential') guarantee of survival in the form of nuclear weapons. This is almost certainly true for Israel, as it was for the apartheid regime in South Africa; and it is probably also the case for Pakistan and North Korea[15]. However, the nuclear option has serious drawbacks. Since it no longer appears to be an option for African states (viz. the recent establishment of a continent-wide nuclear-weapons-free zone[16]) I shall ignore this hypothetical option in favour of the two alternatives: alliances and collective security.

Alliances are either directed against somebody else, i.e. adversarial (often for good reasons, as was the case with the informal alliance of the Frontline States against the apartheid regime); or they are superfluous; or they may, finally, be something completely different *in embryo*, namely collective security arrangements. The latter is, for instance, the case for the SADC, at least as far as intentions are concerned (see appendix). Contrary to alliances, collective security systems include former adversaries, ideally are all-encompassing, if only within a region.[17]

Both alliances and collective security arrangements require forces with longer effective ranges than required for national defence, and certainly longer than what is 'permissible' according to NOD criteria. Without genuine strategic mobility, however, the mutual assistance commitments that alliances and collective security are made of will be mere words. A collective security system will, moreover, need substantial offensive capabilities in order to liberate territory already conquered by an attacker—especially because the latter, in his 'attacker-turned-defender' position, will enjoy some (albeit not all) of the aforementioned advantages of the defence, while the true defenders will have to fight offensively, i.e. at a disadvantage.

Fortunately, this dilemma has a solution: Since it is not individual force components (or weapons) that are offensive, but only larger force 'conglomerates', the requisite mobile forces with offensive shock power may be multinational joint task forces consisting of national contributions that are individually incapable of offensive use. The requirement of collective security may thus be made compatible with those of defensive restructuring and NOD.[18]

NOD in the Third World?

The entire NOD debate has had an unmistakably European flavour to it that could make it unpalatable to countries beyond the European orbit. Among the parochial and eurocentric elements are the following:

- The presumption of a high degree of transparency in military affairs that is not available in most parts of the Third World.
- The preference of most (but not all) 'NOD designers' for high-tech solutions that may be quite unaffordable for most developing countries.
- A certain disregard for economic constraints that are likely to loom large in the future, not only for developing countries but also for the ex-communist states of the former East.
- The assumption of high force-to-space ratios, such as characterised (most of) Europe, but which have few counterparts elsewhere.
- A certain disregard of civil-military relations. The question of the loyalty of the armed forces to the state seemed trivial in Europe, but is a major problem in many Third World states.
- The almost exclusive focus on state-to-state scenarios that was warranted in the Europe of the Cold war. However, many 'weak states' in the South face more serious threats from within than from abroad.

That there are thus gaps in the available NOD literature, however, does not necessarily mean that the 'core idea' of NOD is inapplicable to the rest of the world. It does, however, point to the need for amendments and modifications, for which I shall provide some tentative suggestions.

Low Transparency

The transparency of military holdings and activities was high in Europe, even prior to the break-throughs in the field with CSBMs and on-site inspections, and the Open Skies Treaty. States generally knew how many forces and weapons their adversaries possessed, how they were configured and deployed, and how their use was being exercised. The seminars on military doctrines held under the auspices of the CSCE helped clarify the underlying doctrines and strategic conceptions.[19]

In most of the Third World transparency is much lower, both because of the shortage of surveillance assets, and because of a lack of openness in many states. The recent UN register of conventional arms transfers helps somewhat, but many national submissions are either missing entirely or too unreliable.[20]

Under such conditions of opacity, changes in military strategy as envisaged by NOD may not automatically allay mutual fears—even when materialised in postural changes and amended manoeuvre practices. This does not, of course, speak against making such changes, only highlights the need for parallel efforts at making them known to the respective adversaries, e.g. by means of regional seminars on military doctrines, CSBMs, and crisis prevention centres—as envisioned by SADC (see appendix).

Economic Constraints

Even more so than in Europe, military spending and production in the Third World diverts urgently needed know-how, capital and other resources away from the civilian economy. Hence the need for a reduction of military expenditures to a minimum compatible with national security. This has been acknowledged by the South African government (see the *White Paper* extracts in the appendix), and is even more true for the other, less prosperous, countries in Southern Africa.

In addition to breaking the arms race momentum (*vide supra*) NOD-type armed forces tend to be cheaper than dual-capable forces, designed for both offence and defence. It is simply easier, hence cheaper, to defend one's home ground than to (have the ability to) invade other countries. Such a comparison, however, is not entirely realistic because countries rarely build their armed forces from scratch. They have to make the best of a 'material legacy', i.e. an inventory of weapons and weapons platforms, support systems, barracks, depots, etc. Even though their replacement and/or redeployment might be desirable from a NOD point of view, it will inevitably have to proceed in a piecemeal fashion.

The Independence Imperative

A reliance on 'NATO-type' high technology weaponry would not only exceed the economic means of most Third World countries; it would also translate into a dependence on the suppliers in the industrialised North.

The global centre-periphery structure[21] is mirrored in (and to some extent perpetuated by) the 'global military system' and its 'siamese twin', the 'global military industrial system'.[22] By manipulating the South to emulate the North's military postures, the main exporting countries (above all the USA) may thus secure the lion's share of an attractive and very profitable market at the expense of the Third World.

Hence the attraction of finding military technologies suitable for indigenous production. The 'import substitution' strategy usually recommended requires developing countries to replicate the technologies of the exporting states,[23] but only a handful of Third World countries are in a position to produce aircraft, tanks, ballistic missiles and the like.[24]

The types of weapons required for a NOD-type defence, however, tend to be simpler, hence more suitable for indigenous production, implying that NOD might facilitate an escape from the military-industrial periphery position. On the other hand, there are also drawbacks to the production of small arms, above all the risk that they will end up in the wrong hands (see the chapter by Jacklyn Cock).

The Force-to-Space Factor

Generally, the Third World is much less militarised than Europe, in the sense that armed forces are spread much thinner. Force-to-space ratios are thus usually lower in the Third World, whether measured in terms of troops or weapons per square kilometre (or per kilometre of border). As a consequence, the force requirements of certain NOD schemes might seem absurd if mechanically applied to the Third World—for which they were, of course, never conceived.

This does not invalidate the general notion of NOD, but calls for certain amendments. In most cases, considerable mobility will be indispensable since states can neither defend all their borders simultaneously, nor achieve a meaningful area coverage by means of stationary forces. This poses a problem, since mobility all too easily translates into such border-crossing capabilities that NOD seeks to reduce or abolish.

The 'spider-and-web' notion of the SAS group may provide the clue to escaping this dilemma, since it allows forces a maximum of mobility within, but a minimum of mobility beyond, each state's national territory. Some states might also opt for the above-mentioned selective area defence, around areas that are vital in their own right and/or in a 'checkerboard configuration', i.e. as 'islands' of defence.

Civil-Military Relations

In the Third World (as elsewhere) the main choice concerning personnel structure is between professional armed forces, conscripts and a militia structure, or any combination thereof.

Most (but not all) European NOD advocates have leaned towards a blend of conscripts and militia (home guard) forces, for economic reasons as well as because offensive capabilities would presumably be reduced by the 'popular element'. Furthermore, conscripted forces provide a large 'inflation potential', i.e. a large mobilisation pool which may be useful in a protracted defence against large-scale aggression. Finally, the relatively smaller standing force would tend to minimise capabilities for surprise attack.

When applied to the Third World, however, the picture is less clear. When there is a significant risk of internal armed conflict, or even fully-fledged civil war, to arm the whole population will merely tend to increase the level of violence, should fighting break out. To arm only one side (as is often the case) tends to add to repression and to perpetuate the conflict.

Some of the same problems would speak against the introduction of conscription, which would also add significantly to general militarisation. The professional armed forces fielded by most Third World nations are actually smaller than conscripted armies could possibly be. Also, experience seems to show that a *levée en masse* could still be improvised, if the need should arise, say in the event of an invasion.

One problem with professional armed forces is, however, that they tend to be more pliable tools for praetorian politics that have often been pursued by the officer corps.[25] However, this only underlines the need for tight political control of the armed forces, but says nothing about whether to prefer offensive or defensive forces.

There may be no universally applicable guidelines in this field. Some countries may be better off with professional armed forces, while conscription and/or militias may be a better choice for others. While individual NOD models may presuppose a particular personnel structure, NOD as such is 'neutral' in this respect.

Domestic Threats

European NOD was designed for national defence in the traditional sense, i.e. for defending the national sovereignty and territorial integrity of states against military attack from other states. Such threats, however, may no longer be the most serious ones in Europe, and they almost certainly are not in most regions beyond Europe,[26] which raises the question how a shift to NOD will affect the handling of internal conflicts, such as secessionist movements and/or civil war.

Of course, neither NOD nor any other military strategy will do anything to solve the underlying problem, which is a profoundly political matter. A shift to NOD, however, will not seriously impede a government's ability to quell an armed rebellion (the moral and political justification thereof remaining an open question). The types of weaponry used for counterinsurgency happen to be the same as those which receive a greater emphasis under NOD, while weaponry that is more or less incompatible with NOD (tanks, major warships, combat aircraft, etc.) is anyhow of very limited use for domestic purposes. In a more positive vein, NOD-type armed forces will be eminently suitable for peacekeeping operations, including those which take place within borders, the reason being that the tasks to be performed are quite similar.[27] (See the chapter by Greg Mills).

Current Status of NOD

The concept of NOD originated in the divided Europe of the Cold War, and was, from the very beginning, conceived as an escape from its quandary.

The European Debate

After a first, and unsuccessful, round of the NOD debate in the 1950s, the debate resurfaced in the mid-1970s and first half of the 1980s in response to what were perceived as dangerous new developments in the realm of nuclear strategy. From Germany, the idea spread to the rest of Western Europe, especially to Britain, Denmark and the Netherlands, where it gained a certain political backing. In the United States, interest was all along confined to the academic community and the peace movements.[28]

What placed NOD on the international agenda was, however, the unexpected endorsement of the idea by the Soviet Union in 1986/87, as one element in the 'new political thinking' of Gorbachev.[29] This Soviet (and subsequently Warsaw Pact) endorsement of the NOD idea placed the topic on the East-West agenda.

Inter alia, it paved the way for a Soviet acceptance of the Western approach to conventional force reductions, as eventually manifested in the mandate for the CFE talks: to 'reduce the capabilities for surprise attack and large-scale offensive action', which was what NOD advocates had urged for several years (except for the unfortunate exclusion from negotiations of maritime and nuclear forces).

The CFE Treaty of 1990 was thus viewed as a success for the NOD idea, with the resultant reductions of tanks, APCs, artillery, combat aircraft and helicopters.[30] By historical coincidence, however, this accomplishment was overshadowed by the dissolution of the Warsaw Pact and the USSR, which rendered the CFE limitations largely irrelevant.

A Third Wave?

As was to be expected, these developments produced a noticeable decline of interest in NOD in Western Europe. However, this does not mean that NOD has become irrelevant, since it may well have a hitherto disregarded relevance for other parts (or 'dimensions') of the world such as:

- 'East-East' relations, where the residual offensive capabilities of Russia (inherited from the USSR) continue to pose a threat to neighbouring states.[31] In the former Soviet Union interest seems to have shifted from the defensive restructuring that was embarked upon in the Gorbachev period, to collective security arrangements and improved relations with the West. Nevertheless, the new states have had to establish priorities and decide upon a military doctrine and strategic conceptions. Most have opted for a defensive orientation. There is little or no opposition to this notion, only a reduced saliency of the entire defence question, a small group of supporters notwithstanding. The situation is similar in the former Warsaw Pact countries, above all the Visegrad states (Poland, Hungary, the Czech and Slovak Republics). To the extent that they have made decisions about their future military orientation, they have (at least declaratorily) endorsed the notion of defensive doctrines.
- 'North-South' relations, where NOD-inspired ideas play a certain role in the debate on arms trade regulations and 'counter-proliferation'. It is generally acknowledged that the question whether to sell arms or not depends on whether they will merely help the recipient state defend itself, or increase offensive strength.
- 'South-South' relations: Presumably NOD might contribute to 'defusing' various potential and actual conflicts in the Third World, to which I shall return shortly.

In the post-Cold War period NOD seems relevant for, and is being debated in, several regions around the world.[32] Its attraction seems greatest in the remaining conflict spots, where interstate war is still regarded as a threat; and in former conflict areas, where it may serve as a path to normalisation and peaceful relations.

Defusing Conflicts

In the category of 'hot' conflict spots fall the cases of the Middle East, South and Northeast Asia.

In the Middle East the peace process will undoubtedly require substantial arms control agreements, for which NOD may prove a suitable guideline. This is especially the case for any future settlement between Israel and Syria concerning the Golan Heights. The continued Israeli occupation constitutes not only a violation of international law, but also a latent threat to Syria. On the other hand, it is inconceivable that Israel will return the Golan Heights without reliable security guarantees, such as a build-down of Syria's offensive strength. As a minimum, a settlement presupposes safeguards against the Golan being used for offensive purposes. Likewise, a necessary (albeit, unfortunately, not sufficient) precondition for the establishment of a Palestinian state seems to be that it poses no military threat to Israel, i.e. that its armed forces are strictly defensive.[33]

In Northeast Asia, NOD is immediately relevant for the Korean Peninsula, both for a future process of reunification and for its product. Should the first step towards reunification be a confederation of sorts (as seems likely), it will be absurd for the two sides to continue posing offensive threats against each other. Defensive restructuring will thus have to accompany the gradual (and probably protracted) growing together of the two Koreas. Should reunification, on the other hand, happen swiftly (most likely by the South's absorption of the crisis-ridden North) unified armed forces of very impressive size will emerge, which will, moreover, be available for external use (whereas they are now directed against each other). Without an accompanying downsizing and defensive restructuring of the armed forces, this could well damage the already fragile arms race stability in the region.[34]

Whereas China remains predominantly defensive, recent arms acquisitions and doctrinal changes seem to indicate that she is seeking enhanced power projection capabilities, i.e. offensive reach.[35] This trend may be reinforced by the above development, and may start a chain reaction. Taiwan might, for instance, abandon her defensive military strategy in response. More importantly, however, Japan might reevaluate the unilateral constraints on her military power, in which case her military strength would surpass that of everybody else. A region-wide arms race is thus entirely conceivable, which a defensive restructuring of the armed forces might help avert.[36] There is already considerable interest in the topic in South Korea, some interest in China and an implicit political endorsement of NOD principles in both Japan and Taiwan.[37]

In South Asia, the situation between India and Pakistan is very tense, and seems to have led both sides to acquire nuclear weapons, or at least a nuclear potential. Should another war erupt (most likely over Kashmir), it could thus become extremely unpleasant. A defensive restructuring of the armed forces might help prevent this, as would a further disengagement of forces along the border. In this region as well, there is a considerable interest in NOD, albeit mostly confined to the academic community.[38]

From Conflict Formations to Security Communities

From the category of regions in transition from conflict formations to security communities (see the chapter by Barry Buzan) one could mention (besides Europe) South America and Southern Africa.

Perhaps surprisingly (in view of the long absence of interstate wars on the continent), there is a considerable interest in NOD in South America.[39] The recent abandonment by Argentina and Brazil of the 'nuclear option' and the gradual emergence of a regional institutional framework seem to open up some opportunities for defensive restructuring—which may be especially relevant for the strained relations between Chile and Argentina.

In Southern Africa, the situation seems even more propitious for NOD-type restructuring, especially as far as South Africa is concerned, which possesses by far the most formidable offensive capabilities in the region. A powerful rationale for such restructuring is the desire to forge peaceful relations with the rest of the subregion. This is the topic of the present work.

Notes

1. It is partly based on the author's: 'The Concept of Non-Offensive Defence: Implications for Developing Countries with Specific Reference to Southern Africa', in M. Hough & A. du Plessis (eds.): 'Conference Papers: The Future Application of Air Power with Specific Reference to Southern Africa', *Ad hoc Publication*, no. 32 (Pretoria: Institute for Strategic Studies, University of Pretoria, 1995), pp. 48-128.
2. Palme Commission (Independent Commission on Disarmament and Security Issues): *Common Security. A Blueprint for Survival. With a Prologue by Cyrus Vance* (New York: Simon & Schuster, 1982).
3. Jervis, Robert: 'Cooperation Under the Security Dilemma', *World Politics*, vol. 30, no. 2 (1978), pp. 167-214; Buzan, Barry: *People, States and Fear. An Agenda for International Security Studies in the Post-Cold War Era*, Second Edition (Boulder: Lynne Rienner, 1991), pp. 294-327; Collins, Alan: 'The Security Dilemma', in Jane M. Davis (ed.): *Security Issues in the Post-Cold War World* (Cheltenham: Edward Elgar, 1996), pp. 181-195.
4. Nolan, Janne E. (ed.): *Global Engagement. Cooperation and Security in the 21st Century* (Washington, D.C.: The Brookings Institution, 1994).
5. On the link between NOD and Common Security see Møller, Bjørn: *Common Security and Nonoffensive Defense. A Neorealist Perspective* (Boulder: Lynne Rienner, 1992); Bahr, Egon & Dieter S. Lutz (eds.): *Gemeinsame Sicherheit. Konventionelle Stabilität. Bd. 3: Zu den militärischen Aspekten Struktureller Nichtangriffsfähigkeit im Rahmen Gemeinsamer Sicherheit* (Baden-Baden: Nomos Verlagsgesellschaft, 1988).
6. Boserup, Anders: 'Non-offensive Defence in Europe', in Derek Paul (ed.): *Defending Europe. Options for Security* (London: Taylor & Francis, 1985), pp. 194-209.
7. Huber, Reiner & Rudolf Avenhaus: 'Problems of Multipolar International Stability', in idem & idem (eds.): *International Stability in a Multipolar World: Issues and Models for Analysis* (Baden-Baden: Nomos Verlagsgesellschaft, 1993), pp. 11-20.
8. Borg, Marlies ter: 'Reducing Offensive Capabilities-the Attempt of 1932', *Journal of Peace Research*, vol. 29, no. 2 (May 1992), pp. 145-160.

9. See Kokoshin, Andrei A. & Valentin Larionov: 'Four Models of WTO-NATO Strategic Interrelations', in Marlies ter Borg & Wim Smit (eds.): *Non-provocative Defence as a Principle of Arms Control and its Implications for Assessing Defence Technologies* (Amsterdam: Free University Press, 1989), pp. 35-44.
10. Clausewitz, Carl von (1832): *On War*, edited and translated by Michael Howard and Peter Paret (Princeton, N.J.: Princeton University Press, 1984), pp. 357-366. See also Gat, Azar: 'Clausewitz on Defence and Attack', *Journal of Strategic Studies*, vol. 11, no. 1 (1988), pp. 20-26.
11. See e.g. Mearsheimer, John J.: 'Numbers, Strategy, and the European Balance', *International Security*, vol. 12, no. 4 (Spring 1988), pp. 174-185; idem: 'Assessing the Conventional Balance: The 3:1 Rule and Its Critics', *ibid.* vol. 13, no. 4 (Spring 1989), pp. 54-89; Epstein, Joshua M.: 'The 3:1 Rule, the Adaptive Dynamic Model, and the Future of Security Studies', *ibid.*, pp. 90-127; Posen, Barry R., Eliot A. Cohen & John J. Mearsheimer: 'Correspondence: Reassessing Net Assessment', *ibid.*, pp. 128-179.
12. Grin, John: *Military-Technological Choices and Political Implications. Command and Control in Established NATO Posture and a Non-Provocative Defence* (Amsterdam: Free University Press, 1990).
13. Canby, Steven L.: 'Weapons for Land Warfare', in Bjørn Møller & Håkan Wiberg (eds.): *Non-Offensive Defence for the Twenty-First Century* (Boulder: Westview Press, 1994), pp. 74-84.
14. Møller, Bjørn: *Resolving the Security Dilemma in Europe. The German Debate on Non-Offensive Defence* (London: Brassey's, 1991).
15. Evron, Yair: *Israel's Nuclear Dilemma* (London: Routledge, 1994); Kapur, Ashok: 'Nuclear Development of India and Pakistan', in Jørn Gjelstad & Olav Njølstad (eds.): *Nuclear Rivalry and International Order* (London: Sage Publications, 1996), pp. 143-157; Mazarr, Michael J.: *North Korea and the Bomb. A Case Study in Nonproliferation* (New York: St. Martin's Press, 1994); Howlett, Darryl & John Simpson: 'Nuclearisation and Denuclearisation in South Africa', *Survival*, vol. 35, no. 3 (Autumn 1993), pp. 154-173.
16. Ogunbanwo, Sola: 'The Treaty of Pelindaba: Africa is Nuclear-Weapon-Free', *Security Dialogue*, vol. 27, no. 2 (June 1996), pp. 185-200.
17. Kupchan, Charles A. & Clifford A. Kupchan: 'Concerts, Collective Security, and the Future of Europe', *International Security*, vol. 16, no. 1 (Summer 1991), pp. 114-161; idem & idem: 'The Promise of Collective Security', *ibid.*, vol. 20, no. 1 (Summer 1995), pp. 52-61. For a critique see Betts, Richard K.: 'Systems for Peace or Causes of War? Collective Security, Arms Control, and the New Europe', *ibid.*, vol. 17, no. 1 (Summer 1992), pp. 5-43. See also Weiss, Thomas G. (ed.): *Collective Security in a Changing World* (Boulder: Lynne Rienner, 1993); on regional aspects especially Farer, Tom J.: 'The Role of Regional Collective Security Arrangements', *ibid.*, pp. 153-186.

18. I have elaborated on this theme in Møller, Bjørn: 'Multinationality, Defensivity, Collective Security', *Working Papers*, no. 20 (Copenhagen: Centre for Peace and Conflict Research, 1993).
19. Ghebaldi, Victor-Yves: 'Confidence —Building Measures Within the CSCE Process: Paragraph-by-Paragraph Analysis of the Helsinki and Stockholm Regimes', *Research Paper*, no. 3 (New York/Geneva: UNIDIR, 1989); Krohn, Axel: 'The Vienna Military Doctrine Seminar', *SIPRI Yearbook 1991*, pp. 501-511; Koulik, Sergey & Richard Kokoski: *Conventional Arms Control. Perspectives on Verification* (Oxford: Oxford University Press, 1994).
20. Chalmers, Malcolm, Owen Greene, Edward J. Laurance & Herbert Wulf (eds.): *Developing the UN Register of Conventional Arms* (Bradford: University of Bradford, 1994); Anthony, Ian: 'Assessing the UN Register of Conventional Arms', *Survival*, vol. 35, no. 4 (Winter 1993), pp. 113-129.
21. Amin, Samir: *Le developpement inégal* (Paris: Editions du Minuit, 1973); idem: *L'accumulation a l'échelle mondiale*, vols. 1-2 (Paris: Editions Anthropos, 1976).
22. Kaldor, Mary: *The Baroque Arsenal* (New York: Hill and Wang, 1981).
23. Krause, Keith: *Arms and the State: Patterns of Military Production and Trade* (Cambridge: Cambridge University Press, 1992).
24. An interesting analysis of the global aircraft production system is Forsberg, Randall (ed.): *The Arms Production Dilemma. Contraction and Restraint in the World Aircraft Industry* (Cambridge, MA: The MIT Press, 1994).
25. Central works are Samuel Huntington: *The Soldier and the State. The Theory and Politics of Civil-Military Relations* (Cambridge, MA: Harvard University Press, 1957); Finer, Samuel E.: *The Man on Horseback. The Role of the Military in Politics* (Harmondsworth: Penguin, 1976). See also Millett, Richard L. & Michael Gold-Bliss (eds.): *Beyond Praetorianism: The Latin American Military in Transition* (Boulder: Lynne Rienner, 1995).
26. Ayoob, Mohammed: *The Third World Security Predicament. State Making, Regional Conflict, and the International System* (Boulder: Lynne Rienner, 1995); Job, Brian L. (ed.): *The Insecurity Dilemma. National Security of Third World States* (Boulder: Lynne Rienner, 1992).
27. I have elaborated on these themes in the following *Working Papers* from the Copenhagen Peace Research Institute, COPRI: 'UN Military Demands and Non-Offensive Defence. Collective Security, Humanitarian Intervention and Peace Support Operations' (no. 7/1996); and 'Ethnic Conflict and Postmodern Warfare. What Is the Problem? What Could Be Done?' (no. 12/1996). On peacekeeping within borders see Weiss, Thomas G. (ed.): *The United Nations and Civil Wars* (Boulder: Lynne Rienner, 1995); Ratner, Steven R.: *The New UN Peacekeeping. Building Peace in Lands of Conflict After the Cold War* (New York: St. Martin's Press, 1995).

28. For documentation, see Møller, Bjørn: *Dictionary of Alternative Defense* (Boulder: Lynne Rienner and London: Adamantine Press, 1995).
29. See MccGwire, Michael: *Perestroika and Soviet National Security* (Washington, D.C.: The Brookings Institution, 1991); Holden, Gerald: *Soviet Military Reform. Conventional Disarmament and the Crisis of Militarized Socialism* (London: Pluto, 1991); Bluth, Christoph: *New Thinking in Soviet Military Policy* (London: Pinter/RIAS, 1990); Kipp, Jacob W.: 'Operational Art: The Evolution of Soviet Operational Art: The Significance of "Strategic Defense" and "Premeditated Defense" in the Conduct of Theatre-Strategic Operations', *The Journal of Soviet Military Studies*, vol. 4, no. 4 (December 1991), pp. 621-648.
30. Sharp, Jane M.O.: 'Conventional Arms Control in Europe', in *SIPRI Yearbook 1991*, pp. 407-474 (with appendices, including the treaty itself).
31. The new military doctrine of Russian Federation is not very helpful in this respect, since it retains few of the defensive elements from the past. See Cimbala, Stephen J.: 'Nonoffensive Defense and Strategic Choices: Russia and Europe After the Cold War', *The Journal of Slavic Military Studies*, vol. 6, no. 2 (June 1993), pp. 166-202.
32. To explore this matter has been the goal of the project launched by the present author: a 'Global Non-Offensive Defence Network', funded by the Ford Foundation since 1993.
33. A moderate Israeli example of NOD-inspired thinking is Levite, Ariel: *Offense and Defense in Israeli Military Doctrine* (Boulder: Westview, 1990). More radical is the present author's 'Non-Offensive Defence in the Middle East', forthcoming as a UNIDIR Research Paper. It was prepared for the UNIDIR project on 'Confidence-Building in the Middle East', a project intended as 'track two diplomacy'.
34. I have elaborated on this topic in Møller, Bjørn: 'The Unification of Divided States and Defensive Restructuring. China-Taiwan in a Comparative Perspective', *ibid.*, no. 9 (1996); idem: 'Non-Offensive Defence and the Korean Peninsula', *ibid.*, no. 4 (1995); idem: 'Common Security and Non-Offensive Defence: Its Relevance to the Korean Peninsula', in Bypong-Moo Hwang & Yong-Sup Han (eds.): *Korean Security Policies Toward Peace and Unification* (Seoul: Korean Association of International Studies, 1996), pp. 241-291. A South Korean NOD advocate is Han, Yong-Sup: *Designing and Evaluating Conventional Arms Control Measures: The Case of the Korean Peninsula* (Santa Monica, CA: RAND Graduate Institute, 1993).
35. According to most observers, China still lacks the ability to invade Taiwan. See Starr, Barbara: 'USA Deploys Carriers, But Doubts Invasion Threat Against Taiwan', *Jane's Defence Weekly*, vol. 25, no. 12 (20 March 1996), pp. 17-18. On recent arms acquisitions see Shambaugh, David: 'Growing Strong: China's Challenge to Asian Security', *Survival*, vol. 36, no. 2 (Summer 1994), pp. 43-59; Gill, Bates: 'Arms Acquisitions in East Asia',

in *SIPRI Yearbook 1994*, pp. 551-562.

36. For an elaboration see Møller, Bjørn: 'A Common Security and Non-Offensive Defence Regime for the Asia-Pacific?', *Working Papers*, no. 8 (Copenhagen: Centre for Peace and Conflict Research, 1995).

37. On Japan see Watanabe, Wakio: 'Japan's Postwar Constitution and Its Implications for Defense Policy: A Fresh Interpretation', in Ron Matthews & Keisuke Matsuyama (eds.): *Japan's Military Renaissance?* (New York: St. Martin's Press, 1993), pp. 35-49. On Taiwan see *National Defence Report* (Taipei: Ministry of National Defence, 1994), pp. 83, 101.

38. For an elaboration see Møller, Bjørn: 'A Common Security and NOD Regime for South Asia?', *Working Papers*, no. 4/1996 (Copenhagen: Centre for Peace and Conflict Research, 1996). An Indian advocate of NOD is Jasjit Singh. See his 'Defence Strategies', in UNIDIR (ed.): *Nonoffensive Defense. A Global Perspective* (New York: Taylor & Francis, 1990), pp. 23-39; idem: 'Defensive Security: The Conceptual Challenges', *Disarmament*, vol. 15, no. 4 (1992), pp. 112-125.

39. The most comprehensive work is Cáceres, Gustavo & Thomas Scheetz (eds.): *Defensa No Provocativa: Una Propuesta de Reforma Militar para la Argentina* (Buenos Aires: Editoria Buenos Aires, 1995). See also Proença Júnior, Domicio: 'Prioridades para as Forças Armadas. Uma Visao do "dever-ser" acadêmico', in idem (ed.): *Indústria bélica brasilieira. Ensaios* (Rio de Janeiro: Grupo de Estudos Estratégicos, 1994), pp. 25-72.

2 Regions and Regionalism in a Global Perspective

BARRY BUZAN

This chapter gives a brief overview of regions and regionalism in the post Cold War world. There are three central themes. First is that the ending of the Cold War has given regions more prominence in the overall structuring of international relations, and that this condition looks quite durable. Second is that regionalism, and particularly regional security, tends to involve more diverse, and therefore more complicated sets of issues than it did during the Cold War. Third is that the shift to a more region-based international relations generates very mixed effects: some benign and some malign.

The Logic of Regionalism Post-Cold War

The reasoning behind the first theme—that the ending of the Cold War has given regions more prominence in the overall structuring of international relations—is fairly straightforward. During the Cold War two superpowers projected their ideological and military rivalry into all corners of the planet. Local regions from Europe to South Asia, and from the Middle East to Southern Africa were all penetrated by US-Soviet rivalry, many of them heavily so. This meant that superpower ideology played into local and regional politics, that superpower resources shaped, and often determined, local and regional military balances, and that Cold War alignments greatly affected some patterns of trade and investment. Looked at in global perspective, the Cold War was thus a time when the system level was dominant over the regional one. In neorealist terms, a system structure of bipolarity shaped many of the main features of international relations.

With the collapse of both Soviet power and communist ideology, the primacy of the system level has come to a quite abrupt end. In the absence of overriding powers and system-spanning ideological rivalries, there is a more decentralised pattern of international security, with more room for regional dynamics to operate freely. Two factors reinforce this new freedom from domination: the diffusion of power, and the introversion of the great powers. The sources of power have become much more widely diffused throughout the international system. The Europeans/Westerners achieved their more than four centuries of extraordinary global control because they possessed at least three assets not possessed by the other actors in the system: the political form of the national state, the knowledge and productive power of the scientific and industrial revolutions, and the firepower of modern weapons. All of these assets, as well as the mobilising power of nationalism and ideology, have been thoroughly, if still very unevenly, spread throughout the international system by decolonisation and industrialisation. The result is a huge closure in the gap of military-political power differentials that reached its widest point during the middle of the nineteenth century.

On top of this, and perhaps partly as a result of it, the major centres of power in the international system are all notably introverted. After the Cold War, none of them is willing to take on a strong leadership role in international society, and all of them are preoccupied with their own domestic affairs. The United States still plays some leadership role, but lacks a mobilising crusade, and if not exactly returning to its isolationist traditions, is taking a much more self-interested and restricted view of its interests and obligations. The extraordinary sensitivity of the country to military casualties is a hallmark of its disengagement, as is its current move to cut expenditures on the UN and overseas aid. The European Union has been cast prematurely into a great power role and has not yet even developed adequate machinery for a common defence and foreign policy. Although one of the economic giants, it is too beset by problems of its own development, and pressing issues in its immediate region, to be able to play a leadership role internationally.

Japan is in some ways similar: an economic giant, but as yet almost lacking the internal capability for a robust international role commensurate with its power. Like the EU, it fails to meet Bull's criteria that a great power be: 'recognised by others to have, and conceived by their own leaders and peoples to have, certain special rights and duties ... in determining issues that affect the peace and security of the international system as a whole'.[1] China might be moving towards a world role, but is so far largely confined within its region. Russia is in the depths of painful restructuring and has to come to terms with a whole set of new neighbours. Thus none of the great powers is much interested in playing a strong managerial role in the system, and there are no rivalries amongst them strong enough to drive such engagement. Regional international relations are thus freer to unfold according to their own local logics than they have been for many decades.

It might rightly be objected that the analysis above captures only the military-political aspect of international relations, and ignores a massive economic centralisation at the system level. With the end of the Cold War liberal market ideology found a clear field with no rivals, and has rapidly consolidated itself as the global norm. Deregulation of trade, and even more so of finance, has empowered economic (and criminal) actors in relation to the state, and empowered global markets in relation to both. It is now no exaggeration to speak of a global economy that substantially sets the terms and conditions for investment, trade and production, and also aid (what is left of it), for all peoples on the planet. These two phenomena—the globalisation of the economy, and the regionalisation of military-political international relations—are in my view related. Economic liberalisation has hollowed out the advanced industrial states in ways that make them both less capable of using and less inclined to use force, and less inclined to define their own political interests in terms of widespread political and military engagement abroad. It has also largely removed incentives to make strategic alliances or seek strategic sources of supply.

There is of course also a substantial regionalising tendency in the international economy. Some of this springs from major institutionalising attempts to solve longstanding regional political-military security dilemmas, as most obviously in Western Europe. But much of it, including in part the EU, also stems from concerns about the insecurities of life in the global market. These insecurities are of two types: worry that trade rivalries or financial instabilities will cause a major crisis in the world economy, and concerns that the ferocity of competition in global markets will generate large numbers of losers. Regional responses can meet both fears, the first, by providing a fallback bastion in case of systemic collapse, the second by creating a weightier actor to play in the global game. On both of these counts, economic regionalism[2] has come back into fashion as a result of the widening and deepening of integration in the EU since the late 1980s, and the construction of NAFTA (North American Free Trade Area). The most ambitious of these, the EU, trundles onward despite all of its difficulties, and has unquestionably become the central focus of security in Europe.[3]

These two regional projects at the core of the global political economy have spawned both imitators (AFTA in Southeast Asia, APEC linking Australasia and North America, Mercosur covering the southern cone of South America); and much discussion about other regional economic zones (ECOWAS in West Africa, SAARC in South Asia, SADC in southern Africa, the CIS covering the former Soviet Union). East Asia is a puzzling case, with some interpreting it as lacking formal economic regionalism (and therefore vulnerable) and others seeing it as developing a distinctive informal, transnational model of regional integration. Regionalisation comes in many different forms of integration, with many different degrees of identity, depth and institutionalisation. Perhaps the main difference is between formal, rule-bound, institutionalised versions (EU), and informal versions led by 'undirected processes of social and economic interaction' as in East Asia.[4]

The reasoning behind the second theme—that regionalism, and particularly regional security, tends to involve more complicated sets of issues than it did during the Cold War—arises mainly from the reduced salience of military-political threats that accompanied the ending of the Cold War. This reduction has been very uneven. In places such as South Asia and the Middle East military threats remain high and have not been too much affected by the ending of the Cold War (except in the terms on which arms are available). But for much of the West, and for some other regions (Southern Africa, up to a point Southeast Asia) military security issues dropped sharply from being the central focus of security to being relatively marginal. Where this has occurred, other sorts of security issues, whether economic, environmental or societal, have more room to claim priority on the political agenda. It can also be argued with some force that economic, environmental and societal security issues have been increasing in salience anyway, and that they are claiming more attention even where military fears retain first priority on the security agenda.

This diversification of security issues makes the regionalising process more complicated. The logic of regionalisation has not the same strength across the different types of issues, nor does it necessarily take on the same pattern.[5] Some of the new issues will not produce security regions at all. The group of low-lying states threatened by rising sea-levels, for example, has no geographical coherence and contains states in every continent. Even where economic, environmental and military-political security logics do come in regional form, they may well each define different sorts of regions. When this happens, policy-makers and regional institutions may sometimes succeed in squeezing them all back into a single state-defined region. The process of securitisation can easily link across sectors. Where neighbouring states already perceive each other as hostile, as in the Middle East, then environmental issues (water), societal ones (minorities), and economic ones (oil production and pricing) are much more likely to become securitised as part of the overall package. Where relations are more friendly, as within the EU, then such issues are much less likely to rise above the merely political. Organisations such as the EU, ASEAN or SAARC will naturally try to define issues so as to fit within their geopolitical boundaries. Even where cross-sectoral integration of issues does succeed, the fact remains that in the post-Cold War international system, the logic of regionalism will often reflect a more diverse profile of issues, and be more complicated, than it was during the Cold War.

The reasoning behind the third theme—that the shift to a more region-based international relations generates very mixed effects, some benign and some malign —is largely an empirical observation, and is the subject of the next section. In discussing the de facto pattern of regionalisation in the international system I will use the concept of *security complexes*.[6] The essential logic of security complex theory is rooted in the fact that all the units in the international system are enmeshed in a global web of security interdependence. Because many types of threats travel more easily over short distances than over long ones, insecurity is often associated with proximity. Most states fear their neighbours more than distant powers, and consequently security interdependence over the international system as a whole is far from uniform. The normal pattern of security interdependence in a geographically diverse anarchic international system is one of regionally based clusters, which we label security complexes. Security interdependence is markedly more intense between the units inside such complexes, than with units outside it. Security complexes are about the relative intensity of security relations that lead to distinctive regional patterns shaped by both the distribution of power and historical relations of amity and enmity. The definition of a security complex is *a set of units whose major processes of securitisation and desecuritisation are so interlinked that their security problems cannot reasonably be analysed or resolved apart from one another*. The formative dynamics and structure of a security complex are generated by the units within it: by their security perceptions of, and interactions with, each other. Security complexes not only play a central role in relations among their members, they also crucially condition how and whether stronger outside powers penetrate into the region. Individual security complexes are durable but not permanent features of the international system. The theory posits that in a geographically diverse anarchic international system, security complexes will be a normal and expected feature: if they are not there, one wants to know why.

Security interdependence comes about either by units securitising their relationships with each other (constructing each other as threats) or by desecuritising them (shifting issues from security to normal politics).[7] The internal dynamics of a security complex can thus be located along a spectrum according to whether the defining security interdependence is driven by amity or enmity. At the negative end comes a *conflict formation*,[8] where interdependence arises from fear, rivalry and mutual perceptions of threat. In the middle lie *security regimes*,[9] where states still treat each other as potential threats, but where they have made reassurance arrangements to reduce the security dilemma amongst them. At the positive end lies a *pluralistic security community*,[10] where states no longer expect, or prepare, to use force in their relations with each other. Regional integration (in Deutsch's language, an amalgamated security community) will eliminate a security complex with which it is co-extensive by transforming it from an anarchic subsystem of states to a single larger actor within the system. Regional integration among some members of a complex will transform the power structure of that complex.

Regions Set Free

In the limited space available, it is not possible to do more than sketch what the emerging worldwide pattern of regionalism looks like. In some places the patterns remain almost unchanged from the Cold War; in others they are transformed, sometimes for better and sometimes for worse; and in yet others the new pattern is not yet wholly clear.

Places where the patterns of regional (in)security remain almost unchanged from the Cold War include the Gulf, South Asia, West, Central and East Africa, and the Americas. In many of these cases, the lack of change is explained by the relatively light impact of the Cold War. Since the Cold War did not, with the exception of Cuba, make much impact on regional relations in the Americas, its ending would not be expected to make much impact either. Latin America remains suspended between being a weak security regime and a weak conflict formation.[11] Not even the wave of democratisation in Latin America, or the denuclearisation of relations between Argentina and Brazil, can be much explained by the ending of the Cold War. Although anti-communism was often a refuge for authoritarian Latin governments, the process of democratisation was not strongly connected to the winding down of the superpower rivalry.

In the Gulf and South Asia, the Cold War did make an impact in terms of alliances and arms supply. Both regions fell into the zone of US containment policy against the Soviet Union, and South Asia also got drawn into the Sino-Soviet rivalry. These entanglements lubricated the flow of arms and political support during the Cold War, but they neither created, nor much affected, the deep roots of local rivalry within these two regions. The ending of the Cold War certainly dried up the political supply of weapons, but most of these states could and did afford to purchase what they needed in the buyer's market for arms that unfolded during the 1980s and 1990s. In both regions underlying hostilities supported significant and ongoing attempts on the part of at least two states to acquire options on military nuclear technology (India, Pakistan, Iran, and although thwarted by the UN inspectors, Iraq). Both of these regional complexes (or subcomplex in the case of the Gulf), remained firmly at the conflict formation end of the spectrum, with politico-military fears dominating the processes of securitisation, and little prospect of moving towards desecuritised relations. Both contained some prospect of weak states tipping into failure and possible disintegration (Afghanistan, Pakistan, Saudi Arabia, most of the Gulf Sheikdoms). In the Gulf, there is major potential for disputes over the water resources of the Tigris and Euphrates rivers.

Across the broad swath of states stretching from West, through Central to East Africa, the ending of the Cold War made a difference in terms of reducing the amount of rival great power intervention in the domestic affairs of many states, and also of reducing the politically motivated supply of arms and aid. But it did not much affect the supply of small arms per se, and it left largely untouched the core problem in this area which is the predominance of weak and failed states. It also left untouched the economic failure, which meant that most societies in this area, with or without aid, were not only failing to close the development gap, but were actually losing ground to the growth of their own populations. Because so many of the states in this area are weak both as states and as powers, there has been only faint and rather preliminary formation of security complexes. ECOWAS, with its collective intervention in Liberia, shows elements of security complex formation, as, perhaps more concretely, does the crosscutting set of rivalries that link Sudan, Eritrea, Ethiopia, and parts of Uganda and Zaire. But state failures in Liberia, Sierra Leone, Rwanda and Somalia, and the possibility of several others going the same way (including the two giants Nigeria and Zaire), offers more the prospect of micro-complexes, where substate units such as tribes, gangs and firms become the principal players.

Places where the pattern of regional (in)security has been transformed for the better include Southeast Asia, Southern Africa, and possibly the Middle East. Southeast Asia had been particularly hard hit by the Cold War, suffering major intrusions of ideological and military rivalry, and devastating wars. The complete withdrawal of Soviet power, the easing back of the US presence, and the evaporation of ideological barriers to economic interaction have allowed benign local dynamics to reconfigure the region. ASEAN, a successful subregional security regime, has rapidly begun to absorb its communist former rivals, and is well on the way to providing a security regime, and to a lesser extent an economic region, for all of Southeast Asia. Most of the Southeast Asian states are undergoing rapid economic growth, and ASEAN provides a leading example of successful desecuritisation amongst a group of third world states. Despite this success within Southeast Asia, China may pose a growing military and political threat—more on this in the discussion on East Asia below.

Southern Africa is covered extensively elsewhere in this book. It suffices to say here that the ending of the Cold War coincided nicely with developments in the region to create a desecuritisation as rapid and as profound as that which took place in Europe. Former ideological enemies have become friends, and politically motivated arms supply and intervention from outside the region have largely ceased. The ideological spillover from the superpower rivalry into Southern Africa, which helped to polarise relations in the region, has largely disappeared. A rare instance of nuclear disarmament has helped to take some of the military tension out of the region. As in Southeast Asia a former conflict-based subregional organisation (SADC), has expanded to become a potential security regime for the whole region, covering economic and environmental issues as well as politico-military ones. The region still faces major problems of migration, illegal small arms trade, and economic development, as well as the unresolved civil war in Angola, but there can be no question that its overall security dynamics have been transformed in a largely positive direction.

The Middle East is a possible beneficiary from the ending of the Cold War, but it could also be placed in the category of 'not yet clear'. Like the Gulf (which is a subcomplex within the Middle East), and for many of the same reasons, the mostly Arab states (plus Israel) occupying the southern and eastern shores of the Mediterranean Sea were heavily caught up in the superpower rivalry. The collapse of Soviet power has dried up one of the rival sources of political arms supply to the region and given the United States a dominant influence in most of the Middle Eastern countries. The main fruit of this hegemony has been the peace process between Israel on the one hand, and the Palestinians, Jordan, Turkey and possibly Syria on the other, which if successful could mark a major milestone of desecuritisation in the region. This 'if', however, is still a big one. At the time of writing, with a hardline government newly elected in Israel, the success of the peace process certainly cannot be taken for granted. If it fails, then the rest of the Middle East will, like the Gulf, revert to its former conflict formation mode, with a rich mix of ethnic, religious, political, territorial and water disputes. Because of oil, and because of the US connection to Israel, continued Western involvement in this region is almost guaranteed no matter which way the local (in)securities unfold.

Places where the pattern of regional (in)security has been transformed for the worse include the Balkans, the Caucasus, and more arguably Central Asia. In these places the transformation is self-evident and much commented upon. From a situation of overlay during the Cold War, these regions have been set free, and the result has been an immediate lapse into conflict both within and among some of their constituent states. In both cases, the new regions are partly (Balkans) or wholly (Caucasus, Central Asia) the result of the disintegration of states (Yugoslavia and the Soviet Union). In the Balkans and in the Caucasus, the lifting of overlay unleashed old national and territorial rivalries in regions possessing historical state traditions. In Central Asia, the implosion of the Soviet Union turned a number of provinces into sovereign states possessing virtually no indigenous state traditions. All of these areas have complex and potentially explosive minority problems, and all responded to the collapse of communism by picking up nationalist ideologies. In Central Asia, arbitrary boundaries and minority problems are accompanied by serious environmental issues arising from water shortages, and the legacies of unwise Soviet agricultural policies and uncaring nuclear testing ones. Turkey, Russia, China, Iran and (in the form of oil companies) the United States, all vie for influence in the new international region of Central Asia, whose inexperienced new states (one briefly a substantial nuclear power) have hardly had time to work out their relations with each other, let alone the rest of the world.

The two main places where the new pattern of regional (in)security is not yet wholly clear are Europe and East Asia. Western, Northern and Central Europe of course benefited enormously from the lifting of Cold War overlay and the consequent massive desecuritisation of politico-military relations. They have probably never been so free from major threats to their independence and welfare. All Europeans escaped from the forty-year threat of massive nuclear and/or conventional war in their homelands, and many Central and Eastern European peoples escaped from varying degrees of subordination to Soviet occupation. With the exception of the Balkans, military threats plummeted from the top to near the bottom of the security agenda. But there have been costs, and there are still large uncertainties. Russia, Belarus and Ukraine are all paying a heavy economic, social and political price for abandoning communism and seeking to integrate themselves into the Western political economy. It may be necessary, and there may be a golden payoff, but the transition is long and painful, and the outcome, both political and economic, is uncertain. Western Europe finds its integration process in crisis, buckling under the pressures from nationalist reaction to enlargement and deepening.[12]

The pattern of security relations in Europe has not yet crystallised. Almost certainly the major centre of gravity will be the massive security community centred on the EU. The big question is whether that will form a self-contained security region, or whether it will in some sense absorb Eastern Europe and Russia and the Balkans to create a single super-region either under a security regime (the OSCE), or as some type of conflict formation arising from a revival of mutual securitisation between Europe and Russia. It is not inconceivable that Russia could drift into its own self-contained security region comprising the bulk of the former Soviet Union, thus leaving the rest of Europe largely alone. These questions are all still up in the air, perhaps depending more on domestic developments in both the EU and the successor states to the Soviet Union, than on how well they handle relations between themselves (if these two things can be separated). Europe's future is thus still open. It could end up as a single security region, or as three separate ones (EU, Balkans, and one centred on Russia). It could be largely peaceful, or there could be overall rivalries with some parts (Balkans, CIS) being internally unstable.

East Asia is the other region whose post-Cold War fate is still unclear. Like Europe, it was heavily affected by Cold War overlay, and has experienced a major withdrawal of Soviet power. In Korea, and in the Taiwan Straits, Cold War divisions still persist. Like Europe, levels of industrialisation in East Asia vary greatly, the region is divided into a zone of peace (ASEAN) and a zone of conflict (Northeast Asia), and its security is heavily dependent on the presence of the US. Unlike Europe, East Asia is, excepting ASEAN, weak in regional institutions (though it does claim a distinctive tradition of informal diplomacy). For the first time in modern history this region is largely free from domination by foreign powers. It is composed of several powerful states in varying degrees of industrialisation. Levels of power are rising dramatically, the distribution of power is subject to significant change, and nationalism is strong. The region has a host of historical enmities, border disputes and cultural divides, some very serious (China-Taiwan, the two Koreas, China-Vietnam, the South China Sea). Levels of arms expenditure and military modernisation are rising, and several countries have the means to become nuclear weapons states quickly if need be. Against this, there is a widespread shared commitment to economic development, and substantial regional trade, investment and economic interdependence.

To a Western eye, East Asia bears disturbing resemblances to nineteenth century Europe, with China in the role of Germany as the large, centrally positioned, rising, and potentially hegemonic power, and Japan in the role of Britain, as the offshore advanced industrial country trying to sustain a policy of splendid isolation and global focus. China has conspicuously displayed a willingness to use force in pursuit of disputes with its neighbours (Vietnam, South China Sea, Taiwan). Despite some Chinese participation in ASEAN-sponsored talks, concern about China's rising power and hegemonic ambitions seems likely to link Northeast and Southeast (and in extreme scenarios also South) Asia into a single security complex. There is a distinct possibility that a balance-of-power-based regional security complex will emerge, albeit one mediated by nuclear deterrence, economic interests, and susceptible to whether the United States decides to remain engaged in the region, or reduce its security commitments there.[13] This vision is rejected by those who argue that the parallel with Europe is false, that Asians have their own transnational way of dealing with things, and that the United States will stay in the region as the military-political ring-holder and balancer.[14] Either way it is clear that the military-political dimension of security remains central in East Asia. Quite what the new pattern there will be depends crucially on how China handles its rising power, and how its neighbours respond. It is far from inconceivable that

China might succeed in reestablishing a modern version of its traditional suzerainty in the region.

Conclusion

Probably the best general approach to regional security in the post-Cold War world will be to think in terms of more heterogeneous complexes than we did in the past. Rather than basing security complexes purely on the state, one will need to allow in other types of actors and referent objects as well. In looking at the Balkans, for example, one clearly has a strong mixture of politico-military and societal dynamics. Some of the actors and referent objects are states, but some of them are mobilised ethnic groups. A similar picture could be found within the new regional system(s) emerging from the wreckage of the USSR. Elsewhere the mix might be different. In the Gulf and East Asia, the traditional state-based, military-political dynamics remain strong, but societal actors and issues also play a role, as do economic ones. In parts of Africa and Asia, the state may be giving way to a mix of tribes, mafias, firms and warlords. In this approach one would hope to retain the analytical simplicity of a single form of regional security complex, albeit at the cost of an expansion, perhaps considerable in some cases, of the variety of issues and actors within it.[15]

Notes

1. Bull, Hedley: *The Anarchical Society* (London: Macmillan, 1977).
2. Helleiner, Eric: 'Regionalization in the International Political Economy: a Comparative Perspective', *East Asia Policy Papers*, no. 3 (York and Toronto: University of Toronto-York University, Joint Centre for Asia-Pacific Studies, 1994); Anderson, Kim, & Richard Blackhurst: *Regional Integration and the Global Trading System* (Hemel Hempstead: Harvester Wheatsheaf, 1993).
3. Buzan, Barry, Morten Kelstrup, Pierre Lemaitre, Elzbieta Tromer & Ole Wæver: *The European Security Order Recast: Scenarios for the Post-Cold War Era* (London: Pinter, 1990); Wæver, Ole, Barry Buzan, Morten Kelstrup, Pierre Lemaitre et al.: *Identity, Migration and the New Security Agenda in Europe* (London: Pinter, 1993).
4. Hurrell, Andrew: 'Explaining the Resurgence of Regionalism in World Politics', *Review of International Studies*, vol. 21, no. 4 (1995), pp. 333-358; Helleiner: *op. cit.* (note 2).
5. Buzan, Barry, Ole Wæver & Jaap de Wilde: *The New Security Studies: A Framework for Analysis* (Boulder: Lynne Rienner, forthcoming 1997), chs. 3-8.

6. Buzan, Barry: *People, States and Fear: An Agenda for International Security Studies in the Post-Cold War Era* (Hemel Hempstead: Harvester Wheatsheaf, 1991), ch. 5; idem, Wæver & de Wilde: *op. cit.* (note 5).
7. Wæver, Ole: 'Securitization—Desecuritization', in Ronnie Lipschutz (ed.): *On Security* (New York: Columbia University Press, 1995), pp. 46-86.
8. Väyrynen, Raimo: 'Regional Conflict Formations: An Intractable Problem of International Relations', *Journal of Peace Research*, vol. 21, no. 4 (1984), pp. 337-59.
9. Jervis, Robert: 'Security Regimes', *International Organization*, vol. 36, no. 2 (1982), pp. 357-78.
10. Deutsch, Karl & al.: *Political Community and the North Atlantic Area* (Princeton: Princeton University Press, 1957), pp. 1-4.
11. Buzan & al. *op. cit.* 1990 (note 3), pp. 205-208.
12. Wæver & al.: *op. cit.* (note 3).
13. Buzan, Barry & Gerald Segal: 'Rethinking East Asian Security', *Survival*, vol. 36, no. 2 (1994), pp. 3-21.
14. Mahbubani, Kishore: 'The Pacific Impulse', *Survival*, vol. 37, no. 1 (1995), pp. 105-20; Richardson, James L.: 'The Asia-Pacific: Geopolitical Cauldron or Regional Community', *The National Interest*, no. 38 (Winter 1994/5), pp. 2-13.
15. Buzan & al. *op. cit.* 1997 (note 5).

3 Between Hope and Despair: Southern Africa's Security

JOAO BERNARDO HONWANA

With the end of the Cold War, the international system has lost the spasms—and certainties—of bipolarity, and is adapting to the ambiguities of an emerging multipolar order. Coupled with the demise of apartheid, this has brought about a process of transformation in Southern Africa, i.e. Angola, Botswana, Lesotho, Malawi, Mozambique, Mauritius, Namibia, South Africa, Swaziland, Tanzania, Zambia and Zimbabwe. This is captured in the new and unanimous discourse on democracy, respect for human rights, market economy and common security in the region's political and academic circles.

The change in discourse reveals a more fundamental set of transformations of Southern Africa's political and strategic landscape. Finally liberated from the ideological divisions of the past, the subcontinent has evolved from a region at war to a region at peace, where yesterday's enemies are now partners in the common project of building the Southern African Development Community (SADC). Moreover, within states authoritarianism has been replaced, or is in the process of being replaced, with democratic rule; centralised economic policies with economic liberalism; an emphasis on the security of states, with a focus on the security of citizens.

The instability inherent in changes of this magnitude is compounded by two important external factors. First, the increasing marginalisation of the continent as a whole. African leaders have expressed the fear that Africa 'has moved from the periphery to the periphery of the periphery of the global economy—the permanent political underdog, the world's basket case for which there is little hope'.[1]

Second, the extreme poverty of most African countries, including those of Southern Africa, results in a high level of dependency on foreign aid which, as a rule, is offered under stringent conditions. These conditions invariably include demands for political pluralism and economic liberalism. This powerful foreign pressure creates an unhealthy tension between process and product: in the haste to establish the formal symbols of liberal democracies, the need for these states and societies to develop a corresponding political culture and economic base can be neglected.

This is not to deny the need for political and economic reform. However, democracy stands little chance of success if it is imposed from the outside;

democratic states will only emerge when the societies concerned have taken possession of the concepts and values that underpin democracy, anchoring them in their own specific cultural, political and social universe.

Similarly, the implementation of economic liberalisation programmes through structural adjustment normally sharpens, instead of alleviating, the countries' economic crises, since the search for monetary stability and the holding back of public expenditure extracts an enormous social cost for the millions of Africans who live in conditions of extreme poverty. As a result, their most elementary security requirements, such as access to food, to shelter, to education, to employment, to medical care and to other basic services are not being satisfied. Invariably, this has generated high level of conflict.

So, Southern Africa's future seems to hang between hope and despair. This chapter examines the most recent developments, and outlines the main intra- and inter-state challenges to regional security.

Inter-state Dynamics

In recognition of the new opportunities and challenges of the post-apartheid era, and drawing from the experience of cooperation in the 1980s, the SADC made a substantial progress in the debate around security and the relations between the states of Southern Africa. Thus, by late 1992, SADC had decided that as in the economic sphere, so in the domain of defence and security there was a need for closer cooperation and integration.[2]

Progress in the materialisation of this vision has been slow as the member states were manifestly divided on the character of such cooperation. Some states were of the view that the informality that characterised the Frontline States Organisation and its agencies should be retained in post-apartheid regional security mechanisms. That modus operandi, it was argued, delivered an efficient response to colonial rule and apartheid destabilisation, while respecting the sensitivities around the national sovereignty of member states. These states therefore proposed the creation of an Association of Southern African States (ASAS) which would inherit the functions of the Frontline States and operate as the political and security mechanism of the SADC, maintaining the informal style of its predecessor organisation.

In contrast, other states believed that the Frontline States informality was successful because of the combination of a number of factors which are currently changing. First, apartheid and its strategy of regional destabilisation was the single most important common threat to the survival of the Frontline States and, therefore, a powerful incentive to bring these states together. Second, the struggle against white minority rule was the only item on the regional security agenda, but it is no longer an issue.

Third, leaders such as Julius Nyerere, Kenneth Kaunda, Agostinho Neto, Seretse Khama, Robert Mugabe and Oliver Tambo shared the same vision of how to liberate the sub-continent from white minority rule, which led them to create the Frontline States and the SADCC. Moreover, political and military cadres from Angola, Mozambique, Namibia, South Africa and Zimbabwe, lived and trained together in the refugee and military camps of Botswana, Tanzania and Zambia in the late 1960s and early 1970s. In that process they developed strong and lasting personal friendships, both amongst themselves and with their hosts. After liberation, a number of these freedom-fighters became senior politicians, military officers and security officials in their respective countries. Of that generation of leaders, however, only President Mugabe remains active in the forefront of regional politics. New national leaderships have emerged in some states who do not have that powerful common background and bonding. In addition the current focal point of the common agenda (economic and social development) entails much more competition and potential for conflict among the member states than the national liberation struggle. Under these circumstances, the informal tradition of the Frontline States may not be enough to bring about an effective common approach to defence and security in Southern Africa.

It took nearly three years of consultations to build consensus around the institutional arrangements for regional cooperation in defence and security matters. As a result, the Inter-State Defence and Security Committee (ISDSC) was revitalised and a SADC Organ on Politics, Defence and Security (OPDS) was established. Created in 1983 as a substructure of the Frontline States, the ISDSC was an informal forum gathering together ministers responsible for Defence, State Security and Public Security. Its primary function was to operationalise the decisions taken by the Heads of State and Government of the Frontline States with regard to the common effort against apartheid destabilisation. Over the past few years, the ISDSC has evolved towards a more complex and less informal organisation with the establishment of three sub-committees respectively on Defence, Public Security and State Security, and subordinate sub-structures. The ISDSC is likely to be incorporated into the OPDS, as was agreed upon at the SADC Ministerial Meeting in Gaborone in January 1996 and approved at the head of state and government level in June 1996. The Organ will work to achieve the following objectives, among others:

- to promote political cooperation among member states and the evolution of common political value systems and institutions;
- to cooperate fully in regional security and defence through conflict prevention, management and resolution;
- to promote peacemaking and peacekeeping in order to achieve sustainable peace and security;
- to develop a collective security capacity and conclude a Mutual Defence Pact for responding to external threats, and a regional peacekeeping capacity within national armies that could called upon within the region, or elsewhere in the continent;

• to promote the political, economic, social and environmental dimensions of security.

These developments suggest that a consensus was finally reached that stability in inter-state relations will be best served through the establishment of a collective security regime; only by bringing South Africa, the regional giant, into the fold of common security structures can its power be contained and transformed into a regional asset.

However, practical steps towards the establishment of common security regimes in the region are likely to be slow and tentative. Three factors contribute to this hesitation.

• The scarcity of human and financial resources places a major challenge to common structures since 'the weakness of national institutions is automatically transferred to regional organisations'.[3]

• States are actually reluctant to surrender a measure of sovereignty on security matters to a regional authority. Some of the states in the region were of the view that the informality that characterised the operation of the Frontline States (FLS) should be retained. This led to the creation of the short-lived Association of Southern African States (ASAS), as an instrument to replace the Frontline States in dealing with the region's political and security matters.

• The overwhelming military superiority of South Africa relative to all other SADC member states, despite the obviously friendly intentions of the ANC government towards its neighbours, raises some concerns in regional political and military circles. Those fears are aggravated both by the perception that the new South African National Defence Force (SANDF) is still dominated by the apartheid military elite, and the notion that some western powers are encouraging South Africa to play a 'benign' hegemonic role in securing stability in the region and elsewhere in Africa.

Should this be allowed to happen, the region would be confronted with the ironic reality that the dominance that apartheid desperately sought through military destabilisation and economic pressure might be finally achieved under the umbrella of regional economic and military cooperation.

The Domestic Outlook

In their current format, neither the ISDSC nor the OPDS address directly the more urgent domestic security concerns of the member states. Indeed, as the external military threats, real or perceived, recede, new (and old) internal non-military threats to the security of states and peoples pose a formidable challenge to the region: fragile democracies; the lack of effective governance; unstable civil-military relations; the proliferation of small weapons in private hands; internal political and ethnic conflict; countless refugees and displaced persons; thousands of demobilised soldiers and guerrillas who are destitute; chronic underdevelopment and attendant poverty; and rampant disease and environmental degradation.

A particularly thorny issue in this connection is that of peace and justice in post-conflict situations. It is common knowledge that in conflicts which end with the unconditional defeat of one party, the winner invariably exerts the right to judge and punish the vanquished for the human and material cost of the war. The victor's abuses are conveniently underrated, explained, excused or ignored and the defeated party carries all the blame. Peace comes with a measure of justice, however partial and biased.

From a military perspective, the major internal conflicts in Southern Africa ended inconclusively. Such were the cases in Zimbabwe, Namibia, South Africa and Mozambique. Angola is also moving, painfully slowly, towards a negotiated solution. In all instances, the parties involved accepted that a conclusive military victory was not possible and peace required a measure of accommodation of their respective opponents. In my view, it was this realisation that prompted the political will to seek peaceful settlements.

South Africa and Mozambique illustrate different approaches to post-war reconciliation and justice in Southern Africa. In South Africa, the ANC held the moral high ground, but was far from scoring a military victory; the apartheid regime, in turn, with all its military power, had no domestic nor international legitimacy, was unable to obliterate the liberation movements and could no longer resist the heavy economic pressure of the sanctions. After the settlement the new regime was in a position to impose the establishment of the Truth and Reconciliation Commission, which entailed the granting of indemnity to those individuals who acknowledged the commission of crimes in defence of apartheid or in the struggle against it, and the prosecution of only the 'unrepentant criminals'. This was possible thanks to the unparalleled moral stature of Nelson Mandela, the presence of a relatively sophisticated state, and a vibrant, well informed and demanding civil society. However imperfect, this selective approach to justice has created a fundamental social healing space upon which all South Africans can build a new sense of South Africanness.

Mozambique offers a contrasting example. Here, both the FRELIMO government and the RENAMO rebels were unable to win the war. RENAMO could not claim the legitimacy of a liberation movement, in view of its history and terrorist tactics; the government was rapidly losing the prestige and popular support it had enjoyed in the early years of independence. Moreover, the government was under tremendous domestic and international pressure to engage in negotiations with RENAMO. The peace process was conducted in such a way the real losers were the 'anonymous' people of the land. Their quest for justice failed to stimulate the attention of the authorities, the international community and media. Under these circumstances, the war crimes have been ignored, allegedly to avoid reopening the wounds and for the sake of national reconciliation. In other words, justice was sacrificed for peace. National reconciliation, in these terms, perpetuates a culture of impunity. It may be perceived as merely a compromise between FRELIMO and RENAMO, without any serious attempt to establish harmony and justice among all Mozambicans.

Demilitarisation, Demobilisation and Weapons Control

One important result of the improvement in inter-state relations in Southern Africa is the current wave of drastic cuts in force levels and military spending, which contributes to the emergent climate of regional stability.

South Africa, by far the most significant regional military power, has reduced its defence budget by 51 per cent since 1989 and will downsize the South African National Defence Force (SANDF) from 121,000 to 75,000 over the next five years; Zimbabwe is currently reducing its defence force from 51,000 to 40,000; Mozambique's new defence force is at the level of 12,000, less than half of the planned 30,000; and Angola, under the Lusaka Protocol, will reduce its military to 70,000.[4] Botswana is the only SADC state to manifest a contrary tendency with the recently announced acquisitions of 13 CF-5 aircraft from Canada; and 54 Leopard 1-V Main Battle Tanks, 50 Carl Gustav (84 mm) recoilless guns and 279 DAF trucks from the Netherlands.[5] Some analysts fear that these acquisitions may introduce a measure of instability in the region.

Does this mean that, with the intriguing exception of Botswana, the states of Southern Africa have engaged in a process of demilitarisation? A brief consideration of the concept of militarisation may be useful in assessing the degree to which Southern African states are demilitarising. First, it is important to draw a distinction between the following three interrelated social phenomena: the military *institution*, the *ideology* of militarism and the *process* of militarisation.[6] Some analysts define militarism as 'a set of attitudes and social practices which regard war and the preparation of war as a normal and desirable social activity'.[7] Others view militarism as

> first ... an aggressive foreign policy, based on a readiness to resort to war; second, the preponderance of the military in the state, the extreme case being that of military rule; third, subservience of the whole society to the needs of the army which may involve a recasting of social life in accordance with the pattern of military organisation; and fourth, an ideology which promotes military ideas.[8]

Quite frequently, militarism is also used to describe large armed forces and excessive defence expenditure. This leads to a problem of criteria: how do we define 'large armed forces'? In relation to the total population of the country? To the size of the territory? To the armed forces of neighbouring states? By the same token, how do we measure 'excessive defence spending'? Just as a portion of the GDP? Or as compared to spending in social areas such as health, education and the provision of basic services? More generally, the different meanings of 'militarism' have attracted the criticism that the term is descriptive with very little, if any, analytical value.[9] Jacklyn Cock provides the useful suggestion that militarisation is a multidimensional social process which 'involves both the spread of militarism as an ideology, and the expansion of the power and influence of the military as a social institution'.[10]

Apartheid South Africa presents a well documented typical example of such a process,[11] the central features of which can be summarised as:

- the development of a perception of domestic, regional and international threat, encapsulated in the theory of 'Total Onslaught';
- the promotion of a militarist ideology legitimising the massive use of force by the state to counter that threat, codified in the concept of 'Total National Strategy'; and
- the development of civil-military relations characterised by the extension of the powers and influence of the security forces to virtually all areas of domestic and foreign policy.

In Angola, Mozambique and Zimbabwe, similar processes of militarisation developed as a result of, first, the national liberation wars and, later, the resistance to apartheid destabilisation. As stated earlier, the states in Southern Africa have engaged in significant reductions of force levels and defence budgets. Four interrelated factors seem to have contributed to this:

- The perception of receding external military threats to the countries of the region, as a result of the progress in inter-state relationships;
- the fact that foreign aid, on which most states in the region are heavily dependent, is provided under conditions which invariably include political pluralism, economic liberalism and the reduction of defence spending;
- domestic pressures for increased resources to meet the pressing needs of social and economic development; and
- the presence of governments sensitive to those needs, either because of a genuine commitment to good governance, or to guarantee their own maintenance of power.

These defence cuts have been accompanied by a tendency to commit more resources to the police forces, as a response to the proliferation of small arms in the hands of private citizens and security companies, poachers, crime syndicates, 'vigilante' groups, mercenaries and extremist political formations, in a symptom of what Cock calls a 'privatised militarisation'.[12] In some instances, the sharp rise in organised criminal activities such as poaching (Zimbabwe), and weapons and drugs smuggling (Mozambique), requires that the police be trained and equipped to conduct military-type operations. In other cases, the levels of political violence and instability have required the deployment of a sizeable military force (KwaZulu/Natal). In any event, the distinction that stable democracies make between the roles of the police and the military is blurred, as the policing function becomes militarised and the armed forces are deployed against their fellow citizens.

This suggests that demilitarisation cannot be measured only as a function of reductions in defence spending and force levels. To these indicators, undeniably important, should be added a move away from the employment of military methods to deal with 'civilian crimes' and political and social conflicts; and a significant reduction of the power and influence of the military institution. Further, a comprehensive programme of demilitarisation in Southern Africa also needs to take cognisance of, and address, the question of privatised militarisation. This requires both enhancing the states' capacity to maintain law and order, and resolving the systemic causes of crime and violence. As Jacklyn Cock suggests, transformation is needed at the level of attitudes, social values, practices and relations.

In the current processes of force reductions in Southern Africa, demobilisation typically involves both regular government armies and opposition guerrilla formations which are downsized and merged to establish new, more representative national military institutions. Demobilisation usually comprises three phases:

- the cantonment, registration and disarmament of combatants and selection for the new armed forces;
- the demobilisation of combatants; and
- discharge of former soldiers and support for their social reintegration.

As a general comment, it is important to note that success or failure in demobilisation programmes depends on the context in which they take place.[13] When undertaken in a relatively stable, peace-time situation, demobilisation happens fairly smoothly, as South Africa illustrates. When, on the other hand, it occurs against the backdrop of the spasms of war-to-peace transitions like those of Mozambique and Angola, a successful demobilisation becomes much more difficult to achieve. In Mozambique and Angola, where the opposing sides had occupied different parts of the territory during the war, the obstacles began with the selection of assembly areas: since neither party wanted to give the other a strategic advantage, the assembly areas were often chosen in places with inadequate conditions and difficult access, creating considerable logistical problems. Further, the process was generally marked by a slow pace of cantonment and an even slower pace of demobilisation so that some assembly points soon became overcrowded, with the attendant deterioration of living conditions. Thus, many soldiers and guerrillas stayed in cantonment sites for much longer than initially planned, under stressful conditions, inactive and uncertain about their future. Frustration and anger ensued, resulting in some violent incidents in and around the assembly areas.

However, these were minor problems compared to the daunting, and as yet unfinished, task of ensuring the adequate social reintegration of former combatants. The first difficulty in this regard relates to the issue of defining priorities: in a situation of acute humanitarian emergency and massive poverty, how much human, financial and material resources should go to former soldiers, themselves often responsible (in varying degrees) for the emergency? Is it morally acceptable to privilege the former producers of death? On the other hand, what is the alternative and, more importantly, what is the cost of not doing so?

Another problem has to do with the institutional capacity of post-conflict governments to deliver. A report from the World Bank stresses that demobilisation and reintegration programmes, '... call for substantial capacity (involving providing decentralised benefits to up to 120,000 individuals in some cases) in terms of planning, implementation and overseeing for potential fraud'.[14]

Reintegration programmes normally include the provision of transportation to the area of choice for resettlement, a monetary payment, the provision of agricultural inputs, civilian clothing, building materials and working tools. In addition, such programmes also offer short-term technical training in the fields of agriculture, plumbing, masonry, carpentry, small business management and so on, aimed at providing the demobilised combatants with opportunities for self-employment. The cost of reintegration support schemes presents yet another challenge. Perhaps with the exception of South Africa, the poorly performing economies of Southern African states cannot meet the financial burden of reintegration without external assistance. Nor can they create enough job opportunities to absorb the former soldiers, most of whom resort to violent crime as a means of survival.

The issue of disarmament and weapons control is closely related to demilitarisation and demobilisation in the Southern African context. Angola and Mozambique illustrate the complexities involved therein. In both countries, the negotiated peace settlements included a disarmament component to be undertaken under the auspices of a United Nations peacekeeping force.

The United Nations Angola Verification Missions (UNAVEM I & II) had purely monitoring mandates, while the United Nations Operation in Mozambique (ONUMOZ) had a monitoring and supervision function. This allowed ONUMOZ to play a more active role than UNAVEM in ensuring the implementation of the peace accords. However, in both cases, the UN had no enforcement powers. In addition, the parties to the peace accords did not trust one another and frequently disagreed on the interpretation of the settlement. This resulted in the peacekeepers being unable to obtain accurate information about the quantity, types and location of the weapons of the different armed forces. Thus, the collection, storage and destruction of surplus weapons was fairly ineffective in both countries. In Angola, the failure to disarm the government and UNITA forces meant that both sides had relatively easy access to arms when the hostilities resumed after the October 1992 elections. In Mozambique, a similar failure has contributed to the alarming increase of weapons smuggling into South Africa, as well as the arming of domestic criminal groups.

Conclusion

Southern Africa faces new opportunities and challenges in the post-Cold War and post-apartheid environment. As never before there is considerable potential and political will to ease inter-state tensions, engage in sustainable regional cooperation and development, substantially reduce armed forces and defence spending and develop common security mechanisms. The renewed dynamism of the ISDSC and the establishment of the OPDS are encouraging signs that the states in the region are seeking national security with, rather than against, one another.

This represents a unique opportunity which, however, is overshadowed by considerable obstacles: the lack of human and financial resources, concerns around national sovereignty and the power imbalance between South Africa and all its regional partners. Furthermore, the states that entered the SADC covenant are themselves fairly weak and ill equipped to respond to the demands and pressures of post-conflict peacebuilding, in some instances, and sustainable development, in all cases. Clearly, the solution resides with consolidation of the processes of change. Domestically, states need to build their capacity to address the basic security concerns of their citizens; civil societies need to refine their ability to interact meaningfully with the state in all areas of policy formulation; and the yet fragile processes of national reconciliation need to address the tensions around ethnic affirmation and the access to, and distribution of, power and resources. Collectively, the region needs to strengthen SADC's unity of purpose and objectives, address the factors of inter-state conflict and develop the existing mechanisms of common security.

These are the challenges likely to shape Southern Africa's new journey—one that, one wishes, will be from despair to hope.

Notes

1. See Nathan, Laurie: 'Towards a Conference on Security, Stability, Development and Cooperation in Africa', *Southern African Perspectives*, no. 13 (Bellville: Centre for Southern African Studies, University of the Western Cape, 1992), p. 5.
2. See *Southern Africa: A Framework and Strategy for Building the Community* (Harare: SADC, January 1993).
3. Nathan, Laurie: 'Security and Military Machinery in a Democratic South Africa', paper presented at the SADC Workshop on Democracy, Peace and Security, Windhoek, 1994, pp. 14-15.

4. *International Security Digest*, vol. 3, no. 1 (October 1995); and no. 6 (March 1996). See also the chapter by Jacklyn Cock in this volume.
5. See *International Security Digest*, vol. 3, no. 8 (June 1996); and *Jane's Defence Weekly*, vol. 25. no. 2 (10 January 1996), p. 17.
6. Cock, Jacklyn & Laurie Nathan (eds): *War and Society—The Militarization of South Africa* (Cape Town: David Philip, 1989), p. 2.
7. See Mann, M.: 'The Roots and Contradictions of Modern Militarism', *New Left Review*, no. 162, p. 35.
8. Andreski, S.: *Military Organization and Society* (Berkeley, CA: University of California Press, 1968), p. 429.
9. See, e.g., Smith, Dan & Ron Smith: *The Economics of Militarism* (London: Pluto Press, 1983), pp. 9-13.
10. Cock & Nathan: *op. cit.*
11. For detailed studies of the process of militarization of apartheid South Africa see Frankel, P.: *Pretoria's Praetorians—Civil-Military Relations in South Africa* (Cambridge: Cambridge University Press, 1984); Johnson, S. (ed.): *South Africa: No Turning Back* (London, 1988); Grundy, K.: *The Militarization of South African Politics* (Oxford: Oxford University Press, 1988); and Cock & Nathan: *op. cit.*
12. See the chapter by Jacklyn Cock in this volume.
13. See the World Bank Report: 'Demobilization and Reintegration of Military Personnel in Africa: The Evidence from Seven Country Case Studies', in Cilliers, Jackie (ed.) *Dismissed* (Halfway House: IDP, 1996), pp. 12-26.
14. *Ibid.*, p. 16.

4 Post War Restructuring: The Region's Defence Structures

MARTIN RUPIYA

Following two years of intense debate and an extensive review process by the Southern African Development Community (SADC), a separate Organ on Politics, Defence and Security (OPDS) has been established to succeed the ad-hoc arrangement of the Frontline States (FLS). This development takes place against a background of an outbreak of peace in Southern Africa, following the end of the Cold War and the abandonment of apartheid policies by South Africa.

As a result of the nature of the conflict during the turmoil period, which generally centred on antagonistic groups within and between states, the region's national armies had been structured for offensive operations internally, as well as for cross-border raids in neighbouring states. Conversely, for those not capable of mounting out-of-country operations, their forces were, at the very minimum, configured to challenge an invading force.

The current peaceful environment, characterised by regional political and security accommodation and improved civil-military relations has meant that defence structures have to be reoriented to reflect the new order. While the current dispensation across the region prioritises national reconstruction and economic development, to succeed a credible defence insurance option has to be held in reserve.

However, a closer look at the national defence components expected to cooperate in practical support of the new security organ reveals major deficiencies in critical areas of doctrine, inter-operability, training, communications and equipment. The aim of restructuring, to be implemented at both the strategic and the operational level, will be to establish armed forces which take into account the following realities:

- Democratic environments in which incumbent regimes are accountable to budgetary decisions including transparent defence allocations.[1]
- The global and regional defence and security environment.
- The need to carry out internal security (IS), constitutional duties and limited inter-state regional cooperation for purposes of peacekeeping or enforcement within the framework of OAU and UN Security Council

approved mandates (something which should require state contingents no larger than unit strengths averaging 1,000 men, at the most).

Before considering aspects of the envisaged restructuring, we need to acknowledge certain factors already in operation, which have a bearing on the ultimate result.

First, several *national force levels* have already been determined as a result of the plethora of agreements which ushered in peace in Southern Africa. These figures must be viewed against the total number of combatants that had assembled at independence or when the agreements were struck. For example, Angola and Mozambique each had over 100,000 personnel under arms, from which initial agreements set force levels of 50,000 and 30,000 respectively. Zimbabwe had a pool of over 60,000 from which initially a force of 35,000 was envisaged. But, the statistics below reflects the situation as it unfolds.

Table 1: Country Initial Forces Agreement

	1994/5	1995/6	Future
Angola	82,000	82,000	50,000
Botswana[2]	7,500+	7,500+	10,000
Lesotho	2,000	2,000	2,000
Malawi	10,000	8,000	7,000
Mozambique	12,000	11,000	11,000
Namibia[3]	8,100	8,100	10,000
South Africa	136,000	136,000	90,000
Swaziland	3,000	3,000	3,000
Tanzania	49,600	34,600	25,000
Zambia	24,000	21,600	20,000
Zimbabwe	42,000	41,000	25,000
Totals	376,200	354,800	253,000

From the above it can be gathered that well over 150,000 combatants have been demobilised. The demobilisation process was accompanied by the entry into the region's security equation by the international community in the form of the Commonwealth Monitoring Forces (CMF) in Zimbabwe and British Military Advisory and Training Teams (BMATT) across the region (with missions in Mozambique, Namibia, South Africa, Swaziland, Botswana and Lesotho)[4]; the UN presence, through Resolution 435, in Namibia; the United Nations Angola Verification Mission (UNAVEM); the UN Observer Mission in Mozambique (UNOMOZ); as well as the United States' extension of military aid and joint exercises. This has had far-reaching impacts in at least three important areas.

First, the international community (especially key states in the UN system such as the USA, Canada, France and the UK) has taken over a large chunk of military expenditure from the new governments, as the costs of the above missions amount to nearly one fifth of regional military expenditures.[5]

Secondly, there has been some spin-off from the involvement of the international community in terms of doctrine and structures, e.g. through the various training missions. Essentially, European type, Second World war infantry heavy units have been established with little or no emphasis on support arms or specialisation. There has also been no funding for lethal equipment or its modernisation, which has important implications for the future structures.

Finally the international community has influenced regional defence postures at the strategic level. For example, the United States made it a precondition for normalising relations with South Africa that it dismantled its six primitive gun type nuclear devices. This has also affected the whole region as, significantly, all have now signed the Non-Proliferation Treaty making the area a nuclear-free zone.[6]

Furthermore, anti-personnel mines should disappear from national arsenals within five to ten years, as restructuring armies in the region will have to revisit doctrine and come up with ones that do not require these devices. In this regard, the region's former rogue, South Africa, has already issued a stringent moratorium on production and sale of anti-personnel mines, while President Chissano of Mozambique has indicated his willingness to spearhead a campaign for a region-wide ban, publicly supported by Angola and Botswana.

The above developments in international norms for the conduct of warfare will partly determine how the region proceeds with its current and future security forces restructuring.

Evaluation of SADC National Defence Forces

After assessing the inherent changes as well as the international framework affecting defence restructuring in Southern Africa, the question now arises what the state of readiness is of the components which will be expected to take to the field together? Figures abound of agreed to force levels, but we need to ascertain efficiency levels if regional inter-operability is to succeed.

The fundamental structures of the various armies have been established over the past thirty years. Factors influencing the evolution of national security institutions can be best explained by the manner in which each state secured independence. For brevity, however, these have been grouped into four categories.

The First Group

This category, made up of Tanzania, Malawi, Zambia and the former kingdoms of Lesotho, Swaziland and Botswana all secured their independence through orderly transfer of power by the colonial master, at most preceded by civil disobedience agitation. This had a direct effect on the priority the armed forces received in the subsequent era. However, even amongst this group, there were exceptions.

In Tanzania, the military had attempted to seize power during the transition to African rule and had to be forced back to barracks by the departing colonial power, i.e. Britain. This early civil-military stand off subsequently influenced the incoming government's relationship with the military, as it felt the need to create other sources of power, outside the existing formal military structures. A National Service Scheme and a militia, both with strong party political control, were established. Through these structures, martial skills and centres of control were redistributed amongst a broader constituency within the country. This dispersion also affected the allocation of resources, including basic war material. The net effect was to permanently impair the potential efficiency of the standing force, the Tanzanian People's Defence Force (TPDF).

During both the Ugandan intervention against Idi Amin and the deployment in northern Mozambique under FLS auspices in the mid 1980s, defence experts have perceived that the force did not acquit itself well. Finally, in Liberia, elements were also deployed on peacekeeping duties and elements of this contingent were captured, stripped of all weaponry and marooned for over eighteen months before diplomatic efforts rescued them. Again experts have not been kind with regard to the level of professionalism and efficiency that the TPDF demonstrated in this respect, despite acknowledging the very real problems presented by the international community in not coming through with the funding which had been promised. This then is the organisation which is fast shedding off manpower from 49,600 to possibly 25,000 in the space of three to five years and certainly needs improvements, training and consolidation in various areas before it reaches acceptable levels for regional deployment. While noting deficiencies with regard to regional cooperation tasks, the TPDF is more than capable for the level of internal security duties which it may be called upon to carry out.

Malawi's independence and that of Zambia was achieved following extensive politicisation work and threats of widespread civil disobedience by the nationalists. Leaders in both states, for their efforts, were incarcerated in Southern Rhodesian jails. Independence was secured amidst turmoil in the region, directed against the white minority regimes in Rhodesia, South Africa and the two Portuguese territories of Angola and Portuguese East Africa (now Mozambique).

Soon after independence, Malawi chose the route of non-confrontation and accommodation with settler and colonial powers. This decision affected the subsequent structure of the defence force as it was left largely with internal security duties in a region riven with conflict. Again, as in Tanzania's case, President Banda created the Young Pioneers in 1980 as an organisation which proceeded to challenge the military power base. At the expense of the standing force this youth wing was equipped with better guns, transport, pay, accommodation, radio communication systems, and enjoyed easier access to the politicians. The efficiency of the defence force was consequently impaired.

However, despite this deliberate assault on its efficiency, the force acquitted itself well when deployed in north-eastern Mozambique to safeguard the Nacala rail route under the FLS regional initiative. It was also to prove particularly competent in putting down the Young Pioneers in the run-up to the elections which ousted Banda in 1994. Recent austerity measures have witnessed the defence force being whittled down but the figures involved should not seriously impair its presently acceptable level of efficiency for internal security tasks. There are of course questions regarding its modernisation as recent involvement in peacekeeping duties revealed some structural weaknesses. Basic transport and equipment, including decent salaries were found to be lacking and had to be provided by donors, to enable the force to take to the field on the African continent.

Zambia and Tanzania bore the brunt of assisting the process of decolonisation in the 1960s and the first half of the 1970s. In the case of Zambia, despite the country's bordering Rhodesia, President Kaunda launched his country into the nationalist fray, supporting struggles in Angola, Portuguese East Africa, Rhodesia, South West Africa (now Namibia) and South Africa. This translated into a heightened national security environment which had important implications for Zambian defence organisations. An air defence system comprising ground and air defences was put into place and conventional skills training for the forces was improved. The strategy was to ensure a minimum offensive-defence capability. The force could not hope to retaliate against numerous cross-border incidents by the superior forces of South Africa and Rhodesia but simply demonstrated a local capacity to repulse elements deployed. Consequently, against the deafening background of regional destabilisation, a highly competent, staff trained and defensive organisation was put into place. The value of its competency has of late been demonstrated in peacekeeping operations and reflects an institution which can be considered capable of meeting the envisaged criteria for restructuring.

Botswana has adopted a contrary course to all the others. This country, after maintaining minimum military capability at the height of the decolonisation period, has now embarked on marked increased military preparedness. The acquisition of jet fighters, tanks and armoured vehicles should result in a sizeable increase of manpower. Further, the country is also the only one in the region boasting a huge surplus in foreign currency reserves and is therefore able to pay cash for new weaponry. The expanding force is well trained and motivated, given the generous pay and allowances compared to other counterparts.

However, the perceived and concrete manpower and equipment expansion has raised local tension with neighbouring Namibia over a territorial dispute of the Sidudu islands. Namibian officials have also expressed concern over access to water in their country, presently being affected by perceived untoward behaviour by Botswana. Apart from these negative aspects, which have been loudly voiced, the Botswana Defence Force (BDF) is a reliable anchor on which the new SADC security organ can depend.

Swaziland has an 'adequate emerging force' that is capable of internal security duties. It would be stretched for external deployment that might not leave behind a reasonable reserve. The country has expressed an interest in participating in peacekeeping operations such as monitoring roles, and this type of operations can easily be carried out.

The Second Group: Former Portuguese territories

The second category of independent states emerged following the Armed Forces Movement's coup in Lisbon of April 1974 which directly affected the on-going wars in Angola and Portuguese East Africa. The front runners in both states, the People's Movement for the Liberation of Angola (MPLA) and the Front for the Liberation of Mozambique (FRELIMO), were soon embroiled in cold war and South African destabilisation attempts. Their armies remained largely guerrilla forces, with little time to consolidate and engage in more conventional training. There was little documentation, implementation of regular pay and allowances and proper re-equipping in peace-time. Both armies have had large tracts within both states since independence, which they have never permanently controlled. The advent of the new era, coming through the negotiated treaties, set the current force levels, composition, training and equipment.

In the case of Mozambique, both sides (FRELIMO and the RENAMO rebels) were expected to provide fifteen thousand soldiers each for the new army; however, only a handful have bothered to report. No systematic programmes were mounted to demobilise and reintegrate other elements and the capacity of the existing force to operate inside the country is debatable. There is a lack of communication routes and facilities, accommodation, decent remuneration incentives and transport—the air force, previously armed with Soviet type equipment, is now grounded for lack of aircraft serviceability and an absence of spare parts. The bottom line in the case of this state is that the SADC security organ will have to mount serious supportive programmes to revamp the country's forces if any semblance of regional national reciprocity is to be maintained.

Angola's case is much more complex. Forces which have come together under the Bicesse Agreement of 1988, reinforced by the Lusaka Accords of 1994, have been fighting a civil war which began even before independence in 1975. By the time of writing demobilisation and integration have been suspended as a result of mistrust and proven cases of deceit. Two important armed camps therefore still exist, made up of MPLA adherents and the Movement for the Total Liberation of Angola (UNITA). Consequently, internal security and regional cooperation are beyond the capacities of the incumbent government.

Because the present South African National Defence Force (SANDF), still suffers from lack of representativity—heavily reflecting the former South African Defence Force (SADF), an organisation intimately involved in the Angolan conflict —any future collaboration of forces in the case of Angola must remain in doubt. Any cooperation at present raises questions of rancour, suspicion and mistrust and therefore regional expectations on this score must be tempered with caution.

Events in the Central African Great Lake region affecting Burundi, Rwanda and Zaire, not to mention Tanzania and Zambia, have forced a rethink. The South African forces have begun to demonstrate their positive adherence to the rule of law under the present government, and policy-makers in the region and abroad have begun to reassess their inherent advantages. It is to be hoped that they may be employed to stabilise the rapidly deteriorating security situation north of the Zambezi. The SANDF has excellent communications capable of covering more than half of the African continent. It also has a highly respected separate medical division and logistical capacity able to project and maintain at least a brigade more than 2,000 kilometres from home for periods of about six months. Furthermore, both the naval and air wings have capacities well in excess of Africa's present local requirements, and these assets have come under serious consideration for involvement, under UN and OAU auspices, in the unfolding Central and sub-Saharan crises. With continent-wide and global acceptance of the South African government, the defence institution has already been called upon, in private and diplomatic circles, to come to the fore, as a direct reflection of its capabilities and professionalism, the still undergoing transformation notwithstanding. The urgency has been further underlined by the new phenomena of collapsing states, internecine ethnic blood-letting and the appearance overnight of millions of refugees, as in Rwanda, Burundi and Zaire of late.

Third Group: Zimbabwe, Namibia and South Africa

Independence in all three states involved protracted armed struggles by liberation movements, complemented by negotiated settlements. This had the effect of weakening the ability of the new governments to place at the helm of the security organisations, exclusively, elements of their armed wings as had occurred in Angola and Mozambique. Further, in South Africa and Namibia political power was also assumed in the context of coalition governments, a factor which emphasised accommodation of the other parties and moderation in pushing through certain party based policies. Attempts at force restructuring after the attainment of sovereignty therefore proceeded with varying results.

In the case of South Africa, charges of absorption of only a limited segment of the African National Congress's (ANC) former armed wing, Umkhonto we Sizwe (MK), and Pan-Africanist Congress's former African People's Liberation Army (APLA) have been levelled at the new South African National Defence Force (SANDF). The racial composition of the forces has so far made it unacceptable for deployment on the African continent, let alone in the southern region where it enjoys a particularly negative reputation. In present circumstances, although the generals commanding the different armies are now on speaking terms in the Inter-State Defence and Security Committee there remains tension within the middle and lower ranks of the forces. Political changes have not filtered down to be fully reflected at the security operational level. Problems of the SANDF's force composition can also be anticipated to adversely affect any long term internal deployment amongst the majority of its citizenry who are perceived as also not readily identifying with the present structure. In spite of existing operational capacity the SANDF still needs further fundamental reorganisation and restructuring.

Meanwhile, in Namibia liberation from South African occupation and a not too decisive initial showing at the polls by the South West African People's Organisation (SWAPO), also registered itself in the armed force which emerged. In February 1990 the first infantry battalion drawn equally from People's Liberation Army of Namibia (PLAN) guerrillas and the former South West African Territorial Forces (SWATF) members was established as a nucleus of the new army. Further units were subsequently formed with the assistance of BMATT, adhering to their practices and doctrine as had been experienced elsewhere. Operational experience was gained by limited contingents of this force during peacekeeping duties in Cambodia and Angola.[7] Efficiency reports from both commitments measured up to expectations, reflecting the effectiveness of the foreign military assistance that had been rendered.

In Zimbabwe, despite the achievement of independence with a strategic stalemate on the battle-field, a major part of the then incumbent forces took the immigrant route to South Africa, leaving important posts in the hands of the new government. The incoming government had wished to have in place an armed force made up of at least 80 per cent guerrilla forces and the rest coming from the former Rhodesian forces. In effect, within a year or two following independence in March 1980, this had been more than attained. However, fissures within local nationalists from the 1960s, regarding the Zimbabwe African Peoples Union's former armed wing, Zimbabwe Peoples' Revolutionary Army (ZPRA) and the Zimbabwe African National Union's former military wing, the Zimbabwe African National Liberation Army (ZANLA) resurfaced at this time and threatened to tear apart the new organisation. The December 1987 Unity Accord between the two former political parties agreeing to form a coalition government contributed to the stability which followed.

Subsequent to this hiccup, the Zimbabwe Defence Forces have demonstrated acceptable capability in carrying out required tasks within the country and outside. In the context of external operations for example, the ZNA, some two years after its own emergence, was heavily involved in assisting its former FRELIMO allies inside Mozambique fighting against the South African backed National Resistance Movement (RENAMO). On numerous occasions, the RENAMO Headquarters of

Cassa Banana at Gorongosa was captured and handed over to the Mozambican Armed Forces (FAM), only to be retaken by RENAMO. This was a serious indictment of the local army's capability although demonstrating the growing capacity of the Zimbabwean forces.

Conclusions. What Needs to be Done?

The forces which are available for national internal security as well the envisaged regional cooperation range from those that have not even come together, such as in Angola, to some which can project force thousands of kilometres from home for sustained periods, although still handicapped by an unacceptable composition. Still, others can barely drive a company out of administrative base areas and despite national political accommodation, do not have the ability nor the facilitating infrastructure to work in all parts of their own country, such as in Mozambique.

The existing positive political environment in which southern Africa finds itself, which also extends to the security field, emboldens us to advance some suggestions as to what needs to be done. With such corrective initiatives taken at the regional level, zonal defence cooperation should benefit as will national internal security.

First, the new SADC security organ needs to establish a secretariat, part of whose mission will be to continually evaluate national military efficiency of member states. The body should also come up with a common doctrine, identify and recommend states which specialise in offering skills and capacity in specialist areas along the lines of SADC economic tasking at present. Facilities and regional training teams should be established to take over from the current initiatives, in place as a result of negotiated treaty agreements. The said teams would ensure acceptable maintenance of military efficiency as well as coordinate combined field-exercises, beginning at company level and rising to battalion or regiment levels.

A quick review of the FLS conduct of operations in Mozambique between 1984-8 may serve as an example of not how to do things in future. During this operation, force coordination between the TPDF, ZNA and FAM left a lot to be desired. There was also a complete lack of combat intelligence sharing leading to the large numbers of forces deployed making little impact. Reports of looting and related corrupt practices also reared their heads in zones under the control of the various armies, casting doubt and suspicion on the ability of the forces deployed in their relationship with the local community. During the current re-conceptualisation and restructuring, a deliberate and considered approach to all these issues should enhance and benefit regional civil-military relations as the forces begin to operate within an increasingly democratic and accountable environment.

Finally, in seeking to draw up a restructuring list for policy-makers within the criteria set out above, Botswana, Namibia, South Africa, Swaziland, Tanzania, Zambia and Zimbabwe, all have armed forces which do meet the requirements. Some of them may need cursory revamping but essentially, at present, all carry out effective policing within their borders, are acceptable to their constituencies and can deploy a lightly equipped and armed unit within the region for reasonable periods. Both Malawi and Lesotho, with a little more assistance in the areas of communications, logistics and transport, can also join the above states.

However, Angola, Mozambique and South Africa still need to be restructured in the context of internal acceptability, force representativity, ability to police all parts of their own territories. Other issues such as lack of transport, soldier incentives, training and aspects of doctrine will also need to be addressed to be able to fit in with the region's new demands. Already as a result of political and security-related pressures, a 'Troika' comprising Botswana, South Africa and Zimbabwe has emerged as the vanguard in dealing with the region's problems which is likely to affect the character of the new Organ for Politics, Defence and Security.

Notes

1. McKibbin, Warwick J.: 'An Overview', in Lawrence R. Klein, Fu-chen Lo & Warwick J. McKibbin (eds.): *Arms Reduction Economic Implications In The Post-Cold War Era* (Tokyo: United Nations University Press, 1995), p. 10. See also McNamara, Robert S.: 'A New International Order & its Implications for Arms Reductions', *ibid.*, pp. 267-281; and Ball, Nicole: 'Enhancing Peace & Development: Foreign aid and military expenditure in Developing Countries', *ibid.*, pp. 282-316, both of which focus on the reformed roles of the military in developing countries in the new era.
2. International Institute For Strategic Studies: *The Military Balance 1995/6* (Oxford: Oxford University Press and IISS, 1996), p. 230. President Joachim Chissano, following the dismal call to arms witnessed in his country, called for possible conscription to augment the numbers. South Africa, Malawi, Zambia and Tanzania had their programmes in reducing defence expenditure precipitated by threats of withdrawal of international financing.
3. Pisani, Andre du: 'Democratisation In Post-Independent Namibia: The Role of the Military'. First Draft, presented at the African American Studies Triennial Conference on Southern Africa, held in Maputo, 14-19 June 1996, p. 3.
4. See Rupiya, Martin: 'The Expanding Torrent: British Military Assistance to the Southern African Region', *African Security Review*, vol. 5, no. 4 (1996), pp. 51-59.
5. *The Military Balance 1995/6*, p. 232.
6. Howlett, Darryl & John Simpson: 'Nuclearisation and Denuclearisation in South Africa', *Survival*, vol. 35, no. 3 (Autumn 1993), pp. 154-173.
7. Pisani: *loc. cit.*, p. 2.

5 The Military Requisites of Regional Security Cooperation

CARL CONETTA, CHARLES KNIGHT, AND LUTZ UNTERSEHER

There seems to be a virtual consensus among national leaders in southern Africa that the security of the area's individual nations depends principally on establishing conditions of economic progress and socio-political stability throughout the region. This was recognised explicitly in the Programme of Nations adopted by the Southern African Development Community in 1993 and restated in numerous official documents since then. All regional parties agree that the level of interstate threat in southern Africa is currently quite low, although sub-state actors pose some degree of cross-border military threat and the region as a whole suffers from a variety of transnational problems that impact on military security, such as migratory flows and the illegal market in arms.

Regarding the future security environment, there exists a high level of uncertainty. Sources of instability include serious economic and environmental problems exacerbated by long years of war; ethnic and tribal antagonisms; and internal political instability due to rapid political change, overburdened state structures, or both. The citizens of most nations in southern Africa have been gravely harmed by the social and political conflicts of the last three decades and the accompanying economic dislocations. In many countries new democratic institutions are struggling to respond to the legacies of past conflicts which include high rates of crime and civil violence and the pressing demands of reconstruction. In this light, the most serious and likely of future threats to national security reside in the potential inability of state institutions to respond adequately to the needs of their citizens—a failure that could fracture the civil compact that holds nations together.

Among the most encouraging aspects of the current regional environment is the express desire of all state actors to address the region's problems in a cooperative way and from a common perspective. Yet the experiential and institutional basis for regional cooperation is not yet mature enough to tackle effectively the range and magnitude of problems that beset the region. Also, the impetus for cooperation is restrained by concerns about the profound disparities in power among the region's nations as well as suspicions remaining from the recent wars.

For these reasons most security policy planning and implementation proceeds on a unilateral national basis. Although this circumstance is understandable given the present lack of robust cooperative security institutions and regimes, there always exists the danger that unilateral national policy will undermine the basis for regional cooperation. This concern need not assume ill will on the part of any player. Instead it reflects an appreciation for the ease with which nations can fall inadvertently into the security dilemma, whereby each pursues security in ways that 'beggar their neighbour's'. Extreme care must be taken, therefore, to ensure that each nation's posture (in its particulars) is consistent with and conducive to progress toward greater interstate trust, which is a necessary condition for any far-reaching cooperation. Direct cooperative initiatives—such as joint peace-keeping—are necessary but not sufficient. All aspects of military policy must meet a 'confidence-building' criteria.

In addition to problems related to the security dilemma, there are other ways that adherence to 'old era' military postures and policies could feed regional instabilities and undercut the broader goals of national strategy. For instance, in order to ameliorate the present sources of instability, which could give rise to military threats tomorrow, state resources must be redirected to development programmes. Maintaining 'old era' levels of military funding could pinch this necessary redirection of resources. Moreover, in light of the 1990-1991 Gulf War, military bureaucracies can be easily seduced by the putative promise of ambitious, high-tech manoeuvre warfare—even in those nations that lack the means to effectively employ or support such an approach and that have no urgent or immediate requirement to even try.

Another area of concern relates to ethnic conflict: many countries need to refashion their military organisations so that they neither reflect nor reinforce ethnic divisions and hierarchies, and so that they are less likely to fragment and feed ethnic conflicts. All of these concerns converge in a special requirement to further democratise the process of making security policy. This, because the recent regional-strategic revolution has made obsolete the basic axioms and imperatives that guided military policy since the end of the Second World War. The new era requires a new social consensus on military policy.

This chapter offers a summary of what is required for national military policy to meet the 'confidence-building' criteria. In addition, as an illustration of the kind of national military reform which would facilitate the emergence of regional security cooperation, the chapter specifies an option for restructuring the military of the region's leading economic and military power, the Republic of South Africa.

The primary requisite of effective security cooperation is international trust and confidence. This must be founded on stable regional military relations which, in turn, require stability measures at the level of national military policy, minimisation of imbalances between nations, and a viable institutional framework for multinational cooperation.

National Military Stability

Military stabilisation at the national level can be best achieved by an appropriate and affordable defence establishment and a sufficient, steadfast, and non-provocative defence posture. In addition, military structures must avoid contributing to the aggravation of existing or potential civil conflict.

An appropriate defence establishment is one that is suitable to the particular society it serves. In a region where the legacy of colonialism has frequently distorted the development of military organisations, nations should not imitate foreign structures, but rather build them in accord with the character of the nation and the skills of its people. Furthermore, if a nation's goals include economic renewal, democracy, social harmony, and international cooperation the norms and culture of the military establishment must reflect and reinforce these goals.

An affordable defence will achieve security within existing resource and demographic constraints. In the effort to meet affordability criteria, nations that are confident of their defensive intent can exploit the structural and operational efficiencies of a defensive orientation. These 'home court' advantages include the high morale of troops defending home territory, intimate knowledge of the terrain, shorter lines of supply and communication, and the opportunity to intensively prepare the likely zones of combat. The inherent efficiencies of a defensive orientation also make easier the reconciliation of the various confidence-building defence criteria: non-provocation, sufficiency, steadfastness, and affordability.

At this point in history most southern African nations are looking to spend less on defence and more on social and economic development; the consequence of this choice is that every defence expenditure must be considered in the context of a host of competing demands for resources. Notions of cost-effectiveness become foremost.

Sufficiency refers to how well a defence posture matches a threat matrix. The degree of 'match' involves both qualitative and quantitative aspects of the threat(s). To provide a context for the measure of sufficiency it is important to undertake a broad review of national objectives. This process will help specify what is to be protected and set the level of defence or deterrence certainty that a nation can or wishes to attain. Once objectives are clear, it is possible (although by no means easy) to determine military 'sufficiency.'

In many cases states will discover that they cannot hope to afford the highest degree of deterrence—which requires a transparent and assured capability to quickly and easily defeat any aggression. Furthermore, such a level of deterrence may also be provocative to neighbouring states, contributing to instability. However, lesser objectives may be in reach and desirable—for instance, a capacity to substantially raise the cost of any aggression and buy time for supportive intervention from allies.

A steadfast posture combines qualities of robustness and reliability. Robustness refers to the capacity of a defence array to absorb shock and suffer losses without undergoing catastrophic collapse; instead maintaining a cohesive combat capability. Even when facing an overwhelming level of threat, a robust defence force will degrade gracefully, buying time for regroupment, diplomatic intervention, or outside assistance. As a general rule a robust military posture will not exhibit an over-reliance on concentrated forces and base areas which provide lucrative targets for an enemy. Nor will it depend on a narrow set of technologies which an enemy could counter through a dedicated programme of innovation.

Reliability is the second aspect of steadfastness, and it refers to the capacity of the military to perform as planned with high confidence across a wide variety of 'environmental' circumstances. A reliable defence will avoid the security gamble implicit in 'high risk' operational plans and in dependence on immature or poorly integrated technologies. Reliability is also a function of social relations in the armed forces and the society and of the motivation and training of personnel.

A defence posture is regarded as non-provocative if it embodies little or no capacity for large-scale or surprise cross-border attack, and provides few, if any, high-value and vulnerable targets for an aggressor's attack. These guidelines pertain most strongly to the problem of crisis instability—periods of rising political tension during which the fear of and opportunity for pre-emptive attack may precipitate an otherwise avoidable military clash.

The non-provocation standard also addresses the larger issues of the security dilemma by seeking generally to reduce reliance on offensively-oriented military structures. In so doing it seeks to minimise the threat of aggression inherent in any organised armed force. Such threats often stimulate arms races and countervailing offensive doctrines. By bringing military structures into line with defensive political ends, the non-provocation standard aims to facilitate the emergence of positive political relations and trust among nations. In contrast, any doctrine and force posture which is oriented to project power into other countries is provocative unless reliably restrained by political and organisational structures. A notable negative example is the South African doctrine of 'forward defence' in which South Africa has aimed to fight its wars well north of its borders.

For countries that have experienced serious ethnic and political strife it is of great importance that the national security apparatus does not itself contribute to centrifugal forces.[1] Military functions must be depoliticised[2] and police functions should not be militarised. The composition of forces should reflect the ethnic balance of the nation as closely as possible. Full-time troops should generally serve nationally, while a greater proportion of part-time troops serve locally. Both full-time and part-time (national and local) forces should be thoroughly integrated and interdependent so that national civilian control can be assured even in times of great strain to national political consent.

Implementation of an effective confidence building defence must take into account context, international relations, and a process of optimisation. In considering context, significant portions of the southern African region are remote and sparsely populated. An area-covering force reliant primarily on infantry would require large numbers of troops, thus straining the affordability criteria. Therefore other means of achieving area coverage must be considered, such as infantry/artillery networks[3] mixing the range of artillery fires with relatively fewer infantry and light mechanised forces emphasising missions of reconnaissance and protection of key points and lines of communication.

Forces optimised for defence will nonetheless retain considerable offensive capability on the tactical level. And this capability may have strategic significance from the perspective of smaller neighbours. Thus planning must be sensitive to the provocative nature of many military options, particularly in cases of large asymmetries in power among nations. While recognising that defensive-restructuring on a national basis cannot by itself relinquish all offensive potential, planning options that minimise interstate tension and distrust[4] should be preferred.

The planning problems inherent in the simultaneous objectives of affordability, robustness, reliability, and non-provocation require astute attention to optimisation. An example may be found in planning for the future fighter force of the South African Air Force (SAAF). Currently the priority mission of the SAAF is ground attack—a key component of South Africa's 'forward defence' which seeks to interdict (even, pre-empt) enemy forces before they reach South African borders. By contrast, a confidence building strategy would emphasise control of home air space using air superiority fighters and ground based air defence. A problem presents itself in that South Africa's current inventory of supersonic fighters is not configured for an air superiority role. In the near term it would be very expensive—probably prohibitively so—to either reconfigure these fighters or to purchase a new fighter to fulfil this role. However, defensive restructuring could be achieved in an affordable way through a phased purchase of second-hand mid-life air superiority fighters available on the international market.[5]

Over the next ten years South Africa can replace the greater part of its current supersonic fighter fleet with two squadrons of all-weather air-superiority fighters with considerable life-cycle savings compared to the new aircraft option. In 2009 when the oldest of these jets are approaching the end of their useful lives, the process of modernisation could continue with phased purchase of a more modern air superiority fighter. By setting such a fighter acquisition course South Africa would clearly indicate that it intends to adopt a less provocative air posture, maintain a sufficient and robust fighter capability in the context of regional threats, and achieve these objectives in an affordable way. This illustrates the essence of confidence building optimisation.

Minimisation of Imbalances in the Region

Regional confidence building must take into account the large asymmetries in real and potential military power among states in the region. South Africa is a regional giant: it has four times the GDP and two times the defence expenditure of all other Southern Africa Development Community (SADC) members combined. In light of these realities, there can be no ignoring the hegemonic potential of South Africa. In this context smaller states should emphasise the affordability and robustness of their defence structures; it is beyond their means, individually or as a group, to match South Africa's potential. Smaller states can achieve affordability and robustness in the construction of their national defences by fully exploiting their "home advantages"—which include the opportunity to prepare their territory and infrastructure to support defensive operations. Modernisation must be very selective, avoiding tokens of technological status and instead looking for the occasional 'enabling' technologies that can multiply the effectiveness of the main forces. Moreover, proven technologies are more likely than "cutting edge" technologies to be consistent with the objective of a low risk, robust defence. The overall technological mix of the forces must be realistic in light of resource constraints and suited to the available labour pool. Although taking this course cannot guarantee the deterrence or defeat of large-scale aggression, it can significantly raise the cost to the aggressor and buy valuable time for the nation under attack.

In the case of South Africa, the emphasis should be on reducing its military dominance vis-à-vis other countries in the region while displaying enlightened leadership in cooperative endeavours to improve collective security. This affirmative choice is particularly important in light of South Africa's applied strategy of forward defence which included in the recent past the occupation and invasion of neighbouring countries. South Africa should reduce its active force to the minimum level consistent with meeting immediate threats and preserving the basis for expansion or reconstitution should future threats arise. In our judgement in the year 2001 a full-time force of 50,000 and a part-time force of 100,000 would suffice. This projected force (see the appendix to this chapter) would be about one-third smaller than the South African defence establishment currently plans. Mobilisation of the part-time force should emphasise generation of additional units optimised for defence, rather than strike formations.

Commensurate with the above, the end point of retrenchment and modernisation should be a general reduction in the proportion of strike assets in the force. The structure of long-ranging, mobile forces should reflect missions of patrol and control of areas and lines of communication rather than strike. This means placing lower priority in the force structure composition on highly-mobile protected fire assets such as armoured combat helicopters and tanks. In this approach the army's main standing combat units—elements of a rapid deployment force—would orient primarily toward control of border regions and secondarily toward reinforcement and force allocation tasks. For these missions a mixture of light and medium weight cavalry would be appropriate for the largest component. The air force should orient toward control of the national airspace, placing greater emphasis on air-superiority squadrons rather than fighter-ground attack squadrons. For the navy the primary mission would be extended off-shore surveillance and patrol, requiring minimal investment in new strike assets in the coming decade.

A dispersed home based network making maximum practical use of civilian resources is the most robust and cost-effective manner of organising logistical and medical combat service support. The current South African Medical Service is structured to support long-ranging military expeditions: this posture is unnecessarily expensive and provocative from the perspective of confidence building. Mobile combat and service support assets that are tasked for possible regional peacekeeping or humanitarian operations will, of course, require cross border mobility. Mobility assets should be firmly integrated into the structures of regional cooperative security. This will reassure states in the region that these assets will not be used for illegitimate interventions.

A South African nationalist might well assert that the new RSA has good intentions and no good reason to 'give away' military advantage vis-à-vis its neighbours. However, such a stance fails to appreciate that perceptions and capabilities are as important as intentions in building confidence. It is likely that a greater benefit will accrue to South Africa from secure, stable, and cooperative neighbours than from investment in large national forces well in excess of those needed for any realistic set of threats South Africa faces in the next fifteen years. And, it is a non-trivial effect that reduction of threat perception between nations in the region will make trust and cooperation easier to achieve on the political level.

A Multinational Framework for Cooperation

The future of regional security cooperation rests on the development of a well-resourced cooperative security institution, which could be founded on the already functioning SADC. This chapter does not attempt to specify the components or functions of such a future cooperative security organisation, but instead offers some guidelines for building an effective and stable framework.[6] The primary guideline is that the regional security organisation must endeavour to combine inclusivity with the authority and the capacity to act decisively. This will enable it to use force effectively while claiming legitimacy and also to restrain any particularistic national interests from overcoming multinational consensus. The regional security agency must also be able to draw upon an extensive resource base; having access to a broad range of instruments—political, economic, and military—as well as the resources needed for their decisive use is often a prerequisite for effective action of even a limited type. The credible possibility of escalation of means enables progress at lower levels of effort. The worst policy is to make empty threats, enact porous sanctions, or publicly air the option of military intervention only to quash it for lack of means or will.

It is also vital to prepare for crises well before their event. A particular crisis will likely elicit strong expressions of national interest from specific sets of states. Hence, attempting to resolve general issues of crisis management in the course and context of specific crises virtually guarantees opposition to appropriate principles and measures from some states that might otherwise join the consensus. For this reason, the development of general principles, procedures, and institutions must be vigorously pursued on its own and in a forum independent of and prior to crises.

Multinational participation in military operations should be balanced among participating countries with no one country dominating. Evolution toward multinational unit and command composition should be supported. In order to underwrite reassurance, legitimacy, and restraint, it is especially important that no one nation monopolise projection capabilities. In particular, strategic mobility capabilities should be structured in such a way that their effective exercise depends on multilateral cooperation. Planned roles for rapidly-deployable fighter/attack aircraft, elite paratroopers and special operations forces should be minimised and their composition and support made multinational. Instead, rapid deployment intervention forces should be optimised for peacekeeping or defensive support; both are roles suitable for light to medium weight ground forces. Although it is conceivable that heavier manoeuvre/assault forces drawn from several nations will be needed at some point to repel an aggressor, these should not be supported for rapid deployment. Instead regional security arrangements should rely on national forces (supplemented when needed by multinational defensive support forces[7]), to stop or slow an invader prior to a counter-offensive by later-arriving heavier forces. This approach is both in keeping with goals of regional reassurance and confidence building and with desirable objectives of cost-effective investments in regional strategic mobility assets.

Rather than maintain large forces 'earmarked' for regional interventions, wealthier nations should keep such forces modest in size and place a high priority on helping equip and finance dedicated regional security assets of poorer nations. Over time this will provide for greater equity of participation in regional security cooperation.

Reflecting on the foregoing guidelines it should be clear that achievement of a stable framework for cooperative regional military operations will take time, money, and leadership. In the near term, participation in humanitarian and traditional peacekeeping operations may be the most that is appropriate and affordable. A very different level of military force and institutional functioning is needed for conflict limitation missions (i.e. Somalia and Bosnia) and collective security interventions. Because successful operations of these more demanding types will only be possible after years of investment in cooperative institutional development, there is an ancillary benefit to be had in that nations need not invest in the *military requirements* of these missions in the meantime. Furthermore, premature investment in combat capabilities, especially if concentrated in one or two nations, will beggar the orderly development of an appropriate regional cooperative security institution.

In the end, the viability of cooperative security in the region is dependent on the development of trusting and stable relations among the nations in the region. This condition will not appear overnight, nor can there be any assurance that it will in the foreseeable future. Meanwhile a confidence building approach to national military policy can offer a defence posture that is cost-effective, low in risk, and stabilising both domestically and internationally. On such a foundation nations can extend confidence building principles to emergent regional cooperative arrangements. Such a course will maximise the probability of the emergence of full and equitable security cooperation at a future date.

Appendix: A Confidence-Building South African National Defence Force for the Year 2001

Overall Complement and Composition of the SANDF

Voluntary Full-time Force (FT), including 10,000 civilian personnel	50,000
Voluntary Part-time Force (PT)[8]	100,000
Total Strength on Mobilisation	150,000
Uniform Personnel	140,000

Army

Missions: Full time force: defence of national territory, participation in regional peacekeeping and humanitarian assistance.
Part time force: defence of national territory, border surveillance, rear area protection of objects and lines of communication.

Complement and Composition:
FT: 35,000 (including 5,500 civilians);
PT: 75,000.

Structure: Central command and control, logistics and training elements
- 1 Rapid Deployment Force HQ (FT) with
  - 1 light mechanised (cavalry) brigade (bde)
  - 4 mixed battalions (bns) (Rooikat and Ratel)
  - 1 multiple launch rocket (MLR) bn
- 1 airmobile bde[9] with
  - 2 infantry bns
  - 1 paratroop bn
  - 1 special ops bn
  - 1 engineer bn
- 1 artillery regiment with
  - 1 self-propelled bn (G-6)
  - 1 MLR bn
- 3 Regional HQs, each with:
  - 2 border bdes (each with three infantry bns transported on armoured personnel carriers)
  - 1 light mechanised bde
    - 3 inf bns—majority mounted on armoured infantry fighting vehicles (Ratel)
    - 1 cav bn—mounted on armoured reconnaissance vehicles (Eland) and infantry fighting vehicles (Ratel)

1 artillery regiment (towed—G5)
1 engineer regiment
45 area protection units.

Main equipment:

500 armoured reconnaissance vehicles (Rooikat and Eland)
700 armoured infantry fighting vehicles (Ratel)
900 armoured personnel carriers (Buffel, Casspir, and Mamba)
30 self-propelled howitzers (G-6)
70 towed howitzers (G-5)
130 MLRs (Bataleur)

Air Force

Missions: Control of national air space; defensive air defence; close air support of ground forces; reconnaissance/maritime patrolling; air lift of troops, supplies, and humanitarian aid; participation in peacekeeping missions.

Complement and Composition:

FT: 7,500 (including 2000 civilians)
PT: 10,000.

Structure: 1 Territorial Area Command (plus supporting elements)

1 full time air superiority (A/S) squadron,
1 part time fighter attack (F/A) squadron,
1 part time mixed fighter squadron[10]
1 squadron maritime patrol
3 squadrons heavy transport, tanker, electronic warfare
2 squadrons light/medium transport/liaison
1 full time squadron light/medium helicopter
3 part time squadrons light/medium helicopter

Main equipment:

20 air superiority fighters (new acquisition)[11]
28 fighter attack aircraft (Cheetah)
60 trainers (PC-7, Astra)
10 maritime patrol aircraft (new acquisition: custom outfitted civilian or second hand naval turboprop aircraft)
40 medium to heavy transport aircraft (C-130B, C-160, and C-47TP)[12]
70 medium helicopters (Oryx)
70 armed and unarmed light observation/liaison helicopters (Alouette, Dauphin, and new acquisition)

Navy

Missions: Offshore/oceanic area control; protection of natural resources/environmental monitoring; mine-clearing; search and rescue (SAR); participation in developmental regional maritime co-operative security.

Complement and Composition:
FT: 5,000 (including 1,500 civilians)
PT: 5,000

Structure: 2 half flotillas: area control
1 flotilla: mine countermeasures

Equipment:
3 3,000 ton extended offshore patrol vessels (new acquisition)[13]
3 400+ ton missile patrol vessels (Minister class)[14]
6 mine countermeasure craft (River and Kimberley class)
2 replenishment ships

Medical Service

Missions: Medical treatment of SANDF military personnel; humanitarian aid; participation in peacekeeping.

Complement and Composition:
FT: 2,500 (including 1,000 civilians)
PT: 10,000.

Structure: Less emphasis on (mobile) medical support of troops outside national territory; development of intensified cooperation with and reliance on civilian medical infrastructure.

Equipment:
Increased reliance on stationary (partially decentralised) infrastructure as a cost-effective and optimised environment for practice of modern medicine and application of medical technology.

Main Equipment Items Removed from Unit Assigned Inventory During Five Year Period[15]

250 tanks (Oliphant)

1200 armoured reconnaissance vehicles (Eland)
800 infantry fighting vehicles (Ratel)
700 armoured personnel carriers (Buffel and Casspir)
50 multiple launch rockets (Valkiri)
180 trainers/COIN aircraft (Impala I and II)
40 ground attack fighters (Mirage F-1)
40 medium and light helicopters (Puma and Alouette)
12 attack helicopters (Rooivalk)[16]
6 missile patrol vessels (Minister class)
3 submarines (Daphne class)
various V.I.P. aircraft (substitute civilian charters in the future)

Main Equipment Acquisition During Five Year Period

35 armoured reconnaissance vehicles (Rooikat)
35 armed and unarmed light observation/liaison helicopters
10 self propelled howitzers (G6)
20 air superiority fighters
10 maritime patrol aircraft
3 3,000 ton extended offshore patrol vessels

Affordable Defence: Budget

The long-term planning of the defence budget should reflect the country's investment priorities, while making sure that the forces have robust and well-maintained equipment, operated by well-motivated and trained personnel. The proposed posture would require for the year 2001 circa 7.5 Billion Rand (1995 constant Rand) for a peacetime operational level.

Components	Year 2001 (billion SAR)	Per cent	Year 1995 (billion SAR)	Per cent
Personnel[17]	3.00	40	3.56	34
Operations/Maintenance	1.88	25	3.46	33
Procurement/R&D	2.62	35	3.51	33
Total	7.50	100	10.53	100

Notes

1. See 'Issues of Internal Stability and Democracy', in Project on Defense Alternatives & Study Group on Alternative Security Policy: *Confidence-building Defense* (Cambridge, MA: Commonwealth Institute, 1994), pp. 101-116.
2. For a revealing account of how politicisation of the Iraqi military contributed to general failure of their air defence in both Gulf wars see Biddle, Stephen & Robert Zirkle: "Technology, Civil-Military Relations, and Warfare in the Developing World", paper presented at the American Political Science Association Annual Meeting, Washington, D.C., 3 September, 1993.
3. For a fuller description of an infantry/artillery network as a component of selective area-defence see Conetta, Carl, Charles Knight & Lutz Unterseher: "Toward Defensive Restructuring in the Middle East", *Project on Defense Alternatives Research Monograph*, no. 1 (Cambridge, MA: Commonwealth Institute, 1991), pp. 16-19.
4. The institutionalisation of confidence-building measures (CBMs) can normalise the exchange between states of doctrinal and defence planning information and provide forums for assessing regional impact of various national defence planning options. The notion of confidence building defence (CBD) includes most types of CBMs. But while CBMs emphasise matters of communication and procedure, confidence building defence pays particular attention to the impact of military structures and doctrines on confidence and stability.
5. Appropriate mid-life aircraft to consider, depending on availability and terms, include the Dassault-Breguet Mirage F-1C, the Saab Viggen JA37, and the General Dynamics Fighting Falcon F-16C. By purchasing mid-life aircraft South Africa can further benefit from the experience of other states proving new aircraft and from the likelihood of improvements to electronics/avionics being available at the time of South African acquisition. It should also be noted that moving from the Mirage family to the Saab family of fighters (Viggen/Gripen) might also have particular benefits for South Africa. Saab fighters are designed to operate from dispersed, rough landing strips and for storage in small dimension underground hangars-—both characteristics of optimisation for a defensive role.
6. Details of the institutional requirements for effective United Nations peace operations have been described in Conetta, Carl & Charles Knight: 'Vital Force. A Proposal for the Overhaul of the UN Peace Operations System and for the Creation of a UN Legion', *Project on Defense Alternatives Research Monograph*, no. 4 (Cambridge, MA: Commonwealth Institute, 1995). Many aspects of these requirements in scaled down proportions are applicable to a regional cooperative security agency.

7. Defensive Support forces are structured to rapidly reinforce the defences of a nation threatened by aggression. To allay concerns about regional domination by large powers, defensive support units should be structurally dependent on the overall defensive array of the host nation. This means that defensive support forces emphasise combat support missions such as: reconnaissance, surveillance, and target acquisition; rapid mine emplacement; air defence; artillery; anti-armour infantry; and communications. Although nations contributing defensive support forces to a co-operative security regime will want to maintain their independent capability to protect and withdraw forces, defensive support forces should be understood as specialised contributions to the host nation's defence rather than self-contained expeditionary forces.
8. Assumes substantial internal policing deployments are no longer necessary. If ongoing augmentation of the South African Police is necessary in 2001 force levels would have to be larger.
9. The soldiers of the airmobile brigade will receive special training for out-of-country peacekeeping missions, with the exception of the special operations battalion which normally would not participate in peace operations.
10. This mixed squadron would complete transition to an air superiority squadron by 2005.
11. These could be second hand fighters. Models to consider are the Dassault-Breguet Mirage F-1C, the Saab Viggen JA37, and the General Dynamics Fighting Falcon F-16C.
12. The SAAF transport fleet to be augmented by a civilian transport reserve programme similar to the U.S. CRAF program.
13. These could be new ships of indigenous civilian design and manufacture outfitted with a marine (SAR/ASW) helicopter(s) and with sensors/weaponry transferred from the retiring Minister class missile patrol boats. Another affordable option would be the purchase of small second-hand frigates.
14. By 2006 Minister class vessels would be replaced by 3000 ton extended offshore patrol vessels.
15. Some equipment removed from unit assignment would be scrapped, stored, transferred or sold immediately, others would be phased out. Numbers presented are derived from data in *The Military Balance 1995-1996*, The International Institute for Strategic Studies, London, 1995. IISS data do not consistently account for equipment in storage or inoperative for other reasons. Therefore some of this equipment may have already been withdrawn from service in the SANDF.
16. The Rooivalk is a recently developed indigenous model currently in production. However, this attack helicopter has no real place in the force structure and strategic posture proposed here. Although South Africa could include one squadron in its rapid deployment force, such a unit would add to the strike assets of the SANDF during a period in which confidence

building goals call for a relative reduction of strike assets. In addition, an attack helicopter squadron is a very expensive military asset to operate and maintain. South Africa would likely be better off placing this holdover from a discarded offence-oriented defence strategy in storage. Any emergent threat that would warrant activation of these aircraft would develop with sufficient warning to allow for training of crews in combat manoeuvre support operations.

17. Relative to the historic pattern of SADF budgets there is a greater weighting on personnel. This is due to a greater percentage of the force serving full-time. In addition to the increased salary costs of a more professional military, the relative share of maintenance costs will decrease as large amounts of obsolete, maintenance-intensive equipment that outfitted the larger part-time force of the past is phased out of inventory.

6 A Postmodern Military: Mission Redefinition and Defensive Restructuring

ROCKLYN WILLIAMS

The political and strategic environment in Southern Africa has vastly changed since the late 1980s. The end of the Cold War, the unfolding of what is, in retrospect, a remarkable transition in South Africa, and the optimistic emergence of new democracies elsewhere in the Southern African region, are key indicators of this trend. The armed forces, as with other actors and institutions in society, are themselves undergoing a process of dramatic and intense strategic, cultural and normative transition in the light of these factors. Virtually no arena is spared the embrace of this transition be it civil-military relations, strategy, doctrine, force design and posture.

National Defence Posture, in particular, has been the subject of considerable debate in recent years. Configured around a strong offensive profile, it is now called upon by the Constitution, the Defence White Paper and the policy perspectives of the dominant party to be 'primarily defensive' in its posture and orientation. This could, theoretically, be seen on a sliding scale anywhere between a high tactical offensive threshold on the one hand, to a totally defensive threshold on the other.

This chapter examines the question of defence posture through the lens of non-offensive defence (NOD) and argues that a much higher premium needs to be placed on defensive mechanisms and strategies for a variety of political reasons. The political and economic realities of the Southern African region, the exigencies of the present policy environment, and the 'logic' of emerging South African civil-military relations, impel defence planners towards a much more serious consideration of defensive strategies than has hitherto been the case. However, it also indicates that a totally defensive posture in the 'purist' and absolute sense of the word is not possible in the short-to-medium term in South Africa for political and practical reasons.

What Is A South African Defence Force For?

Perhaps it would be a moot point to examine the nature of conflict in the late 20th century in general and the forms it assumes in Sub-Saharan Africa in particular.

Conflict within this scenario translates itself mostly, and with very few exceptions, into intra-state conflict either between opposing political or civil groups, or between the central government and secessionist or guerilla movements. The determination of roles, missions and tasks, and the planning and design of force structures for the armed forces in these contingencies is, thus, a very different conceptual and practical exercise to planning for classic threats.

Indeed, it is precisely in these arenas that the present SANDF finds itself deployed: an increasing internal stability role, maintenance of forces to protect the authority of the civil power from unconstitutional attack (be it guerilla or secessionist styled), protection of the country's borders against drug smuggling, arms smuggling, stock theft, and isolated acts of banditry. Yet the notion of a classic modernist defence force, configured to protect the country against an external conventional threat, continues to reign supreme in the minds of the SANDF planners and strategists.

A more realistic approach would be the design of multi-functional forces that are capable of executing a wide range of identified roles for which they are specifically budgeted and designed. The 'balance' of these forces should be determined by precisely those roles and functions which a specific Defence Force is required to execute in its specific environment.

The dominant thinking within the South African defence community acknowledges that a real tension appears to be developing between the likelihood of executing the primary functions (increasingly remote) and the urgency of participating in the secondary functions (an existing and increasingly pressing reality). However, the orthodox answer to this dilemma by defence planners is provided by a response familiar to most modern strategists namely: 'We design and budget for the primary function and we execute the secondary functions with the collateral utility derived from our primary force design'.

Apart from the fact that historical evidence tends to militate against the retention of armed forces only configured for their primary role (notwithstanding nervous protestations from defence planners regarding 'insurance policies' and the like), political realities, following fast on the heels of fact, seem to be suggesting likewise. President Mandela in his opening address to parliament in 1996 praised the armed forces for their involvement in the internal stability, their success in handling the integration process and their involvement in the region—not once mentioning their role in preserving territorial integrity and sovereignty.[1]

Parliamentarians and the Treasury support the allocation of scarce funds to the Defence Force on the basis of the secondary tasks it can execute. They appear increasingly reluctant to release monies for the maintenance of forces that do nothing else but train for a hypothetical enemy. Increasingly the South African Department of Defence feels compelled to justify its role in light of its contribution to the Growth and Development Strategy—a justification that sees its emphasis on its traditional brief receding.

It seems likely, therefore, that the armed forces of the future will be increasingly configured around non-traditional roles and secondary functions, and that these roles will encompass regional security, peace operations, internal stability (with the latter eventually being taken over by the police), protection of the civil power against unconstitutional action, border protection, and maritime protection. Although forces will be maintained for preservation of territorial integrity and sovereignty, these will tend more towards cheaper, lighter and less technologically sophisticated forces with a strong emphasis on reservist and part-time components. The resulting national defence posture will, almost certainly, undergo the following changes:

- A shift away from the primary function towards the secondary functions in terms of planning, budget and force design.
- A shift from a force that has a strong offensive conventional posture towards a defence force increasingly configured towards more defensive secondary roles.
- The retention by the force of a relatively high level of operational manoeuvrability and mobility given the low force-to-space ratio within the country and the region, and the inevitability of extensive involvement in regional (and possibly international) peace support operations. The retention of this range, while not equatable with the offensive capabilities of the present force, will equip a future force with a tactical offensive capability. Limiting the extent of this capability within the present constitutional provision for a force that is 'primarily defensive' will be examined in great detail below.

It is within this broader framework that theories of defensive restructuring and NOD should be situated. The reconfiguration of the roles, missions and tasks of the armed forces will invariably, and decisively, impact upon the National Defence Posture of the armed forces and the nation.

NOD and South Africa: Reviewing Policy Positions

In light of the strong defensive orientation of South Africa's major policy documents, surprisingly little has been written on NOD in an academic context. That which has been written has remained either strongly normative in content stressing why NOD 'ought' to be introduced without providing detailed analysis,[2] or has largely attempted to apply European NOD principles to an African environment,[3] or has concentrated on the regional dynamics of NOD without detailing force design and strategic implications.[4]

However, the principles of NOD remain explicitly and implicitly pronounced within the policy positions of both South Africa and the Region. The following demonstrate South Africa's orientation:

• The Interim Constitution calls on the Defence Force to 'be primarily defensive in the exercise or performance of its power and functions' (227.1f).
• The Draft White Paper on Defence similarly states that the Defence Force shall be 'primarily defensive' in posture, doctrine and orientation.[5]
• The ANC's guidelines as the ruling party, contained in 'Ready to Govern', makes a stronger call for the Defence Force to be 'defensive in orientation, posture and strategy'.
• The Joint Military Coordinating Council agreement reached by all armed forces and their political principals signatory to the military integration process reflects similar principles:

> • Strategically Defensive but operationally and tactically offensive.
> • The RSA will promote common and mutual security in the region through mutual confidence and trust.
> • Conflict shall be resolved primarily by diplomatic means.
> • To discourage an arms race.
> • To strive to enhanced shared responsibility for regional security and regional co-operation.
> • To promote and play a role as a deterrent force for the region.
> • To participate in regional and international peace support operations.
> • South Africa will adopt a non-threatening force structure in relationship to the region.
> • The Reconstruction and Development Programme and the Growth and Development Strategy stress the importance of socio-economic development and political stability to the growth of both the country and the region. Indeed, the ethos of the RDP remains solidly situated within the framework of 'new thinking on security'.

Within South Africa, this defensive policy orientation is the product of an amalgam of factors. The first is the political culture of the ruling party, the African National Congress (ANC). Historically, the ANC has been strongly influenced by the principles of both Ghandian passive resistance, with its emphasis on non-violent forms of struggle, as well as exhibiting a strong Christo-centric value system. The former was vividly demonstrated in the passive resistance campaigns of the early 1960s and the Defiance Campaign of the 1950s—traditions which were to resurface again in the 1980s with the emergence of the United Democratic Front. The latter was partially a product of the fact that the early ANC, in some senses, grew out of the churches, with many of its founding members being religious leaders.

Secondly, both liberation movements, the ANC and PAC (Pan-Africanist Congress), were based largely in Southern Africa prior to their unbanning. Their facilities in Angola, Zambia, Botswana, Mozambique and Zimbabwe were frequently attacked by former SADF forces. In addition the countries within which they were based were extensively destabilised by repeated SADF incursions into their territories and the ongoing activities of rebel groupings such RENAMO and UNITA. The effects of destabilisation on the Southern African region were vividly manifest to a generation of leaders who, upon their return to senior positions within the South African body-politic were acutely conscious of the need for development, cooperation and mutual security within the region.

Thirdly, most major groupings in civil and political society in the post-1990 negotiation period supported the necessity of expanding the definition of security to incorporate a range of non-military factors in its ambit. The root causes of insecurity were seen to be primarily non-military by nature—unemployment, poverty, underdevelopment, lack of democratic participation etc. (as reflected in the RDP document). The military component of security was seen as ancillary and subordinate to this broader strategy, and the role it played was supportive to this process of political and socio-economic development.

Fourthly, the politics of negotiation and compromise lends itself towards a consensual resolution of disputes. The very values upon which NOD is premised-—tolerance, confidence-building, dialogue and transparency—provided the normative framework for the South African transition and continue to provide the normative basis for the Interim Government of National Unity. The cultural and ethical predisposition of the present political culture, therefore, inclines in the direction of NOD-type solutions.

NOD and the Region: Regional Security and Confidence Building

A high degree of political and normative unity existed within the Southern African region prior to the results of South Africa's non-racial and democratic elections in April 1994. Largely this was due to the debilitating effects of South Africa's dominance of the region and the coordinated response required to counter this hegemony. Partially this was due to the common political histories of the countries of the region—most were British colonies and had travelled similar roads in their respective struggles for independence.

Concepts of common security thus emerged as a result of a number of initiatives in the region. The Frontline States grouping established in the 1970s was an informal regional grouping that sought to promote and strengthen regional security in the wake of South Africa's repeated forays. When SADC was established in 1992 it provided for seven areas of cooperation, including peace and security. The 1993 SADC 'Framework and Strategy for Building the Community' called for the adoption of a 'new approach to security' which would include, amongst others, the adoption of non-offensive defence doctrines.[6] Subsequent meetings of SADC in July 1994 and early 1995 reaffirmed this commitment to a more defensive posture for the region:

Concepts of demilitarisation and non-offensive defence were inherent, if not explicitly spelt out, in these proposals: for example, the ministers recommended that 'in view of the reduced tensions in the region, military force levels and expenditure should be reduced to the minimum level required for territorial defence'.[7]

These principles were to receive concrete expression with the establishment of the Inter-State Defence and Security Committee (ISDSC) in 1995 on which all SADC member states are represented. The ISDSC is divided into ten sub-committees dealing with operational, intelligence, aviation, medical and related areas. The responsibility of these committees is to investigate, recommend and coordinate activities on a wide range of issues including cross-border crime, illegal immigration, peace support operations and intelligence sharing. These committees are fully functioning and meet on a regular basis.

At a political level both South Africa and the region make for fertile ground within which the principles and practice of NOD can be nourished. The policy dynamics of the 'New South Africa', the letter and spirit of regional cooperation, and the urgent imperatives of socio-economic development and regional reconstruction confirm this observation. However, the extent to which this reality is compatible with the emerging defence-related needs of the country is examined in further depth below.

Civil-military Relations in the Post-1994 Period

All debates concerning the review of present South African defence posture will have to take cognisance of a salient reality: ultimate power and decision-making in this regard resides in parliament. Civil-military relations during the pre-1990 period were characterised by the high level of militarisation in the executive, the lack of transparency with regard to national defence matters, and the exclusion of civil society from the policy decision-making process. The emergence of F.W. De Klerk as President in 1989 witnessed a partial civilianisation of the executive and heralded a move towards the liberalisation of the political process as demonstrated by the initiation of negotiations and the unbanning of the liberation movements.

The post-election period has witnessed the robust emergence of both political and civil society as the major players within the political process. A vivid phenomenon of the transition has been the real shift in power from the executive to the legislature. Nowhere is this more manifest than in the parliamentary committees where the departments of state are held accountable for their budgets, their policies and their actions.

The influence of the Joint Standing Committee on Defence and the Portfolio Committee on Defence will play a major role in determining the final outcome of the defence posture debate. More than three quarters of the Joint Standing Committee on Defence consists of ANC members who have, on a number of occasions, committed themselves to the principles of defensive orientation as outlined in their party's policy guidelines. The decisions of the Committee on the posture to be adopted by the National Defence Force will, in effect, be the deciding factor in determining which variant of posture will prevail.

Equally significantly, and in keeping with the new ethos of transparency and accountability within the national political debate, has been the convening by the Ministry of Defence of a National Consultative Defence Review Process. The aim of the Defence Review is to determine, in a consultative manner, the defence needs of the country, the strategies whereby these can be accomplished and the resources required to equip defence in the future. A wide range of actors from parliament, political society, the state and civil society are involved in the process and the intention is to produce a medium to long-term review of defence needs which is consistent with the electorate's sentiments in this regard. The outcome of this process will have a critical impact on the structure, strategy, force design and budgetary implications of the defence force of the future.

Already the Defence Review has made pronouncements on posture as reflected in a separate chapter entitled 'Defence Posture and Doctrine'. The main tenets of this chapter include the following:

> The doctrine of the SANDF should therefore reflect the international prohibition on acts of aggression; the exercise of the right to self-defence in a manner which is consistent with international law; a defensive posture at a strategic level; and the employment of the SANDF as a measure of last resort.
>
> The policy of non-aggression and the constitutional commitment to international law, which outlaws the initiation of armed hostilities by states, preclude the option of pre-emptive strike. Counter-offensive action against an attack, however, is a legitimate exercise of the right of self-defence.
>
> In the light of the above, the doctrine of the SANDF will be based on a strategic defensive posture with sufficient capabilities to protect military and economic assets against offensive action by an aggressor. Further, capabilities to reverse the effects of offensive actions are required. The SANDF must be able to halt, contain, and roll back such actions. Accordingly, appropriate offensive capabilities will be required at an operational level.
>
> This approach will be completed in times of conflict by government spelling out clearly the threshold for offensive action by the SANDF. In practice this may take the form of appropriate exclusion zones or similar mechanisms[8].

At the time of going to press, a heated debate was taking place between the parliamentary defence committee and the South African Department of Defence over the inclusion of the clause that ruled out the right of pre-emptive strike. The parliamentary committee was overwhelmingly inclined in favour of retaining the clause, whilst the Department of Defence maintained that ruling out a pre-emptive strike option limited the SANDF unduly, and that the decision to use a pre-emptive strike should rather be the prerogative of the Commander-in-Chief on the basis of the information he/she had at his/her disposal in a particular situation.

Not to be ignored is the new government's Growth and Development Strategy which commits itself to ensuring growth, employment and social services for the country's population. Defence has been targeted as an obvious avenue via which funding for reconstruction and development can be secured. In the face of a declining budget, the defence force's capacity to maintain relatively sophisticated offensive options may be limited.

South African Defence Strategy and Structure At Present

As outlined in the Constitution the posture of the National Defence Force is primarily defensive and it may be employed for six possible functions: preservation of territorial integrity and sovereignty; for service in compliance with international obligations; for service in preservation of life, health and property; for service in the maintenance of essential services; for service in upholding law and order, and for service in support of any department of state for purposes of socio-economic upliftment.

In terms of the JMCC agreements outlined above, the Defence Force remains strategically defensive but operationally offensive. In addition to its territorial and rear area protection responsibilities, its offensive threshold remains high and it must possess deep interdiction capabilities. The operational strategy of the Defence Force, therefore, reflects a synthesis of defensive and offensive components. An overview of the strategies and force structures of the respective Arms of Service confirms this observation.

The SA Army's role in Territorial Defence and Mobile Operations

The mission of the SA Army is defined as the rendering of landward military services to the RSA. In addition to standard support elements (HQ, Support and Training institutions) which provide both static and mobile support to the Army, its structure consists of the following:

- A rapid deployment force: This consists of both an airborne and ground component both of which have the responsibility for neutralising any enemy threat within or without the country's borders. The Force consists of a mixture of mechanised infantry, parachute, motorised infantry, armour, artillery and support elements (engineers, signals, maintenance units etc). Its functions include holding and capture of ground, launching of pre-emptive strikes, conducting mobile defence and conducting major offensive operations.
- A special forces brigade consisting of three Special Forces units specialising in landward and amphibious special operations.
- Three part time force divisions consisting of one operational division and two reserve divisions with the responsibility of acting as the primary mobile force for the land battle. The responsibility of these mobile forces are to act as the second line of conventional defence after the RDF and to reinforce

forces already committed to the land battle. Equipment possessed by the division includes artillery regiments, anti-aircraft regiments, mechanised infantry battalions, motorised infantry battalions, armour regiments and standard support units.

• Territorial forces entrusted with the responsibility for providing rear area protection services within their various areas of responsibility. Their responsibilities include the provision of reaction forces that can, amongst others, ensure the safeguarding of the local population, the protection of the country's borders and the protection of national key points. Units are light motorised infantry equipped with armoured personnel carriers and flatbed trucks.[9]

From an appraisal of the South African Army it is evident that it possesses a combination of both offensive and defensive capabilities. The role of its Territorial Forces are similar, in many respects, to the 'spider-in-the-web' model of the Study Group Alternative Security Policy.[10] The forces are, however, much lighter than the 'spider-in-the-web' model, are geographically more dispersed, and do not possess the anti-amour and artillery capabilities referred to in the model. In the Mobile Forces, the Rapid Deployment Force and the Special Force Brigade, the Army possesses limited offensive capabilities (most probably not in excess of 400-500km beyond the RSA borders), with a relatively high tactical offensive threshold. The equipment utilised by the Army is mostly mobile including both combat and support items, has a flexible logistic system, and possesses ranges of anything between 250km for the Olifant Tank to 1,000 km for the Ratel ICV series. Furthermore, the Mobile, RDF and Special Forces complements are not dependent on the Territorial Force network for logistical support allowing them considerable manoeuvrability in the field (the Ratel Logistic system, for instance, can support both mechanised infantry and armour for up two weeks over ranges of approximately 2,000kms).[11]

The South African Air Force: Light Offensive Capabilities?

The South African Air Force has seen considerable reductions in both its equipment and force levels during the 1990s. At present the SAAF administers two main fighter bases and five permanent bases administering some 36 squadrons and related flying institutions.

The two main fighter bases are 1 Squadron located at Hoedspruit consisting of Mirage F1AZ (strike fighters with a secondary air-to-air role), and 2 Squadron located at Louis Trichardt consisting of Cheetahs (a mid-life update of the Mirage 11CZ and EZ fighters). In addition 8 Squadron at Blomefontein consists of Impala MKII which are used in a light attack role (30mm cannons and capacity of up to 1 814kg bombs or rocket pods). In addition the SAAF possesses in-flight refuelling capabilities in the form of Boeing aircraft.

Apart from its fighter capabilities, the SAAF possesses a number of helicopter squadrons consisting of a mixture of Oryx medium helicopters and Alouette light helicopters based in Natal, the Western Cape and the Northern Transvaal. It also possesses air transport squadrons (C130, C160 and Dakotas) which have considerable range within and without the RSA. In addition to these capabilities the SAAF also has an electronic signal intelligence capability in the form of Boeing 707 aircraft. On analysis it appears that the SAAF has a light offensive fighter role and possesses considerable range with regard to its transport fleet. Although not overwhelmingly offensive, it possesses a definite tactical offensive capability.

The South African Navy: Defensive by Default?

The Navy is the smallest of the Arms of Service and has been the victim of budgetary neglect since the 1970s. Its major systems include the following:

- The Strike Craft Flotilla : nine strike craft (six of which are maintained in the cycle) equipped with surface-to-surface missiles and a variety of other guns. The range of the strike craft are, at economical speed, 5,800km.
- The Submarine Flotilla consisting of three Daphne class submarines with a snorkling range of 7,200kms.
- The Mine Counter Measures Flotilla consisting of four mine counter-measures vessels, three hunters and one sweeper.
- Independent vessels consisting of one hydrographic vessel, and two combat support replenishment vessels.

The Navy thus possesses considerable range in terms of all vessels although armaments are light in comparison.

The South African Medical Services: Field Support for the Arms of Service

Unlike most modern militaries, the SANDF possesses an additional Arm of Service known as the South African Medical Service. Established in 1981, the SAMS is responsible for providing centralised military medical facilities to all Arms of Service. Although largely a support service, and although not inherently capable of independent offensive action, many of the SAMS function have been configured to provide support to mobile operations over long distances.

This manoeuvrability is reflected in its operational medical support capability. It supports the ground forces of the Rapid Deployment Force via its Medical Rapid Deployment Force organisation, and both the airborne RDF and the Special Force Brigade with a Special Medical Battalion Group. The Part Time Forces Division is supported by different Citizen Force Medical Battalion Groups.

Can Non-offensive Defence Be Applied in South Africa?

South Africa constitutes a ripe environment for the application of NOD at many levels. This is testified to by the following:

- The emerging regional ethos which is premised on cooperation, development, mutual security and non-threatening defence postures. This is reflected formally, in the various policy positions and deliberations of SADC, and informally, in the common history and shared values of the region itself.
- The emerging civil-military relations in the country which ensure that the armed forces are not only subordinate to elected government, but that defence needs are commensurate with the requirements of the country.
- A declining defence budget which limits the ability of the armed forces to invest in and purchase sophisticated weapons systems and equipment.
- A policy environment that inclines towards the strengthening of the defensive component of national defence posture.
- A likely shift towards secondary functions in light of the requirements of the country, the region and the continent and the consequent de-emphasis on the primary function.
- The fact that, contrary to the opinions of many military planners, South Africa possesses sufficient strategic depth within which a defensive posture could be established. It should be born in mind in this regard that strategic depth refers to a range of factors in addition to physical distance that include geography, exploitation of terrain, and dispersal of forces.

However, certain factors could well militate against the adoption of a NOD posture including the following:

- Notwithstanding the likely emphasis which will be placed on secondary functions in the future, the armed forces are still constitutionally mandated to provide for the defence of the territorial integrity and sovereignty of the nation. Large areas of the country (the West Coast and the Northern Cape for instance) are characterised by an exceedingly low force-to-space ratio which is exacerbated by the under-populated nature of the countries adjacent to it: Namibia and Botswana. It could be argued that a limited tactical offensive capability is necessary in order to secure these borders.
- Countries of the Southern African region have made repeated requests to South Africa for assistance in various defence and defence-related fields. An evident example in this regard is the question of maritime assistance, most notably assistance in fisheries protection. Honouring these and other commitments will require the maintenance of forces which have considerable range and manoeuvrability.

• A similar argument pertains to South Africa's involvement in peace operations. It is highly likely, and is already emerging, that South Africa will provide the bulk of the logistic and support requirements for regional peace initiatives and for regional involvement in peace operations. Yet again the defence force will require equipment with range and operational manoeuvrability.

• The costs to the defence force to reconfigure its force design will be considerable, particularly if investments in anti-air capabilities and early-warning and surveillance systems is made. Relocating bases, particularly Air Force bases, further into the hinterland will be unrealistic.

• Much will depend on the leadership role which the country assumes explicitly within the region and the continent. If it is to be an assertive profile, committed to the development of the region and the protection of its interests, the country will require forces that are, to a certain extent, both commensurate with this vision and acceptable to the region as a whole. It is probable, therefore, that these forces will require reach, range and the operational capabilities required to project this influence.

From these considerations a number of options can be derived, which are briefly outlined below.

Considering Options for a South African National Defence Posture

A number of options with regard to the possible institution of NOD models within the South African context are considered in this section. Considerable work still needs to be done in this area particularly at the level of force design, doctrinal implications, and human resource implications. For purposes of practicality certain extreme options—the 'no army' scenario and the highly offensive model for example—have been excluded from this overview. The models referred to below use South Africa's present force design as a basis. Three variants in the models can be discerned: those with a strong domestic defensive orientation which is configured around domestic roles and tasks, those with a strong regional orientation in terms of their roles and tasks, and those models that combine both regional and domestic responsibilities.

It is important to draw a distinction at this stage between the offensive capabilities which a particular force design may possess and the operational manoeuvrability of that force design. Operational manoeuvrability is not synonymous with offensive capability and there is a level at which the two should be decoupled. The following example is pertinent in this regard. An air force transport fleet may, hypothetically, possess a range of 6,000 km. This would equip the force in question with the ability to transport personnel and material over vast distances. The ability of the force to maintain offensive operations within these areas, however, depends on its logistical ability, its equipment and the training of its personnel.

The 'Core Force' Options

The 'Core Force' options derive from a consideration of the concept of the 'Core Force' as proposed by the Department of Defence within the 1996 Defence Review (see Appendix A). The 'Core Force' argues for a 'balanced' force capable of executing a wide range of tasks in response to a variety of contingencies.

The first option that requires consideration relates to the present concept of the 'Core Force': the maintenance of those capabilities that are required to execute present responsibilities, whilst also maintaining those core capabilities that can, with appropriate warning, be expanded into a War Force if required. The Core Force basically proposes the maintenance of the present SANDF with some alterations—strengthening the SAAF fighter capabilities and acquisition of corvettes for instance. It remains predicated on the roles and missions as outlined in the Constitution and accords with the strategy as outlined in the JMCC. The 'Core Force' proposes that the Defence Force be configured around its primary capabilities: the basis upon which the SANDF will execute its functions of peace support operations: the maintenance of law and order in cooperation with the SAPS, disaster relief and other tasks is its conventional capabilities. The Core Force envisages the following:

- Intelligence capabilities to ensure early warning against possible risks and threats.
- Strategic interdiction capabilities to impair enemy efforts including fighter aircraft with appropriate reach, in-flight refuelling, surface combatants, submarines, and special and air mobile forces.
- Landward defence capabilities to counter conventional attacks from overland. These forces should be highly mobile and largely self-contained.
- Landward defence capabilities to counter special operations over international borders. Such capabilities should provide coverage and area defence.
- Area defence capabilities to counter air attacks, including both fighter capabilities to strike against launching sites and bases, as well as localised anti-aircraft defence capabilities.
- Maritime defence capabilities to counter attacks from seaward and attacks on seaward trade including mine clearance capabilities and capabilities to act against air, surface and submarine attacks.
- Command and control capabilities commensurate with the above.
- Support capabilities including operational medical support and air and sea transport capabilities as well as logistics, personnel and training capabilities.
- Such other capabilities as decided by the executive for defined secondary functions.

In relationship to the region it is clear that the Core Force remains offensive at the operational level. Few, if any, of the region's armed forces can match the Core Force with regard to its cross-border offensive capabilities. Indeed in terms of sheer size and force levels, the Core Force remains a formidable opponent in the region. It does, however, possess strong defensive elements as outlined in its emphasis on area protection.

The second option is a hypothetical option and consists largely of the 'Core Force' concept with the following distinguishing features:

- It is strongly defensive in design and orientation as demonstrated by its Territorial Defence role.
- It possesses a tactical offensive capacity to strike beyond the country's borders given the low force-to-space ration in the border areas and adjacent countries although this is limited to a 200km-300km range.
- Its peace support operation capability is 'meshed' into the regional security structures and agreements that are emerging within the region thereby reducing the capacity for South Africa to use this force independently of the region.

This model is premised on the retention of a strong defensive element in force design, the commitment of the force to an increased regional role—but a role that is characterised by its interdependence on and close configuration with the other forces of the region, and the maintenance of a cross-border offensive capability that is justified in terms of the low force-to-space ratio in certain areas of the country. Weaponry is suitably configured with less of a reliance on certain weapon types: medium battle tanks, in-flight refuelling capabilities and submarines for instance.

'Pure' NOD options

Option 1 is strongly defensive in orientation with a regional peace support operations commitment. Its features are:

- Totally defensive in strategy with no offensive capabilities beyond the country's borders.
- The application of a selective area defence to compensate for the non-existence of a tactical offensive capability in certain parts of the country (Northern Cape for example). In areas that are characterised by low force-to-space ratios, judicious use of strategic depth and defence-in-depth is utilised.
- A regional peace operations commitment that is entrenched in regional security structures. This is similar to the revised Core Force option.
- Continued use of the armed forces in secondary functions. This option allows for the maintenance of a purely defensive capability, whilst allowing

the force the ability to fulfil its regional and international commitments.

Option 2 is a variation on Option 1 and consists of a totally defensive posture, with selective area defence, involvement in secondary functions and no involvement in peace operations.

Option 3 is the 'purest' of the NOD options in that it argues for a totally defensive function with total area coverage and no involvement in either peace operations or secondary missions.

The Regional Option

The Regional option argues for the adoption of totally defensive postures by all countries of the region but the maintenance of a limited operational offensive capability to deter would-be aggressors to the region. This would entail substantial interdependence and cooperation within and amongst all forces of the region. Whilst all participating states would possess defensive postures, the combined posture of the region to external adversaries would be offensive (although the level of offensive would depend on the combined capabilities of the forces and the political intentions of the region).

Conclusion

It is evident that much detailed thought and planning needs to be given to the question of South Africa's national defence posture and the extent to which this is reflected in doctrine, force structure, force design and force levels. Whilst it is unlikely that South Africa will adopt a totally defensive posture in the NOD sense of the word, it is clear that the emerging political realities within both South Africa and the region will require a revision of fundamental aspects of South Africa's offensive capabilities. Such a redefinition will have to take account of South Africa's regional responsibilities and profile, its legitimate defence interests and the practical and fiscal realities of reconfiguring force design.

It seems almost certain, and is indeed desirable, that South Africa's future armed forces retain a high level of mobility and operational flexibility. This is a reality dictated by the exigencies of the African operational environment. It also appears likely that the South African armed forces will increasingly find themselves inter-linked via a series of regional security arrangements with the armed forces of the region. This 'meshing' of South African military capabilities with those of the region (a process that will develop incrementally) will make the adoption of an operationally offensive posture by South Africa increasingly difficult to justify.

Whilst neither the provisions of the Interim Constitution nor fiscal realities allow for the adoption of a totally defensive posture, it is clear that regional and domestic political realities will impel the South African armed forces towards a more defensively oriented posture than has been the case either historically or currently.

The present debate concerning the application of NOD models to the South African environment have largely been confined to the level of principle and theory. Indeed the intellectual debate concerning posture has, until recently, been dominated by traditional schools of argument which have somewhat uncritically posited offensive theories as being the only postures worthy of serious military consideration. Considerable work, therefore, needs to be done in order to ensure that NOD and related defensive approaches are operationalised in such a manner that they not only stimulate defence debate, but also assist defence planners in determining a defence posture that is capable, credible, affordable and consistent with both South Africa and the region's requirements.

Notes

1. 'President's Address to Parliament', Cape Town, 9 February 1996.
2. Nathan, Laurie: *Changing the Guard* (Pretoria: Human Sciences Research Council Publishers, 1995).
3. See the following in this regard: Williams, Rocklyn: 'The Institutional Restructuring of the South African Armed Forces', *Strategic Review for Southern Africa*, vol. 15, no. 2 (November 1993).
4. Cawthra, Gavin & Mohlolo Siko: 'South Africa: Prospects for Non Offensive Defence in the Context of Regional Security', in *NOD & Conversion*, no. 33 (1995), pp. 18-25.
5. 'Draft White Paper on Defence' (Pretoria, 31 January 1996).
6. Cawthra & Siko: *loc. cit.*
7. *ibid.*
8. *Defence Review* (1996), pp. 13-14.
9. 'The National Defence Force in Transition', *Annual Report*, Financial Year 1994/95 (Military Printing Unit, 1995).
10. SAS & PDA (Project on Defense Alternatives): *Confidence-building Defense. A Comprehensive Approach to Security and Stability in the New Era. Application to the Newly Sovereign States of Europe* (Cambridge, MA: PDA, Commonwealth Institute, 1994).
11. 'The National Defence Force in Transition', *loc. cit.*

7 Defence Restructuring for the South African Navy: Uncharted Waters

ROBERT W. HIGGS

South Africa is strategically situated at the tip of Africa, abutting three oceans yet also part of the Indian Ocean Rim, the South Atlantic Rim and the Southern Ocean[1] down to the Antarctic. In addition, South Africa is suitably positioned to influence events along the Cape Sea Route, whose significance fluctuates in proportion to the perceived reliability of the Suez Canal, which remains a major East-West passage.

South Africa has a coastline of some 3,000 km which spawns four major and three lesser ports. These ports serve the South African economy as well as the economies of her landlocked neighbours. 95 per cent of South Africa's imports and exports in terms of tonnage, or 80 per cent in terms of value pass through South African ports. More than fifty per cent of South Africa's GDP is generated through its maritime foreign trade and sea fishing industry.[2] Currently, the sea as a source of riches including minerals and protein is becoming more contested.[3]

South Africa's history over the past 500 years has been significantly influenced by foreign powers by way of the sea. Towards the end of the 15th century Portuguese explorers discovered the sea route to India via the southern tip of Africa. In the 17th century the Dutch established and maintained a half-way replenishment station at the Cape using Dutch sea power, and towards the end of the 18th century the British used the sea to colonise parts of Southern Africa.

The British used their vast sea power to consolidate and expand their interests locally and also into the Indian Ocean and beyond.[4] During the Anglo-Boer War at the turn of the 19th and 20th centuries Great Britain was able to secure the services of 230,000 troops from her empire[5] to defeat the Boers. These troops who were transported to South Africa by way of the sea, won a decisive land battle.

During the World Wars of the 20th century the trade routes and ports around South Africa were threatened by foreign powers. Germany laid minefields off the South African coast during both wars. In addition, German surface raiders and U-boats and Japanese submarines sank or damaged over 160 Allied ships in the region during the Second World War.[6]

During the 20th century seaborne trade allowed the economy of South Africa to prosper. This development was protected first by the British Royal Navy and then later by the South African Navy. During the Suez closure of the late 1970s there was a significant increase of shipping activity around the Cape resulting in an additional load being placed on both South African ports and the associated ship repair facilities. As world opinion turned against South Africa because of her domestic policies, it is argued that the existence of the SA Navy, and particularly its submarines, prevented South Africa from being blockaded.[7]

South Africa can therefore, as a result of her geostrategic position, history and present dependence upon the sea, most certainly be considered to be a Maritime Nation. Maritime Power is therefore of fundamental importance to South Africa to protect and promote her national maritime interests. From a strategic national security[8] point of view, South Africa's maritime interests are arguably just as vital as her non-maritime interests. A democracy with a population of 42 million people, a GDP of more than R400 billion, friendly countries on landward borders, yet strategically vulnerable and critically dependent on its maritime trade routes for more than half of its GDP, South Africa maintains the capability to promote and protect those maritime interests.

Access to global resources and foreign markets and the protection of our own interests from unwarranted foreign interference or manipulation must be assured. Therefore, in 1996 and in the foreseeable future, it would seem prudent for our fledgling democracy to allocate equal consideration to maritime defence as to landward defence.

The Changing Environment

In his recent book, *High Seas: The Naval Passage to an Uncharted World*, Admiral William A. Owens, US Navy, emphasised how important it is "...to inculcate the idea that change is a constant. Uncharted passage is the environment of the future.... we must be aware that we walk a narrow path between the dangers of mindless adherence to outmoded concepts and fashionable acceptance of change for the sake of changing".[9] This pronouncement of caution is certainly most pertinent to the uncharted waters which South Africa and the Southern African Region are presently entering.

The dramatic changes which occurred on a global scale with the demise of the Cold War and regionally with the ending of apartheid and the establishment of a fully fledged democracy in South Africa have given rise to a new set of strategic perspectives in South Africa. Previously engrained biases of the "Fortress South Africa" are systematically being replaced by new realities where the country is no longer regarded as being a pariah, but is being welcomed into the international brotherhood of nations. This has been manifested in many ways including invitations to (re)join many international organisations including the United Nations (UN), the Organisation of African Unity (OAU), the Southern African Development Community (SADC) and the Commonwealth.[10]

The changes to the strategic environment together with associated military developments have resulted in a reassessment of the functions of the military in the new society. Traditional South African concepts of security have been rewritten to include a much broader dimension, while the role of the military is being focused into a much narrower area. This development is understandable and was predicted many years ago by groups who rejected the concept of a militarised society. However, as the function of the military was expanded in the past to encompass a broader sphere, significant elements of the military were reduced.

As national strategy led South Africa into her "fortress" of isolation, traditional naval elements of the force design became neglected, for example anti-submarine warfare amongst others. South Africa moved into a unique paradigm where the keyword became "survival" of an abnormal society in an abnormal set of circumstances. As this became more evident and the concept of using the security assets of the state to promote and ensure democratic interests and to create greater prosperity became more remote, the security assets of the state were prioritised towards the land battle and the deteriorating internal situation.

Maritime elements in general and the Navy in particular ultimately became the stepchild of the defence force as a victim of budgetary neglect.[11] Despite the severe financial constraints which prevented the navy from renewing ageing equipment, the Navy managed to exist on its limited budget. However, today the threat of block obsolescence[12] looms ominously on the horizon.

The introduction of the 1996 White Paper on Defence brought with it another dimension to which the SANDF had to adapt. The defence posture for the SANDF was defined as being "primarily defensive".[13] This pronounced strategic intent is consistent with the new emerging common security environment which exists in the Southern African region today and is entirely appropriate.[14] On the other hand, what is posture? For this debate posture is defined as the combined (maritime) strategic intentions, capabilities and vulnerabilities of a country including the strength, disposition and readiness of its armed (maritime) forces.[15] But what does it mean to be primarily defensive with specific reference to the maritime environment in the South African context?

A "Primarily Defensive" Posture

A "primarily defensive posture" could be regarded as having a dual aim including the building of confidence and positive relationships; and the reduction in defence spending to an appropriate and responsible level avoiding an arms race.

The first purpose of building confidence and positive relationships in a region is entirely fitting today and in the future of Southern Africa. If the posture of South Africa is perceived by the rest of the region to be non-provocative and confidence enhancing, then it could be assumed that the balance of the countries would not perceive themselves to be in jeopardy and allow them to associate themselves with the common destiny of the region.[16]

Simultaneously, however, as the region is still politically volatile and security institutions are not very strong, the possibility of intra-state conflicts giving rise to inter-state hostilities cannot be ruled out. These circumstances would expose the region to foreign interference. It would be imprudent to ignore this possibility because of the potential impact of such interference.

The second purpose of the pronounced "primarily defensive posture" would be to reduce defence spending to appropriate and responsible levels, avoiding an arms race so that the bulk of funds could be used for socio-economic development. The level to which defence spending should be reduced is difficult to define and would be a function of, amongst other factors, long lead times for creating capabilities, high start up costs and uncertainty in international relations. For this reason it is imperative to ensure that South Africa maximises her defence value from her defence budget.

Strategic intent is signalled on the political level and South Africa's strategic intent is reflected by pronouncements in the new constitution and White Paper on Defence. At this level it is made very clear that South Africa intends pursuing peaceful relations with other states.[17] In addition, relations with neighbouring states are for the first time now based on friendship and cooperation.[18]

However, as South Africa is the major state in the region and arguably the major state in Sub-Saharan Africa, the states of the region and the sub-continent will increasingly look to South Africa to give them a lead in many spheres. South Africa ultimately will engage in Africa for a number of pragmatic reasons. This engagement will help inspire international confidence in the continent and will require both international diplomatic skills and the means with which to back it up.

Centuries of experience have demonstrated that a navy is one of a country's preferred means for supporting diplomatic initiatives.[19] As such, the use of the SA Navy in support of South African international and regional initiatives will add credence to South Africa's strategic posture and commitment to both international and regional peace and stability.

The Offensive and the Defensive Forms of Warfare

There is presently much debate on the changing nature of warfare with particular reference to a new strategic environment, a new era of defence and phenomenal technological developments. But if this were an exhortation, I would probably take my text from Alfred Thayer Mahan's words "From time to time the superstructure of tactics has to be altered or wholly torn down; but the old foundations of strategy so far remain, as though laid upon a rock".[20]

Warfare does not change its nature. It is, and always has been organised violence conducted for political ends; the second objective, that of being political, is critical to the definition because it distinguishes war from crime.[21] And also in today's terms it is not easy to improve upon Carl von Clausewitz's definition: "War is thus an act of force to compel our enemy to do our will".[22]

How do the offensive and defensive forms of warfare relate to each other? Paradoxically, in the "defensive" there are significant elements of the "offensive" and in the "offensive" there are significant elements of the "defensive". According to Clausewitz, the defensive form of warfare is intrinsically stronger than the offensive despite its negative object. However, he defines a battle as being defensive if one awaits the attack: "...the appearance of the enemy in front of our lines and within range". He qualifies this further by saying that "...if we are really waging war, we must return the enemy's blows and these offensive acts come under the heading of defence.... So the defensive form of war is not a simple shield, but a shield made up of well-directed [offensive] blows".[23] As such the offensive and the defensive are intricately interwoven into a seeming contradiction.

Mao Zedong writes in his "Strategy in China's Revolutionary War" that the primary problem in strategy is how to conserve one's strength and await an opportunity to defeat the enemy. He saw passive defence (defensive defence) as a spurious kind of defence and active defence as offensive defence or defence through decisive engagements as the only option of any consequence.[24] His concept of battle further relates to good intelligence and military capabilities, allowing the commander the position from which he may relate, gauge and regulate his engagement in the battle by integrating the offensive and the defensive.

I submit that these two approaches described above relate to the "primarily defensive posture" espoused by the White Paper where an operationally effective and efficient use of offensive actions underpins the strategically defensive posture. Strategically or on the theatre level one may have a defensive posture, but to give credence to that posture one may need a shield made up of the ability to deliver well-directed blows. This ability to deliver well-directed blows is the chief means which a joint commander may use to influence the outcome of a battle.

A purely defensive response to any form of armed aggression would be very demanding on own forces which could result in high costs for the defender for a relatively modest investment by an adversary.[25] This inherent ability to gain and hold the initiative is also critical to ensure that confidence and morale are established amongst one's own forces.

This combination of strategically defensive intent while maintaining the ability to succeed at the operational level by offensive means, where necessary, is termed "primarily defensive". However, a problem with both Clausewitz and Mao Zedong is that their thinking was influenced directly by their respective environments. They both suffered from a distinct lack of salt behind their ears. The problem is how to relate these concepts to the maritime environment.

The Nature of Warfare at Sea

Naval strategy differs vastly from strategy on land primarily because of the nature of the maritime milieu and also because of the intrinsic capabilities of naval platforms and weapon systems. Naval strategy is not only concerned with deterrence of aggression and defence against the incursion of the territory of a state. It is primarily about the use of the sea for passage of goods and people for both economic and military reasons and ultimately also to ensure the exploitation of riches in and under the sea. Similarly, naval forces may be necessary for a particular offensive action, but they are not sufficient on their own. It is an army which must ultimately occupy the ground.[26]

What is the difference between the "offensive" and the "defensive" at sea? Does the Clausewitzian paradigm of the defensive being inherently stronger than the offensive hold true at sea? It is argued by Gray that the offensive is the stronger form of war at sea because there is no "terrain" in the conventional sense and therefore forces should be optimised for operational offensive actions even if the strategic objectives are defensive. This is not necessarily a contradiction of Clausewitz, but rather a qualification because of the nature of the maritime environment.

The irony of today's post Cold War environment is that the roles which are required by naval forces participating in UN sanctioned enforcement operations or operations encompassing the evacuation of non-combatants are those forces which are deemed the most "offensive" or "provocative", being amphibious landings and strike warfare! However, in the final analysis of naval warfare despite an "offensive" or a "defensive" posture which is adopted at the strategic, operational or tactical levels, the success of the doctrine depends on the ability to *attack* a particular target which is on, over, or under the sea or a target ashore.[27]

The geographical and legal character of the sea adds another dimension to the debate. The sea covers two thirds of the surface of the earth and a large percentage of it is "international". The sea divides and yet also joins all people and even where there is national jurisdiction, warships have right of passage. Oceans are by and large an international environment or a "commons of the world" and naval forces may thus be deployed in this international commons without interfering with another state's sovereign rights. There is no equivalent for this on land. Therefore, the notion of area defence based on a national community with an inert posture upheld by short range weapons is in contradiction to the attributes of the maritime community. Democratic nations dependent on trade with limited ports, coasts and coastal forces will without fail have significant interests in far off maritime affairs. Ultimately those nations with only coastal forces will live under the umbrella of those responsible nations who contribute to international maritime stability and free trade.

At first glance and measured against a landward value system, navies may seem to be both provocative and offensive. This is primarily because they have the inherent ability to operate in enemy controlled territory for sustainable periods on self-propelled platforms which may be very well endowed with self-defence capabilities. This could be considered to be provocative to the extreme! However, these characteristics are less destabilising at sea because of the nature of the maritime environment.

One of the most central uncertainties associated with posture at sea is the intrinsic mobility and flexibility of naval vessels. In attempting to classify the system to be offensive or defensive, the dilemma is whether one should concentrate on the potential of the platform or of the weapon systems. If one uses the convenient measure of range where "short range" is good and "long range" is bad, what happens when one arms a "short range" platform with a "long range" missile system? In addition, how would one classify a "short range" platform with a "short range" weapon system which has been sent on a very offensive and provocative mission? Another complicating distinction between a navy and most other elements of the armed forces is that a navy must be "maintained". It cannot be "constructed" to meet a contingency at short notice. It requires highly skilled personnel and is capital and technology intensive.[28]

Would one consider a frigate to be "offensive" or "defensive"? A frigate is a multipurpose combatant with an emphasis on anti-air warfare or anti-submarine warfare, but also with capabilities in many other disciplines. In addition they are the smallest surface units which may be deployed autonomously for a number of military tasks. Their capabilities allow them to be used to cover a wide range of military, constabulary or benign tasks. They are particularly good at maintaining a "presence" when naval forces are used in a general way involving deployments, port visits, exercising and routine operating in areas of national interest. This serves to remind local inhabitants and the users of the sea of the effectiveness of the navy and the state that owns it. When a stronger message is required, these vessels could be used as part of a carefully tailored force with an offensive ability which could act as a signal of will and strategic intention of greater concern or to encourage a friend or ally.[29] According to landward terms, these platforms could be considered to be most offensive by virtue of the nature of their range, endurance and weapon systems. However, in the context of the maritime environment, and in accordance with the purpose for which they are employed, frigates would not be perceived to be overly provocative.

Would one consider a modern conventional diesel-electric submarine to be "offensive" or "defensive"? A modern conventional submarine is capable of sustained underwater operations and constitutes a major sea denial system.[30] Submarines are essentially immune to most of the threats that surface ships face, in particular to current surface-to-surface missiles (SSM) and air-to-surface missiles (ASM). The submarine has developed into a platform that is hard to trace, uses its weapons sparingly, reserving them for either the tactically or strategically optimal moment of kill, dropping back into silence immediately thereafter.[31]

Modern submarines have an excellent anti-submarine and anti-ship capability and can operate independently or in support of surface forces. The inherent stealth, mobility, firepower and endurance they bring to a battle space allows them to dominate many mission areas in their own right as well as contribute in a big way to overall force effectiveness. A submarine is a force multiplier. Without submarines, a navy would have to have a considerable number of surface combatants with incomparably higher sophistication and cost considerations to provide the same deterrent and defence value. The submarine's non-provocative value is enhanced by its unique ability to control its visibility. Submarines stationed off distant coasts have consistently provided military planners with information required to formulate necessary contingency plans. They can provide locating data on key communications facilities, covertly monitor, record and send commanders real time status of both military and commercial shipping. They can monitor embargo compliance, examine the status of military forces and in general keep the commander-in-chief in the picture with dynamic and unfolding events in troubled parts.

Submarines do not disturb the environment in which they work.[32] The antagonist has no idea that he is the subject of this continuous surveillance and preparation effort and as such is not provoked into retaliatory action. On the other hand, the same leader knows when an aircraft or surface ship attempts the same mission. "Submarines can sometimes be better instruments of diplomacy than surface ships. If there are problems in your area you can just quietly announce that you are conducting submarine exercises there. Everyone gets the point.[33] In fact, a submarine can be both covert and non-confrontational.

What of Mine Warfare and Mine Countermeasures Vessels (MCMV's)? Mines form the foundation of most "defensive" postures even though they can be used for both offensive and defensive purposes. Mines can provide a cheap and cost effective method for helping to defend your harbours and harbour approaches. Similarly they can be used against your harbours, harbour approaches and certain parts of your trade routes in a most effective manner by a poor and unsophisticated adversary. They can also be used indiscriminately and therefore illegally. Once again it is the context and the purpose for which they are used to deny the potential adversary the use of that piece of sea which is important in the debate.

MCMV's are possibly the most innocuous of all naval vessels. They help keep shipping flowing and have little offensive potential. Yet if mines are used for defensive purposes, then their capacity to neutralise those mines could be deemed to be very aggressive. Another factor to be taken into account in the debate is the fact that it is difficult for any MCMV force to clear mines quickly.[34] By and large, it is difficult to classify mines and MCMV's as being overly provocative.

Ultimately each specific and unique situation must be contextualised as an integrated function of the entire strategic and operational situation so that potential mismatches between capability and posture can be determined and evaluated in context.

Strategic Vulnerabilities of the Nation

When one appraises the posture of a state it is imperative to contextualise the strategic vulnerabilities of that state. For example, the British rely on their ability to control the English Channel for security purposes and the existence of any dominant power along the European lowlands has in the past caused the British to take decisive military action. Therefore, a reasonable British capability to ensure their interests in the English Channel is not deemed to be unduly provocative, despite the immense offensive capabilities associated with such a force.

As deduced earlier in this paper, South Africa is a maritime nation. South Africa is critically dependent on her trade routes. Most serious consequences would occur if, for example, the ports of both Durban and Richards Bay were to close simultaneously and for a lengthy period. It could result in an economic catastrophe if the closures continued for a lengthy period because the impact on the balance of payments and the GDP would be severe and unemployment would increase with many firms being reduced to bankruptcy. A recent report on the consequences of the unplanned closure of a major South African port[35] by Transport Research Associates of Stellenbosch states that "It would be in the interests of the government to re-open the ports whatever the resource cost of doing so, as soon as possible.[36] In addition South Africa has an Exclusive Economic Zone (EEZ) encompassing more than 1.1 million square kilometres including the possessions in the Prince Edward Island Group in the South Atlantic and its associated EEZ. The fishing and mineral deposits inside the EEZ currently provide jobs for 18,000 directly and indirectly support 100,000 people. The 1994 fishing catch was valued at R1.5 billion, the diamond sector turnover R80 million, the Mossgas project R825 million, together with tourism and shipbuilding and repairs totalled R10 billion or just under 3 per cent of GDP.[37]

The dependence of South Africa on her international trade routes as well as her growing maritime assets make her strategically vulnerable primarily because of her position of geographic isolation from her trading partners and from potential allies with any significant maritime ability.[38]

International and Regional Perceptions of South Africa's Maritime Posture

During a recent National Maritime Strategic Conference on "Navies in Peace and War" the South African Deputy Minister of Defence, Ronnie Kasrils, stated that the demands for South Africa to become more involved in the area of regional security have become greater. South Africa, one of the few states with a naval capability, is being urgently called upon to curb the pillaging and compromising of Africa's maritime resources. Mr Kasrils stated that this concern for the maritime environment was not only limited to coastal states, and that a recommendation that landlocked states become involved through some of their military serving on South African ships was enthusiastically endorsed.[39]

Similarly, the South African Minister of Defence, Joe Modise, to *Jane's Defence Weekly*, stated that other nations need help in protecting their coasts. "They come openly to us to request South African support and assistance. They complain that the marine life in their waters is being plundered by foreign ships. They are not even talking about security problems or some future military threat. The region wants and needs our support, particularly Mozambique, Tanzania and Namibia".[40]

The sentiments currently being expressed in the region are that of confidence and trust. The procuring of maritime assets against this backdrop would instead of being perceived as being "provocative" by the neighbourhood, rather be welcomed as assets of the region. Measured against the purpose of a "primarily defensive posture" (having the dual aim of the building of confidence and positive relationships; and the reduction in defence spending to an appropriate and responsible level), the prudent procurement of maritime assets to maintain modest balanced maritime capabilities would seem appropriate for South Africa in 1996.

Capabilities

The capabilities of a navy and as such the force design of such a force will depend on the primary (wartime) tasks. These tasks include the defence of maritime communications (trade routes and ports), territory and offshore assets. Peacetime roles would, amongst others, include patrolling, evacuation, surveillance, influencing, diplomatic showing of the flag, disaster relief, search and rescue, fishery protection duties, pollution control, customs and excise (contraband), the combating of piracy, and support of scientific programmes, specifically hydrography.

However, to be operationally effective within the environment in which it is expected to operate, there needs to be a critical mass of certain classes and sizes of platforms.[41] Within the context of reduced budgets, it is imperative for a navy to be cost effective. Both in the "bang for the buck"[42] argument and also organisationally, South Africa cannot afford to design or redesign a navy without taking cognisance of the "defence value per Rand" concept and as such, in accordance with international post-Cold War trends, will have to focus on multipurpose and force-multiplier platforms. Organisationally, the SA Navy will have to be cost effective, meaning getting the best return on human resources and naval systems and for this there is an optimum size.

To obtain maximum defence value and simultaneously to have an efficient organisation, the design of a navy must take into account the interaction between the three dimensions of maritime warfare. The uniqueness of these three interrelating environments (air, surface and sub-surface) allows the maritime commander opportunity to optimise his position by asymmetric means against a potential aggressor who does not have the capability to operate effectively in all three of the environments. It is this balance which ultimately is the greatest hedge to counter the assumption that we cannot predict with certainty the pattern of the war for which we prepare ourselves.[43]

South Africa protects its maritime interests by securing access to the region through its ports of entry, by guaranteeing its maritime sovereignty, through patrolling its sea lanes and EEZ, guarding its harbours, fish stocks and natural resources under the sea bed, and by ensuring the safety of international maritime traffic around its coasts. The main ports for trade are Durban, Richard's Bay, Cape Town and Saldanha Bay, with Simon's Town as the main naval base. It is of vital importance that these ports should be kept open to shipping during times of war or tension. The present lack of finance for defence matters has determined that only two critical areas can be defended. To this end two local maritime defence areas have been planned, one based on Durban/Richard's Bay and the other on Cape Town/Saldanha Bay/Simon's Town.

A compact, robust and balanced naval force representing basic maritime defence capabilities and optimum defence value for the Rand has been designed to defend these two local maritime defence areas. This force, which supports the White Paper's "primarily defensive posture", comprises of four conventional submarines; four corvettes; six strike craft; four minesweepers; four minehunters; two inshore patrol vessels; 39 harbour patrol boats and a combat support ship. This force can be divided into two smaller forces to defend each local maritime defence area and is supplemented by medium range maritime patrol aircraft. It can be regrouped to be utilised for other purposes. This force has the ability to deal with limited contingencies in the air, surface and sub-surface dimensions and will enable South Africa to maintain the core naval capabilities and expertise to be able to expand if and when necessary.

Conclusion

South Africa is both geographically and historically a maritime nation which has vital maritime interests. By virtue of the nature of its economy, South Africa is strategically dependent on maritime trade. South Africa is emerging from a position of isolation where its military focus was directed towards protecting itself from hostile neighbours to the north and a deteriorating internal situation. In a process of democratisation South Africa is now re-engaging with the region, the continent and the world. New security realities are emerging and the country is taking cognisance of these realities. Capabilities must be commensurate with the "primarily defensive" defence posture. In the maritime environment this includes elements of intent, capability and strategic vulnerability. The political and strategic intent of South Africa is clearly friendly. Any maritime capability can be offensive or defensive by nature depending on the mission for which it is employed. Therefore it is necessary to take additional steps to ensure that your neighbour does not feel provoked by investing in broad confidence building measures. If your neighbours are encouraging you to develop and maintain a credible maritime capability, then doing so can develop confidence and stability in the region. If your neighbours understand that more than 50 per cent of your GDP is dependent upon maritime trade routes, it is easier for them to understand why it is prudent for South Africa to maintain the ability to promote and protect its maritime interests. To ensure good defence value on a limited budget, it is prudent to maintain balanced capabilities using force multipliers with sufficient critical mass in numbers. South Africa should therefore strive to redress the present imbalance between the maritime and non-maritime spheres by investing in an appropriate, affordable, compact, robust and balanced naval force with the ability to deal with limited contingencies in the air, surface and sub-surface dimensions, maintaining core naval capabilities, expertise and the ability to expand when necessary.

Notes

1. The Southern Ocean contains critical elements of the start of the food chain and South Africa has legitimate interests in large areas of this immense ocean.
2. Siko, Mohlolo: 'South Africa's Maritime Interests and Responsibilities' (SA Navy Publications Unit 1995), p. 6.
3. Higgs, Robert W.: "The United States and Sub-Saharan Africa", *Naval War College Review*, vol. 49, no. 1, sequence 353 (Winter 1996), pp. 90-104. In the developed world, marine economic resources are jealously protected by sovereign states with naval and other maritime law enforcement assets. As developed countries become more concerned about the depletion of their fisheries, they can be expected to protect rigorously what is legally theirs forcing less scrupulous into the rich zones of sub-Saharan African States where there is a maritime power vacuum. See also Hinds, Lennox: "World Marine Fisheries: Management and Development Problems," *Marine Policy* (September 1992), p. 395.
4. Simpson-Anderson, R.C.: "The Future of Sea Power", *Navy International*, vol. 101, no. 1 (January 1996), p. 29. The author is the Chief of the South African Navy.
5. Mahan, Alfred Thayer: *The South African War* (New York: Peter Fenelon Collier & Son, 1900), p. xvii.
6. Simpson-Anderson: *loc. cit.*, p. 29.
7. *Ibid.*
8. National security can be defined as a country's psychological freedom from fear of foreign attack. See Kegley, Charles W. Jr. & Eugene R. Wittkopf: *World Politics. Trend and Transformation*, 5th edition (New York: St. Martin's Press, 1995), p. 371.
9. Owens, William A.: *High Seas: The Naval Passage to an Uncharted World* (Annapolis, MD: Naval Institute Press, 1995), p. 177.
10. *South African White Paper on Defence*, p. 20.
11. See the chapter by Rocklyn Williams in the present volume.
12. Block Obsolescence is a military term used to describe a complete system of antiquated equipment which is of dubious value, about to be discarded.
13. *South African White Paper on Defence*, p. 20.
14. Nathan, Laurie: *Changing of the Guard* (Pretoria: HSRC Publishers, 1994), p. 48.

15. Collins, John M.: *Grand Strategy: Principles and Practices* (Annapolis: Naval Institute Press, 1990).
16. Møller, Bjørn: 'Non-Offensive Defence and the Korean Peninsula', *Working Papers*, no. 7/1995 (Copenhagen: Centre for Peace and Conflict Research, 1995), p. 3.
17. *South African White Paper on Defence*, p. 6.
18. *ibid.* p. 22.
19. Edmunds, Martin & Greg Mills: *Unchartered Waters-A Review of South Africa's Naval Options* (Johannesburg: South African Institute of International Affairs and Lancaster: Centre for Defence and International Security Studies, Lancaster University, 1996), p. 72.
20. Mahan, Alfred Thayer: *The Influence of Sea Power upon History, 1660-1783* (Boston: Little, Brown, 1890), p. 88.
21. Gray, Colin S.: 'The Changing Nature of Warfare?', *US Naval War College Review*, Spring 1996, p. 9.
22. Clausewitz, Carl von: *On War*. Michael Howard & Peter Paret, eds. and trans. (Princeton, NJ: Princeton University Press, 1976), p. 75.
23. *Ibid.*
24. Mao Tse Tung: *Selected Military Writings of Mao Tse Tung* (Beijing: Foreign Languages Press, 1967), p. 105.
25. *Defending Australia*. Defence White Paper 1994 (Canberra: Ministry of Defence, 1994), p. 29.
26. Booth, Ken: 'NOD at Sea', in Bjørn Møller & Håkan Wiberg (eds.): *Non-Offensive Defence for the Twenty-First Century* (Boulder: Westview Press, 1994), pp. 98-114.
27. Grove, Eric: 'Naval Technology and Stability', in Wim Smit, John Grin & Lev Voronkov (eds.): *Military Technological Innovation and Stability in a Changing World. Politically Assessing and Influencing Weapon Innovation and Military Research and Development* (Amsterdam: VU University Press, 1992), pp. 197-213.
28. Edmunds & Mills: *op. cit.*, p. 15.
29. *The Fundamentals of British Maritime Doctrine (BR 1806)*, p. 175.
30. Sea denial is the condition short of full sea control that exists when an opponent is prevented from using an area of sea for his own purposes. See *ibid.* p. 235.
31. Ya'ari, Yedidia "Didi": "The Littoral Arena: A Word of Caution," *Naval War College Review*, Spring 1995, p. 17.
32. However, if the submarine is discovered the political consequences could be grave.
33. *Time Magazine*, 12 February 1996.
34. Grove: *loc. cit.*
35. Transport Research Associates: *The Consequences of the Unplanned Closure of a Major South African Port* (Stellenbosch, March 1996), p. 26.

36. The report further states that the use of the ports of Richards Bay and Durban are not indispensable to the economy of South Africa and that other ports could well be developed to accommodate the traffic, although that would take several years to achieve.
37. Edmunds & Mills: *loc. cit.*, p. 19.
38. To further realise the complexities of the South African maritime situation, it is necessary to comprehend distances and transit times between the borders and major harbours of the country. A Frigate will take 64 hours to transit from the Orange River Mouth (the western maritime border) to Ponto do Ouro (the eastern maritime border) and 33 hours to transit between Cape Town and Durban, two of the major ports on the western and eastern seaboards, at 25 knots. A conventional submarine will take 160 hours to transit from the Orange River Mouth to Ponto do Ouro and 82 hours to transit between Cape Town and Durban, at 10 knots.
39. 'We Live in a Tough Neighbourhood'. Extracts of an Address by Mr Ronnie Kasrils, Deputy Minister of Defence on the occasion of the 1995 National Maritime Strategic Conference, at Simon's Town on 26 October 1995, *Salut* (March 1996), p. 14.
40. *Jane's Defence Weekly*, vol. 25, no. 1 (3 January 1996), p. 32.
41. Edmunds & Mills: *loc. cit.*, p. 14.
42. "Bang for the Buck" is a term which is used to denote combat value for the resources which are spent on Defence. The Chief of the South African National Defence Force, General Meiring is accredited with having coined the South African equivalent of "Rumble for the Rand".
43. Wylie, J.C.: *Military Strategy: A General Theory of Power Control* (Annapolis, MD: Naval Institute Press, 1989), p. 70.

8 South Africa and Peacekeeping: Is there a role in Africa?

GREG MILLS

> Since democratic changes in South Africa, hailed worldwide as the 'political miracle', there are great expectations of the role South Africa can and must play in helping to achieve peace and stability in Africa and elsewhere. The issue is widely debated in South Africa. There are those who argue that South Africa has its own problems and must solve these and not become involved outside its borders. There are others who argue that the country must be involved within the context of SADC. (South African Deputy Minister of Foreign Affairs, Aziz Pahad, July 1995).

> The nervous calm was shattered by small arms, rockets and mortar-fire..... There appears to be no clear objective in the combat and the pattern of today's events seems to be repeated on an almost daily basis. When we asked some of the fighters about the announcement of a cease-fire made by the various faction leaders in the past few days, they just laughed and said: 'There was no cease-fire'. Many of these fighters are young children and all wear a rag-tag assortment of clothing. Some did not even have proper weapons, walking around with pipes, swords even power tools. The atmosphere among them is almost that of children playing a game. But for the civilians of Monrovia, the spiral of violence that has laid waste to the city.... has meant nothing but misery (Bob Coen, CNN Reporter, Monrovia, 19 May 1996).

> Watching a coast as it slips by.... is like thinking about an enigma. There it is before you—smiling, frowning, inviting, grand, mean, insipid, or savage, and always mute with an air of whispering. Come and find out (Joseph Conrad, *Heart of Darkness*).

In July 1995, the South African Institute of International Affairs (SAIIA) and the Institute for Defence Policy (IDP) jointly staged a conference on the subject *South Africa and Peacekeeping in Africa.* This event was the largest of its sort yet held in Southern Africa, and brought together a diverse group of military, government, academic, and civilian personnel. The popularity of the event reflected the topicality of South Africa's potential participation in global peace-support operations, particularly in Africa.

Since the transformation of South Africa's global status from pariah to participant, so the calls for and expectations of South Africa's continental role have incrementally increased. The South African National Defence Force (SANDF) does have applicable experience in such operations, albeit locally, particularly in the townships of the East Rand in Gauteng. In the region, South Africa's contributions to peace-support efforts in Angola (*Operation Genesis* in 1992), Mozambique (*Operation Amizade* during the elections in October 1994) and Rwanda (through the supply of humanitarian assistance in 1994-95) has given the SANDF and the Department of Foreign Affairs (DFA) a taste of the operational environment. Preventive diplomacy actions have, since April 1994, included the defusing of the political crisis in Lesotho (1994), the threatened derailment of the Mozambican elections (1994), facilitating contact between interested parties in the Angolan conflict (such as with UNITA's Dr Savimbi's visit in May 1995), and, most recently, the process of democratisation in Swaziland. But there is a considerable degree of experience still to be gained in operating both in a multilateral environment and under the spotlight of the international media. Moreover, any deployment will probably occur in partnership with African nations, and within embryonic organisational structures.

This chapter examines the potential for South African participation in peacekeeping operations in terms of the domestic, regional and international environments in which such involvement may occur.[1]

The International Context

South Africa faces calls for involvement in peace-support operations, not only at a time when the very future of the United Nations (UN) is under debate, but when the effects of the passing of the Cold War are visibly being displayed in various crises that appear to befall the nation-state system, especially in Africa. The last ten years have witnessed a huge increase in the number and scope of peacekeeping missions. In 1987, the UN was involved in five such operations with a total deployment of 10,000 military personnel; by 1994, this had increased to 17 operations with a deployment of over 70,000 members. Importantly, too, there is a trend towards intervention in intra- rather than inter-state conflicts: of the five UN missions in 1988, only one was related to an intra-state conflict. Of the eleven operations established since January 1992, nine were concerned with intra-state conflict situations. It is notable that an estimated 70 per cent of this deployment was in Africa. This led to a growth in the UN's peacekeeping budget from US$400 million in 1990 to more than US$3.5 billion in 1994.

Table 2: African Peacekeeping Missions, 1994-1996

Country	Personnel	Annual Cost (US$m.)
Angola (UNAVEM III)	6,184	200
Liberia (ECOMOG)	11,000	-
Liberia (UNOMIL)	84	36
Mozambique (UNOMOZ)	5,760	327
Rwanda (UNAMIR)	5,500	98
Somalia (UNOSOM II)	19,224	1,000
Western Sahara (MINURSO)	350	40

Notes: UNOSOM II, the successor to the UN Transitional Authority (UNITAF, which had reached a peak strength in 1993 of 37,000 troops from 25 countries) was terminated in March 1995; UNOMOZ in November 1994.

The full-strength of around 7,000 troops for the third UN Verification Mission in Angola (UNAVEM 111) will only be reached in mid-1996.

The final troops of UNAMIR left Rwanda in April 1996.

The status of both the seven-nation West African Economic Monitoring Group (ECOMOG) and the UN Observer Mission in Liberia (UNOMIL) was unclear at the time of writing given the renewed outbreak in fighting in April 1996.

The Value of Peace Operations Today

The value of peace-support operations is today being questioned in a very public manner. Headlines of 'Can blue helmets keep the peace?', 'United Nations —disunited purpose', 'Shamed are the peacekeepers', and 'Shades of impotence behind the UN's neutral sky blue' are indicative of the level of public disenchantment over the UN's abilities and activities.

The rapid expansion in the number, scope and cost of such missions has also occurred at a moment when there is a crisis of funding in the UN. As of October 1994, the UN was owed US$2.5 billion in bad debts, of which US$812 was for the regular budget and US$1.7 billion for peacekeeping operations. This reduced to around US$2.1 billion in mid-1996. The United States is the largest debtor, owing US$1.5 billion in 1996.

In order to keep the UN's other activities and myriad of agencies functioning (which costs US$400 million monthly), the peacekeeping budget is raided regularly—to the tune of US$200 million in 1995. Although contributors to UN operations are guaranteed payment (after the first 60 days, payment at a rate of US$988 per person for infantry and US$1,279 for engineers and specialists), the lack of cash in the UN's peacekeeping kitty has meant that these states (which include some of the poorest in world-terms) are in essence subsidising the UN's general functions and thus ironically, indirectly, the United States and other bad debtors.

Yet although the very worth of peace-support contributions is being questioned, these are seen by many as one of the most necessary areas of UN activities. Indeed, speaking at the SAIIA in February 1996, the former UK Ambassador to the UN, Sir David Hannay, noted that: 'UN peacekeeping missions have taken more than their fair share of criticism for some recent failures. As is often the way in a media-dominated world, the shortcomings have overshadowed the successes. And yet these successes are real and they were not easily achieved. In Africa, the Namibia and Mozambique operations stand as models of their kind which brought peace, free and fair elections and respect for human rights to countries which had known none of these before'.[2]

Undoubtedly, as the human catastrophes in Angola, Liberia, Burundi, Rwanda, Somalia and the Sudan all exemplify, there is a massive demand for peace-support activities in Africa. Yet now peace-support goes beyond just peacekeeping, and covers a whole gambit of conflict prevention and resolution activities. This extension of activity has, in turn, sparked a fresh debate as to our understanding of peacekeeping today.

Understanding Contemporary Peacekeeping

Before 1948, peacekeeping was largely a matter of upholding a peace that had been agreed to. In the aftermath of the Cold War, the experiences in Somalia, the former Yugoslavia and Cambodia pointed to a more ambitious sense of mission in which there were some major setbacks. And now, in a third phase where there is a loss of confidence in the *modus operandi* of peacekeeping and on the abilities of personnel to absorb these responsibilities, the pressures on South Africa to assume a major role in Africa are growing. To complicate the issue, there is still great sensitivity over apartheid South Africa's role in the sub-continent, to the point that the Angolan government refused *all* parties which had been involved in military activities in that country permission to participate in the current peacekeeping activities, including South Africa. The irony does not end there, however. The role of South African mercenaries in Angola and Sierra Leone, principally through Executive Outcomes (EO), has complicated and tainted South Africa's potential contributions to creating and ensuring peace and stability in an impartial manner.

The calls for South African participation are coming at an awkward time. Not only is the new nation itself involved in a process of nation-building and reconciliation, but African states are becoming increasingly marginalised from international concerns and actions of the international community—so-called 'African fatigue' or 'Afro pessimism'. This has meant that more and more this will have to be managed by African states themselves—even though there are likely to be increasing needs for outside intervention in African states, not only to quell violence but, more importantly, to build structures capable of sustaining peace.

The continuous flux in the theoretical debate about the exact typology of peacekeeping missions serves also to complicate and confound, and thus it is not surprising that much of the contemporary discussion in South Africa has centred around the terminology, categorisation and classification of peace-support operations. At the military level it makes sense to distinguish between three major types of peace support operations:

- Support to diplomacy, i.e. conflict prevention under Chapter VI of the UN Charter involving both civilian and military forces; diplomatic peacemaking to settle ongoing conflict through mediation, conciliation and even sanctions; and post-conflict peacebuilding to strengthen a political settlement.
- Peace enforcement, i.e. classical military action under Chapter VII of the UN Charter designed to restore peace.
- Peacekeeping, i.e. the containment, moderation and/or termination of conflict through outside intervention. Put simply, keeping the warring factions apart.

It should thus be clear from the above distinction that peace-support operations do not necessarily involve the deployment of troops. The emphasis is, first, on the diplomatic means of avoiding conflict through diplomacy and crisis management. Only if this action fails, does the emphasis shift to the humanitarian aspects so as to give assistance to the innocent victims of conflict. This should occur alongside military and ongoing political action aimed at quelling conflict (peace making and peace enforcement) and, once this has been achieved, peacekeeping. Only once the dust has settled and political accommodation achieved, can post-conflict peace building efforts begin. *An Agenda for Peace*, the report by the UN secretary-general, Boutros Boutros-Ghali, released in 1992, recognises in the above stages the centrality of the UN to peace-support operations. The report has since served both as a basis for debate and as a guideline for the range of peace operations.

Given the diversity of problems experienced by the principal powers in the UN involved in peace support missions (the US, UK and France), the debate has also included questions about the criteria for involvement to avoid involvement in untenable and unsolvable conflict situations. Impossible goals have, in the last decade, often related to attempts to create peace to which the major warring factions are not yet committed. Such circumstances demanded a clear articulation of the goals and limits of missions. Following the failure of the mission to Somalia, the Clinton Administration outlined this approach in the Presidential Decision Directive number 25 (PDD-25) issued in May 1994. This document contains the fundamental principles on which future US-UN cooperation would be based, principles of extra-territorial military involvement similar in concept to the earlier Weinberger Doctrine. Washington would only consider joining peacekeeping operations if strict conditions were met, which included:

- The establishment of a clear military mission.
- The consent of all parties involved.
- The availability of sufficient money and troops.
- A clear exit strategy.
- The crisis had to be a threat to international peace and security.
- The need for standardisation of training and equipment, and the careful coordination of the parties involved are also seen as critical for the success of peacekeeping operations today.

The Regional Environment: The Contemporary Security Architecture

The regional environment is the principal influence on the nature and areas of possible South African involvement in peacekeeping operations. South African participation will, it seems, only occur with both the connivance of and through regional bodies, notably the Southern African Development Community and the Inter-State Defence and Security Committee (ISDSC). And the region is likely also to be the most obvious area of future deployment—whether this be in terms of actual physical deployment (as in Mozambique and Angola) or humanitarian and peacekeeping/building operations, or through participation in conflict prevention or mediation diplomacy (as in Lesotho and Swaziland).

With regard to the former, there have been considerable shifts and developments in African security architecture. Central to this has been the reconfiguration of the Organisation of African Unity (OAU) and SADC and the now-defunct Frontline States (FLS) grouping.[3] Numerous meetings were held throughout 1995 to discuss the proposed establishment of the Association of Southern African States (ASAS) as a successor to the FLS. The Foreign Ministers of the FLS/SADC met on 3 March 1995 in Harare and recommended that ASAS be created as a political arm of SADC and as a mechanism, as Deputy Minister Aziz Pahad put it, 'for dealing with conflict prevention, management and resolution in Southern Africa'. At this meeting it was proposed that a separate military and political sector each be created. Guided by the principles set out at the Foreign Minister's July 1994 Windhoek Summit document which called for the establishment of a *sector* on Conflict Resolution and Political Cooperation and the drawing-up (under Article 22.1 of the SADC Treaty) of a Protocol on Peace, Security and Conflict Resolution, the ASAS was designed to strengthen OAU initiatives and the UN's *Agenda for Peace* in the promotion of conflict prevention, mediation, democratisation, peacemaking and peacekeeping.

But the organisational structures are still not settled. The expected formation of ASAS as the regional association for peacekeeping/conflict prevention duties did not materialise out of the SADC Heads of State summit in South Africa in August 1995 as a result, it seemed, principally of Zimbabwean intransigence over leadership of the Association. The August 1995 summit reviewed the decision by the SADC Council of Ministers to replace the FLS with the ASAS and to create a permanent security sector, but deferred the decision so as to ensure that an appropriate institutional framework was in place 'to avoid duplication and to create a common regional agenda'.

With the change from the Southern African Development Coordination Conference (SADCC) to SADC in 1992 and the shift in emphasis from 'development coordination' to 'development integration', SADC now sees itself as having a wider political function in the region. On 18 January 1996, the SADC Ministers of Foreign Affairs, Defence and Security met in Gaborone and agreed to recommend to their heads of states the creation of a SADC Organ for Politics, Defence and Security. This was reiterated at the Summit of SADC Heads of States of Government in Gaborone in January 1996. No less than fourteen objectives have now been defined for the Organ—given regional capacities, little more than an ambitious wish-list of roles and responsibilities. These range from: the development of a 'common foreign policy' to mediation in 'inter-state and intra-state disputes and conflicts', the operation of an 'early-warning system', the development of 'a collective security capacity' and conclusion of 'a Mutual Defence Pact', to addressing cross-border crime and the promotion of 'peace-making and peacekeeping in order to achieve sustainable peace and security'.

These recommendations were adopted by the SADC Summit in Gaborone in June 1996. The Organ will operate at the Summit level, though it is designed to operate with greater flexibility and informality than the other SADC sectors. Military intervention is, however, seen only as a final resort. The ISDSC, which before 1994 had operated as a coordinating mechanism for the liberation movements, will operate under the SADC Organ. This Committee has now taken on greater responsibilities to promote regional stability through security cooperation through its three sub-committees: one each for the military, police and intelligence community.

South Africa is, in all of this, going to find it important, but difficult, to balance the need to be seen to be assisting Africa with the need not to be seen as the regional bully in dominating events simply on account of size and force capability. A joint approach to security enabling smaller powers to play equal or leadership roles alongside the larger nations is crucial to avoid the negative implications of such sensitivities. A most visible exchange of ideas around potential cooperation has occurred through the ISDSC, until October 1996 under the chairmanship of South Africa's Defence Minister Joe Modise, and in which army, air force and naval sub-committees meet regularly to discuss issues of standardisation and interoperability. The SANDF has reportedly accepted the inevitability of its involvement in peacekeeping operations, and is already liaising with Southern African states in combined planning and exercises. Major-General S.E. Du Toit, Deputy Chief of Staff of Operations has noted: 'It is now important for members of the ISDSC countries to get together and decide on certain peace-support issues. These include responsibilities of the different countries as far as geographic location is concerned, doctrine and standard operating procedures, command and control, training, tasks, standardisation of equipment, logistic support, medical services, and communication and signals'. He pinpointed Rwanda, Mozambique and Angola as 'basically the areas in which we can be employed most effectively'.[4]

African experience will no doubt also be instructive to the SANDF in spite of its considerable range of experiences. Conditions in Africa are in many areas clearly unlike anything outside of the continent and unfamiliar even to many South Africans (see the earlier quote on the Liberian conflict), where certain past sensitivities around the SANDF could be best masked through the use of a heterogeneous African force.

Although South Africa (along with other parties previously involved in the Angolan conflict) was prevented from assisting with UNAVEM III, the regional contribution to the peacekeeping mission has been substantial. Of the almost 7,000 troops committed, Zimbabwe has supplied 879 and Zambia 300 (Brazil, India, Rumania and Uruguay are the other largest contributors with 1,125, 1,095, 892 and 856 troops respectively). South Africa has been involved to the extent of supplying logistical backup. In September 1995, SA Air Force planes ferried tents and other equipment for the UNITA quartering areas in Huambo.

The Organisation of African Unity has, in the light of the move towards intervention internationally in intra-rather than inter-state conflict—which was traditionally outside of the OAU's ambit of operation—more actively attempted to mediate in internal conflicts through the Mechanism for Conflict Prevention, Management and Resolution which was established within the OAU at the July 1993 Cairo summit. This was a radical departure from the OAU's previous *ad hoc* attempts at finding solutions to conflict.

This Mechanism has been adopted and channelled through the so-called Central Organ for Conflict Prevention, Management and Resolution (COCPMR). A number of shortcomings with the operationalisation of this mechanism led, in 1995, to the creation of an Early Warning Network based on a coordinating facility to be located in a Conflict Management Centre at OAU Headquarters. This Centre is to be equipped with a Crisis Management Room which will, on a 24-hour basis, monitor crisis situations in Africa. The other notable area of deficiency in the operation of the Mechanism was in peacekeeping, where the increasing reluctance on the part of extra-African powers to become involved plus a lack of an OAU force, have created problems in meeting the demands for a peaceful environment in which to enable a diplomatic solution. As a result, the African Heads of State and Government have requested OAU member-states to earmark and train units of their national armies for this purpose.

The COCPMR and the Early Warning Mechanism was the subject of a consultative meeting held in Addis Ababa in January 1996. The seminar looked at how the creation of a facilitatory system for expediting information on situations in member states could assist in giving the right warnings prior for the need for peacekeeping missions. Of course, the major problem with such an Early Warning System remains the fundamental conflict between the need for more information and timely action on the one hand, and the possible clash with sovereign interests on the other. Discussion on intra-state situations is fine, for as long as it does not involve discussion of your state. Political will is a paramount requirement for the operationalisation of the system.

Greater awareness of the limitations and failings of peacekeeping missions will presumably be reflected in their future size, scope and mandates. Funding remains a perennial and worsening problem, which is exacerbated by the current bout of 'Afro-pessimism'. Second, there is an increasing realisation that arms control, particularly that of light (small) arms, has to go hand-in-hand with peace-support measures. The one cannot succeed without the other. In every area of the peacekeeping operations of the UN in 1995-96 (Somalia, Liberia, Rwanda and Angola) attempts were made to stem the flow of arms into the area of conflict. But given the numbers of weapons already in circulation in Africa, more will have to be done than simply to prevent the flow of new armaments. Only 165,000 of an estimated 1.5 million weapons were accounted for in Mozambique following the cessation of hostilities.[5]

Confidence-building measures, including principally economic growth, will have to operate in tandem with strict penalties in order to both encourage and police arms control. Landmines remain a similar danger to the social fabric of nations, particularly as these weapons remain even after the reasons for their deployment have long passed. An estimated 10 million remain unaccounted for in Angola and two million in Mozambique.

The Domestic Context: The South African Challenge

South Africa faces its own peculiar internal challenges in meeting the regional and international responsibilities of peace support operations. These relate to the nature of the transformation process of South African government, and the (re)formulation of policy. The Defence White Paper, *Defence in a Democracy* (of May 1996) makes specific provision for the utilisation of SANDF units in peace support missions. The document notes:

> As a fully-fledged member of the international community, South Africa will fulfil its responsibility to participate in international peace operations. There are two types of operation in which the SANDF may become involved: i) peacekeeping, which entails military operations undertaken without resort to force and with the consent of the major parties to a dispute in order to monitor and facilitate the implementation of a peace agreement; and ii) peace enforcement, which entails the application or threat of force, pursuant to international authorization, in order to compel compliance with resolutions or sanctions designed to maintain or restore peace and order.[6]

Clearly taking its lead from President Bill Clinton's PDD-25, the document goes on to note that South Africa will only become involved in 'specific peace operations' if certain conditions are met:

> • There should be parliamentary approval and public support for involvement, and appreciation of the associated costs and risks, including the financial costs and risk to the lives of military personnel.
> • The operation should have a clear mandate, mission and objectives.
> • There should be realistic criteria for terminating the operation.
> • The operation should be authorised by the United Nations Security Council.
> • Operations in Southern Africa should be sanctioned by SADC and should be undertaken together with other SADC states rather than conducted on a unilateral basis. Similarly, operations in Africa should be sanctioned by the OAU.

Quite fairly, questions should be asked about how realistic such criteria are for peacekeeping operations generally, and especially in Africa. Although there is today a commonly accepted consensus that 'soldiers should not do the work of politicians and should only be called in to make or keep the peace once it has been created, this argument is unrealistic where there is no agency to take over from the military. And while militaries might not want to intervene without a definite time frame for involvement, Somalia, Liberia and arguably Rwanda all indicate that peace-support operations *per se* are a messy and long process, in which the military should expect to stay around a long time and where, in the absence of civilian authorities, they might also be expected to carry out operations for which they were not initially trained.

It is notable that the Department of Defence has taken the lead from the Department of Foreign Affairs in setting the foreign policy agenda rather than appearing as the handmaiden of foreign policy. As one example, in January 1996 Defence Minister Joe Modise announced that the SANDF was soon to take part in peace-support operations the cost of which would be offset against the country's US$100 million UN debt. He noted: 'South Africa is also committed to participation in United Nations peace operations, and we have a direct responsibility in this regard following the cancellation of our debt'.[7]

The most recent enunciation on South African foreign policy and peacekeeping was made by Deputy Director-General (multilateral affairs), Abdul Minty, at the conference on 'Africa: Crisis and Challenge' in Johannesburg during May 1996. Speaking of the global expectations of South Africa, he noted that there was 'a great deal of misconception about the capacity of South Africa and the role it could play'. Minty drew a picture of South Africa where the high cost of transition had mopped up the expected post-apartheid dividend, where South Africa would be guided by foreign consensus in making its foreign policy decisions. Minty argued that while there was enormous pressure on South Africa to play a role in peacekeeping missions, it was not keen to do so. 'We can provide logistical support', he is reported as saying, and 'we will provide troops as a region, not individually'. He noted that neighbouring countries had far wider experience in this field. Although he conceded that SADC had proved a disappointment in backing South Africa over its stance on Nigeria, Pretoria would refuse to move and work out an African and regional role without the Development Community. The challenge for South Africa is thus not only to develop a clear foreign policy position and consensus on the country's involvement in peace-support operations, but also to get to grips with its African role (and geography).[8]

In 1994, African nations contributed around eleven per cent of troops used in UN peace missions, and there is little doubt that South Africa is expected to contribute its part. After all, it is the only African military in sub-Saharan Africa with the logistical and technical capacity to sustain a large peacekeeping intervention. It is estimated that the SANDF (at 70,000 in 1999) could probably muster a peacekeeping force of 8,000 troops for a limited period (around 3-4 months), and for longer sustain a combat group numbering some 2,500. Clearly questions of: why, where, how and when it should contribute will have to be answered in due course. The justification for involvement can vary from those who think that peacekeeping could earn foreign exchange, it could imbibe a sense of military professionalism and pride, it could provide an excuse for the continuation of a technologically-sophisticated and well-equipped defence force, or simply that peacekeeping is 'the right thing to do'. Certainly the South African public are in favour of a peacekeeping role for the SANDF: a poll carried out by the Institute for Defence Policy and the Human Sciences Research Council in 1996 showed that almost two-thirds of respondents wanted 'the country to have a peacekeeping force that can be utilised externally to help other countries maintain peace'.[9]

The SANDF does have considerable experience in the sort of tactical operational environments generally found in peacekeeping through its peace support missions particularly in the South African townships such as Katorus and in KwaZulu-Natal. The SANDF currently has some 55 companies of troops involved in border and area protection on a full-time basis: a total of 7,337, of which around 2,000 soldiers are tasked with border security patrols and operations. But herein lies the catch. As the SANDF 'downsizes' to its optimum force level of around 70,000 (Army 55,000; Navy 5,478; Air Force 10,480), it is likely that greater and greater demands will be made on the SANDF in its internal security function, whether it likes it or not. The crime wave in South Africa shows little sign of abating, and the police force is still wracked by a combination of transformation and the difficulties of policing in a hostile environment. Consider, for example, some of the following about the South African crime and policing situation:

- South Africa is popularly considered to be the 'murder capital of the world' with, according to the World Health Organisation 44 murders per

100,000 people compared to Russia's 30 per 100,000 in next place. Violent crime is thus one of the most serious problems facing the Government. Murder, car-jacking, armed robbery, gun-smuggling and drug-running have all reached alarming levels, while political violence continues especially in KwaZulu-Natal. White collar crime has also become a serious concern.

• Our police, for so long denigrated at the sharp-end of upholding apartheid, face an impossibly difficult, demanding and complex job. The strains and stresses on not only performing this job but coping with the transformation of the old SA Police into the SA Police Services, has taken its toll. For example, the number of police retiring early due to stress or injury has risen steadily since 1992: 664 police members retired last year due to stress and 566 following injuries. Four years earlier the figures were 265 and 272 respectively. The suicide rate for policemen in South Africa is 200 for every 100,000 members compared to only 22 in the United States. 12 police officers were killed in South Africa in 1995. Today, 50-60 per cent of police duties are taken up with attending to domestic violence, and dramatic changes in societal values will be necessary to change this situation. South Africa is also relatively under-policed: the number of police officers has risen from 52,590 to 102,340 over the past ten years, while the population has risen from 23 to 41 million. Including civilians, there are 140,541 police members. There is a ratio of 2.5 policemen per 1,000 of the population, which compares unfavourably with the European average of 3.5.

• The prisons are jam-packed. There is prison accommodation available for 94,697 prison inmates countrywide. However, today prisons hold 25 per cent more than this figure, with 117,989 prisoners. Almost 30,000 of this number were prisoners awaiting trial. This points to the need to build new facilities, and, of course, to reduce the number of prisoners by reducing crime and the reasons to resort to crime.

• Crime is related, at one level, to a lack of opportunity for South Africans. This relates in turn to the failure of South Africa's Reconstruction and Development Programme (RDP) and to the massive increases in population. This situation is exacerbated by regional immigration into South Africa, with a veritable flood of illegal immigrants which is leading to a xenophobic reaction by some who see their jobs and opportunities at risk, and consequently posing serious problems for the police force and politicians who attempt to balance regional and domestic sensitivities.

• Efforts to solve regional problems such as the flood of immigrants across the borders and other regional problems of gun, drug and vehicle smuggling and the related problems of organised crime syndicates, all demand regional action. But there are questions about how best to manage this and what fora to use—multilateral and/or bilateral, and so on.

• Finally, with South Africa's opening up to the world, we have also opened ourselves to a globalised criminal 'industry'. According to Assistant

> Commissioner Neels Venter, 'Since South Africa emerged from international isolation, it has increasingly become a transit point and now a consumer market for many types of rich man's drugs'. There are an estimated 136 drug syndicates, 112 vehicle related syndicates, 85 commercial/fraud rackets, and 71 diamond and gold related syndicates.[10] This obviously demands international solutions in concert with international agencies such as Interpol and the newly-formed Southern African Regional Police Chiefs Cooperation Organisation (SARPCCO), and using the most up-to-date international techniques to track and apprehend criminals.

The issue of and need to combat crime is critically important when considering the economic fortunes of South Africa. There is, firstly, a link between rates of crime and the attractiveness for local and foreign investment, particularly direct foreign investment which is so essential for creating jobs in South Africa. The business-initiated crime project recently showed that, after market growth, political and social stability was the most important factor influencing foreign investment decisions. At another level, crime is also a deterrent to tourism, an important foreign revenue earner for South Africa. Secondly, there is a link with encouraging emigration of skilled South Africans because of crime. Lastly, there is a link between South Africa and the region, where instability in one threatens to spill-over and engulf the other. And, in this regard, South Africa's stability and prosperity is inextricably linked to the improving fortunes of Southern Africa.

There have, of course, been positive events in South Africa which do offset the rather bleak picture detailed above[11] There has been stabilisation and in some areas a decrease in crime from 1994 to 1995—including murder (up 1.8 per cent) and attempted murder (+0.4 per cent); aggravated robbery (-11.5 per cent); and commercial/white collar crime (-13.3 per cent, though this is probably significantly under-reported). This stabilisation stems essentially from a greater sensitivity to and understanding of factors conducive to crime, including: improved intelligence gathering and statistical information, a new milieu more tolerant of policing and less of criminal behaviour, and a better understanding of the role of urbanisation and problems with old methods of policing. But despite these improvements, it is clear that with a declining defence budget (which went down 2.7 per cent in nominal terms and eight per cent in real terms to R10.2 billion in 1996 compared to the previous year), the SANDF is going to have to play an internal security role and with dexterity 'juggle' all these demands. According to the SANDF's Chief of Staff (Finance), the defence force budget is now 51 per cent lower than in 1989-90 while the percentage allocated to staff costs had risen from 18-33 per cent because of integration costs. The SANDF is still the most effective and balanced military force in Africa south of the Sahara. But gaps are beginning to appear due to funding cuts: the maritime patrol capacity, the strike-aircraft, and the long-range transport force all require replacements in the near future if these capabilities are not to be lost.

Conclusion

There is now a pervasive awareness throughout all sectors of South Africa that national, regional and international security concerns are indivisible: that 'security and development in Southern Africa are two sides of the same coin'. This is evident in South Africa's willingness to contribute to peacekeeping operations, in assisting with policing in Southern Africa (through, principally, the Southern African Regional Police Chiefs Cooperation Organisation as a sub-committee of the ISDSC), as well as through Pretoria's contribution, *inter alia*, to the Non Proliferation Treaty (NPT) review conference in May 1995 and its participation in the Zone of Peace and Cooperation in the South Atlantic (ZPCSA). South Africa's armed forces have moved from an offensive (destabilisation-type) posture to a defensive one; from confrontation to cooperation; and from an individual or unilateral focus towards ensuring security to a bi- or multilateral approach. It is apparent, too, that Pretoria will preferably contribute to operations with SADC, and the formation of the new SADC Organ for Politics, Defence and Security must be viewed as a positive and necessary step towards facilitating such involvement. Institution and capacity building remain an important challenge to African states, and not just in the security realm. In April 1996, it was announced that South Africa had voluntarily donated R12.6 million to the UN to be used for UN peacekeeping activities in Africa. This donation was reportedly made in appreciation of the UN's role in the democratisation of South Africa, and for the General Assembly's decision in December 1995 to forgive South Africa's multi-million dollar membership arrears accumulated while the apartheid government was suspended by the organisation. But although the stage is set for South African military involvement in UN peace-support operations on a much larger scale than before, South Africa's policy-makers will undoubtedly do their best to resist this inevitable contribution as they strive to combat South Africa's own development challenges and to create effective and accepted security forces.

Notes

1. The chapter is based on a paper presented at the conference on 'Southern Africa: Is Regional Integration Possible' held at Wilton Park, United Kingdom, 3-7 June 1996; and on the chapter on 'South Africa and Peacekeeping', which appeared in the *South African Yearbook of International Affairs, 1996* (Johannesburg: SAIIA, 1996), pp. 213-222.
2. Hannay D: 'UN: An Agenda for Reform', *International Update 6/96* (Johannesburg: SAIIA, 1996). For a general background on South Africa and peacekeeping operations, see Cilliers, Jackie & Greg Mills (eds.): *Peacekeeping in Africa* (Johannesburg: IDP and SAIIA, 1995); Shaw, M. & Jackie Cilliers (eds.): *South Africa and Peacekeeping in Africa* (Johannesburg: IDP, 1995); and Smock, D.: *Humanitarian Assistance and*

Conflict in Africa (Washington, D.C.: United States Institute of Peace, 1996). For a critical analysis of PDD-25, see Finkelstein, L.S.: 'PDD-25: A New Failure of Nerve?', *Swords and Ploughshares*, vol. 9, no. 2 (Winter 1994-95), pp. 12-16.

3. See Cilliers, Jackie: 'Security in Southern Africa', *South African Yearbook of International Affairs, 1996* (Johannesburg: SAIIA, 1996), pp. 202-213.
4. See the feature on the SANDF in *The Star*, 10 May 1996, particularly the points made under the heading 'Getting ready for international peacekeeping duty'.
5. These figures were supplied by the former US Ambassador to Mozambique, Ambassador Dennis Jett, in October 1995.
6. See *Defence in a Democracy: White Paper on National Defence for the Republic of South Africa* (May 1996). For details on SANDF force levels, see *The National Defence Force in Transition*. Annual Report Financial Year 94/95.
7. *Natal Mercury*, 2 February 1996.
8. See 'Mute SA dashes the hopes of African democrats', *The Sunday Independent*, 12 May 1996.
9. See the report in *The Star*, 5 August 1996.
10. Venter, C.J.D.: 'Staunching the Flow of Drugs'. Paper given at a conference on *War and Peace in Southern Africa: Crime, Drugs, Armies and Trade*, co-staged by the SAIIA, World Peace Foundation and the Institute for Defence Policy, Jan Smuts House, 4-6 August 1996.
11. De Kock, C.: 'Policing the Cities: South Africa and the United States', *ibid.*

9 The Cultural and Social Challenge of Demilitarisation[1]

JACKLYN COCK

This chapter argues that a commitment to a comprehensive programme of demilitarisation is essential to the stability of the Southern African region and involves more than institutional defence restructuring. It also involves new forms of social integration, solidarity, identity and citizenship. It means creating alternative cultural values and meanings; in particular it involves eroding the ideology of militarism which views violence as a legitimate solution to conflict and an effective means of obtaining and defending power. This emphasis on the social and cultural aspects of demilitarisation is illustrated in the focus on the problem of light weapon proliferation in the region. Light weapon proliferation is used as an indicator of both a privatised militarisation and of a level of social disintegration, demonstrating that demilitarisation goes beyond the restructuring of state institutions to involve the recasting of social relations in a much broader project of transformation in the region.

Changes in the nature of armed conflict in the post Cold War world have not only led to shifts in the global flow of weapons but to dramatic changes in the social organisation of violence. In the predominant form of armed conflict—intra-state conflicts involving light weapons—'it is members of the opposing group who are seen as the enemy, not the armed forces of a hostile state'.[1] The boundaries of these opposing group identities are socially constructed and defined. Whether in a global or regional context, the issue of light weaponry involves social relationships that are structured around diverse interests and identities, values and beliefs, group loyalties, social institutions, social practices and cultural meanings.

It is debatable to what extent NOD is relevant to this situation. Møller has pointed out that NOD designers have focused almost exclusively on state-to-state scenarios. He poses the question of 'what effect a shift to NOD would have on the

---

1 The paper has benefited from the critical comments of Alison Bernstein, Gavin Cawthra, Penny McKenzie, Peter Bachelor, Laurie Nathan and Rocky Williams. I am grateful to all of them for giving up their time.

handling of internal conflicts, such as secessionist movements and or civil war'. His answer is a pessimistic one that '... neither NOD nor any other military strategy would do anything to solve the underlying problems, which is a profoundly political matter'.[2] This paper tries to suggest a more positive answer if NOD is conceptualised as part of a broad process of demilitarisation that involves social, cultural and economic as well as political dimensions.

Demilitarisation in Southern Africa

In Southern African the meaning of demilitarisation is framed by four social and historical processes concerning violence. The first social process is the armed conflicts in the region in the past thirty years and ineffective disarmament and demobilisation in post-conflict peace building. The second related social process involved a broader and more encompassing trend—militarisation during the 1976-1990 period as the apartheid state mobilised resources for war at political, economic and ideological levels.[3] A powerful indigenous arms industry and a widespread ideology of militarism which views violence as a legitimate solution to conflict are among the legacies of this process.

Since the 1980s there have been two further linked social processes concerning light weaponry: the first is what Klare has termed the 'privatisation of security'[4] as increasing numbers of citizens have lost confidence in the capacity of the state to protect them, and have come to rely on individual gun ownership and private security arrangements. This trend is linked to the fourth social process in which the current problem of light weapon proliferation is grounded: the 'commoditisation' of violence as increasing numbers of citizens come to rely on criminal violence of various kinds as a means of livelihood. In this process light weapons are a means of subsistence as well as profit. Small arms are also currency in black market transactions throughout the region. Another aspect of this commoditisation of violence is increasing arms exports through the South African state's arms procurement agency, ARMSCOR.

An indigenous de-militarisation movement should involve the kind of mass mobilisation that marked the anti-apartheid struggle. It essentially involves recasting social relations and building new cultural meanings and values. Demilitarisation involves a shifting of power and resources away from military elites. It is anchored in a broadened concept of 'national security' which encompasses economic, social and ecological factors. In this broadened concept of national security high defence expenditure has been compared to dismantling a house in order to erect a fence around it. Demilitarisation should involve not only cuts in defence spending, but reductions in force levels and restrictions on arms exports as well as the conversion of the arms industry to civilian production. It should involve the conversion of the 600,000 hectares of land presently controlled by the SANDF to development purposes. It should also involve effective civilian controls through a civilian defence secretariat and powerful parliamentary defence committees, as well as the restructuring of the SANDF in the direction of NOD and common security.[5] But demilitarisation should not be limited to these institutional aspects; it also involves dismantling the ideology of militarism and specifically uncoupling militarism from nationalism and from masculinity, a question posed most sharply by Virginia Woolf sixty years ago when she asked, 'how can we alter the crest and spur of the fighting cock?'

Many young South Africans understand weaponry as emblematic of manliness; this militarised masculinity cuts across diverse cultures as the following statements illustrate:

> Buy weapons, collect weapons and clean your weapons. The boer and his gun are inseparable (Afrikaans resistance leader, Eugene Terre Blanche).
> The call to ban the bearing of weapons is an insult to my manhood. It is an insult to the manhood of every Zulu man. (King of the Zulus addressing a rally)
> A Zulu man without a traditional weapon will be regarded as a half man. In my village a man has to carry a weapon even if he goes to the shop, so that everybody should see that it is a man that is walking (Zulu migrant, Johannesburg, 1991).
> This is my rifle; this is my gun. This is for fighting; this is for fun (former SADF conscript).

The former SADF was an important source of ideas about what behaviour was appropriate for white South African men. A number of SADF conscripts have emphasised that the core of military training was to inculcate aggression and equate it with masculinity. They report that the army cultivated a form of masculinity that involves insensitivity, aggressiveness, competitiveness, violence and the censure of emotional expression.[6] Many thousands of white South African youths were exposed to these messages about their gender identity.

This linkage between militarism and masculinity is frequently harnessed to an ethno-nationalism. Many of the men possessing light weaponry have deep seated fears and insecurities that are grounded in racial and ethnic identities which are antagonistically defined. For many South Africans ethnic identities are the strongest source of social cohesion. As Drew Forrest has written of the Zulu emphasis on cultural weapons (rawhide shields, clubs and spears):

> Support for the carrying of weapons is often seen as a simple call to arms, but it is more than this ... it is a deliberate attempt to mobilise politically around symbols of nationhood.[7]

This politicised ethnicity often involves a dehumanisation of the 'enemy' and feeds into an ideology of militarism. This militarised masculinity is one reason why the social mobilisation necessary to create a demilitarisation movement is particularly difficult in South Africa. During the process of 'elite-pacting' which marked South

Africa's transition from authoritarian rule, an alliance of militarists from the various armed formations, but particularly the SADF and MK was firmly established. No strong grassroots anti-militarist movement emerged during the 1990-1994 period to challenge this alliance.

One reason for this is that since 1961 resistance to apartheid has been militarised; 'peace' has been widely interpreted to mean acquiescence and a denial of the legitimacy of armed struggle against the apartheid regime. MK was often depicted by the apartheid state as a 'phantom army'; but what it lacked in resources and personnel, was offset by its powerful ideological presence. During the 33 years of its existence, MK soldiers were heroised and its episodic military actions were eulogised. This may be connected to the historical linkage between military service and citizenship in South Africa. In 1986 on the occasion of the 25th anniversary of MK, Oliver Tambo lamented that 'our people have been deliberately deprived of the skills of modern warfare and denied access to weaponry'.[8] This denial was particularly contentious during World War II when 74,000 African volunteers were deployed in non-combatant roles and prohibited from carrying arms. Z.K. Matthews wrote at the time:

> It is argued that the taking up of arms is not the only way in which a citizen may serve his country, but the African looks upon that as the highest symbol of citizenship and consequently as long as they are refused that privilege, they feel that it is sufficient announcement to them regarding their future place in the body politic of South Africa.[9]

This prohibition on arms was understood to involve a denial of African manhood as well as citizenship.[10]

The link between military service and citizenship deepened during the 1976-1990 period when conscription was extended to all white, male, South Africans with the length of military service among the longest of the 76 countries in the world which then practised this form of defence 'manpower' procurement. Because conscription was framed in race and gender-specific terms, the organisation formed to oppose this policy—the End Conscription Campaign—had a limited impact.

The outcome of these social processes is a militaristic nationalism in South Africa which links prestige in international relations to military power. Subverting this requires the erosion of current antagonistic ethnic identities and the creation of a common society bound by shared values of peace and justice, democratic participation, equality of economic opportunity and respect for cultural diversity. The need for a cultural shift which encompasses these values is clear with regard to the problem of light weapon proliferation. This problem is deeply embedded in the social fabric; the solution requires a change in attitudes, values and social practices of the core social groupings involved; in other words, a recasting of social relations.

The Problem of Light Weapon Proliferation

The Southern African region is awash with light weapons. In South Africa the level of violent crime linked to this proliferation threatens the consolidation of democracy. In Mozambique, northern Namibia and Angola the proliferation of light weapons, especially anti-personnel landmines, threatens to subvert social and economic reconstruction. This proliferation is largely the legacy of armed conflicts in the region which contributed to the creation of high levels of poverty and social dislocation, as well as deep seated ethnic, racial and ideological antagonisms. The proliferation problem is exacerbated by South Africa's arms manufacturing capacity which was developed during the apartheid era. The declared intention of the new government is to increase arms exports by 300 per cent in the next five years.

The proliferation of light weapons in the region is an indicator of a privatised militarisation. In a sense this is partly a consequence of an incomplete process of public demilitarisation that has been underway in Southern Africa for some time. This paradoxical relation suggests, not that public demilitarisation is inappropriate, but that it needs to be broadly conceived to go beyond the political level—beyond the restructuring of state institutions—to involve a transformation of social relations and cultural practices and understandings.

The problem of light weapon proliferation is essentially social. Discussions of the problem that are framed in legal or technical terms are analytically deficient. It is argued here that the issue revolves around social relationships, values, beliefs, practices and identities. The demand for light weapons is socially constructed; the supply is socially organised. Ultimately the problem of the proliferation of light weapons in the region requires a social solution; the mobilisation of a demilitarisation movement that addresses both micro and macro-level disarmament.

The main source of this proliferation is leakage from the various armed formations involved in past armed conflicts in the area. This conflict has involved both wars of liberation against colonial powers and post-independence civil wars. In three countries of the region—Angola, Mozambique and Zimbabwe—the post-independence period witnessed the continuation of armed conflict due to ethnic or ideological differences.

In both Angola and Mozambique, as well as in the wars of liberation in Namibia and Zimbabwe, the apartheid state, specifically the South African Defence Force (SADF), the South African Police (SAP), their surrogate forces and the apartheid arms industry played a crucial part in opposing these liberation movements. A 'boomerang effect' is behind much of the current problem of criminal violence in South Africa as it is fuelled by light arms from South Africa flowing back into the country, particularly from Mozambique, but also from Namibia and Angola. Furthermore not all of the negotiated settlements which marked the end of these conflicts in Mozambique and elsewhere involved effective disarmament and thus large quantities of light weapons have been released onto the black market. However any attempt to deal with the problem must be grounded in an understanding of the factors which create a demand for light weapons.

The Demand for Light Weapons

There are general cultural meanings, social practices and economic motivations among the various social categories that possess light weapons that shape their demand. Such categories include extremist political groupings, criminal networks, hunters, poachers, mercenaries, Self Defence Units, the security forces, citizens and private security firms.

- Many (though by no means all) of these actors rely on their weaponry for subsistence. In some cases weaponry is a requirement of their formal occupational identity; in others it is connected to the way light weapons have become a form of currency throughout the region. The outcome of this linkage between weaponry and livelihood is an attachment that will be difficult to dislodge.
- Many of these actors define themselves as soldiers fighting a 'war'.
- Many share a gender identity that involves a militarised masculinity.
- Many of these actors accept an ideology of militarism which views violence as a legitimate solution to conflict, and a means to both obtain and defend power. This involves a range of social practices including leisure pursuits such as hunting, war games, toys and films. None of these are insignificant in the light of Mann's definition of militarism as 'a set of attitudes and social practices which regards war and the preparation for war as a normal and desirable social activity'.[11]
- For many people light weapons are important symbols of liberation. Whereas, as Ellis has argued, the machine gun was a crucial means of colonial conquest and European domination, the AK 'is more than a weapon; it has become a symbol. The Maxim represented the power of the imperial armies, while the AK has become an icon for many of the anti-establishment insurgent, freedom fighter, and terrorist organisations that exist today'.[12]

Any attempt to control the proliferation of light weapons has to deal with these cultural meanings, social practices and economic motivations. There are eight main (and often overlapping) categories of state and non-state actors who possess light weapons for various reasons.

Political Extremists

These are organised groups with an ethnic base within South Africa seeking greater political power, autonomy and economic resources. There are two distinct groups of such political extremists—the white right and the Inkatha Freedom Party (IFP).

Both mobilise around a politicised ethnicity—an Afrikaner identity in the case of the white right, and a Zulu identity in the case of the IFP.

There are strong separatist pressures in KwaZulu-Natal; Inkatha has always pushed for the maximum federal devolution of power to the province, but its proposals for a new provincial constitution included a provincial army and envisaged virtually an independent state. Violent conflict between IFP supporters and the ANC in this area peaked during the 1990-1994 period but continues today. The weapons involved are mainly AK-47s, but include G3 assault rifles, R5, R4 and R1 rifles.

Elements within the white right are demanding session and territory for an independent Afrikaner homeland or '*volkstaat*'. After 1990 white, right wing organisations began mobilising armed commandos countrywide. The leader of the Afrikaner Resistance Movement, Eugene Terre Blanche, said on many occasions that his organisation was training Afrikaaners for armed combat for the day the ruling National Party handed over power to the ANC. Another afrikaner leader, Robert van Tonder declared, 'The Boer Volk would start shooting on the day the Volk's right to decision making for itself was removed'.[13] Some of these right-wingers have engaged in random racist shootings. The best known of these was Barend Strydom who randomly shot 23 black people, killing six, in the centre of Pretoria in 1988.

Considerable quantities of light weapons have been obtained by white right-wing groupings in thefts from various military bases and state armouries. These thefts occurred largely between 1990 and 1994 and some of the weaponry was used in right-wing political violence prior to the April 1994 elections. In June 1995 it was reported that a right-winger arrested as a suspect in the murder of a progressive church leader was also linked to the discovery of an arms cache in a cave near Groblersdal in 1994. Most of these weapons had been stolen from the Swartkops air force base in March 1994. This suspect was also linked to a makeshift explosives factory discovered on a farm near Bronkhorstspruit earlier in 1995.[14]

According to a number of informants there are links between these white right-wing groups and elements of the IFP. One informant maintained that the predominant weapon in political conflict in Natal until recently was the 'kwasha': a home made gun constructed from metal tubing which fires conventional ammunition. 'From 1994 the pattern started to change. ... IFP and ANC supporters now have serious fire power .... IFP supporters own G3s, R-4s as well as AKs'. This informant maintained that gun running in Natal is a massive commercial operation with the demand coming largely from IFP supporters who are supplied by white right-wing elements with connections to the SADF and the SAP.

Criminals

There has been a dramatic decline in political violence in South Africa since 1994.[15] However this decline has been paralleled by an increase in criminal violence involving light weapons. For many this criminal activity is a means of survival; it is in this sense that there has been a commoditisation of violence. Recent economic strains in South Africa have deepened the vulnerability of marginalised social groups who have come to depend on banditry and criminal violence for a livelihood. At the same time there is an anomie that is characteristic of a society in transition; the repressive forms of social control of the apartheid system have not been replaced by legitimate forms of social control and cohesion.

There has been a dramatic increase in violent, recorded crime in South Africa such as murder, armed robbery, car hijacking and sexual assault since the political transition began in 1990. The World Health Organisation points out that South Africa's murder rate of 53.5 murders for every 100,000 people is more than five times that of the USA. Johannesburg recently became the 'murder capital' of the world, with 9.3 murders each day.[16]

The extent of violent crime is best illustrated by the fact that several satellite police stations in the Johannesburg area have been closed on the grounds that they are too vulnerable to gang attacks and are not safe for policemen. For example in June 1995 a group of four bandits surrounded a satellite police station in Alexandria township, disarmed and shot a policeman before making off with 'five weapons: an R1, an R5 and three service pistols'[17]

The AK is the symbol of criminal violence, but less than three per cent of all murders in 1992 were perpetrated with AK-47s.[18] In 1994 only 7.63 per cent or 458 of the 15,999 murder cases reported involved automatic weapons—a category which includes AK-47s, R1 rifles and sub-machine guns.[19] This statistic would suggest that the obsessional focus on AKs in the South African media is an ideological hangover from the demonisation of ANC guerrillas that was widespread during the apartheid era.

About two-thirds of the firearms seized by the South African Police Service are of non-Eastern block origin, suggesting that the great majority of crimes committed with firearms are committed with firearms of domestic origin. These are either legally owned weapons used for an illicit purpose, or weapons that are stolen from their legal owners. Clearly, legally owned weapons are a large part of the problem.[20]

As Shaw has pointed out, the availability of weapons 'erodes one of the key requisites of democratic transitions, the State's ability to monopolise the instruments of coercion'.[21] It is in this sense that the extent of criminal violence linked to the proliferation of light weaponry threatens to subvert South Africa's consolidation of democracy.

Since many people in South Africa feel that no strong central authority exists that can protect them, there has been a 'privatisation of security' and increasing numbers of both black and white citizens have come to rely on individual possession of firearms. Affluent citizens have increasingly sought protection from security firms which advertise 'Immediate Armed Response'. The social equivalent of this privatisation of security in impoverished black communities was the establishment of Self Defence Units (SDUs).

Self Defence Units

Self Defence Units were established by the ANC as a response to the violence of the apartheid state. Both members of Umkhonto we Sizwe (MK), the armed wing of the ANC, and SDU members tended to define themselves as soldiers fighting a 'war' against the apartheid regime and its supporters. SDUs continue to exist in diverse, fragmented forms and define themselves as 'defenders of the community'. They were established in many areas on the Reef during the 1990-1994 period when political violence peaked in what was widely understood as a 'war'.[22] During this time there was a notable failure on the part of the South African Police (SAP) to protect the private rights of black citizens against violent attack. The SAP was widely viewed as either partisan or ineffective. According to an ANC document:

> In many instances weapons are acquired in crime ravaged areas simply to protect and to provide security for members of households threatened by criminal elements and political opponents. At the level of the (black) community, both self-defence units (SDUs) and hostel residents' associations demand access to firearms for the same reason, to protect themselves on account of the fact that they have limited or no faith in the Security Forces' willingness or ability to protect them'.

Until recently, because of difficulties in the licensing procedures, black citizens were forced to obtain firearms through the illegal arms market (see below).

SDUs were initially armed with knobkieries, spears and home-made weapons, but later obtained access to a variety of firearms including AK-47s, and R4 rifles.[23] Rosenthal found that SDUs were not armed by MK, but by gun-runners operating in terms of commercial rather than political interests.

Poachers

Poaching is an increasing problem in Southern African and poachers are an important criminal category involved at both the supply and demands ends of the illegal arms trade. According to two informants there are strong linkages between the illegal arms trade and poaching with ivory and rhino horn frequently exchanged for weaponry. Poachers are also a source of demand for illegal weapons. The National Parks of Zimbabwe recovered a number of weapons, mainly AK-47s and rounds of ammunition between July 1984 and July 1995, during which period 954 rhino and 458 elephants were known to have been killed by poachers.[24] According to one source from the International Union for the Conservation of Nature in Zimbabwe, the AK-47 is the preferred weapon of poachers and is used to shoot elephants, hippos and rhinos. This is because the weapon does not rust, is simple mechanically, robust and quick to reload, enabling marksmen to shoot twenty rounds in thirty seconds. According to this informant 'there has been over the last fifteen years a major impact on wildlife populations in the Southern African region as a result of the proliferation of light automatic weapons'.

It is alleged that most of the poachers in Zimbabwe and Mozambique are ex-combatants. In South Africa the head of the SAP's Endangered Species Unit maintained that in 1995 all the arrested poachers had been in the possession of AK-47s, 'apart from one case in possession of an R4 rifle stolen from the military base in the Kruger National Park'.

The overlap between different social categories is evident in the fact that there have been numerous reports that the former SADF was involved in poaching. A US investigation concluded that members of the SADF in Angola and Namibia were 'actively engaged in killing and smuggling of wildlife species—including rhinos and elephants—for personal gain and profit'. The SADF was also involved in poaching in Namibia on a scale which led to dramatic falls in the populations of springbok, elephants and black rhino. It is also well known that SADF support to RENAMO in Mozambique was paid for with ivory and that 'tens of thousands of elephants were slaughtered by UNITA forces in southern Angola to pay for military assistance provided by the SADF'. Evidence submitted to the Kumleben Commision of Inquiry suggests that the SADF was involved in illicit ivory and rhino horn poaching in Angola and Namibia until at least 1986.[25]

Hunters

The culture of brutality referred to above is illustrated by the fact that SADF involvement in poaching was not always confined to hunting animals; there was an investigation by the SADF in 1991 into a report that a 'group of officers' shot 12 Bushmen in Angola 'when they failed to find game on a hunt near their base'.[26] Hunters are a significant social category who create a demand for light weapons. Big game hunting is a growth industry in South Africa. Tourists from America, Germany, France and Spain are drawn to the South African farms by the low value of the Rand, by the selection of 31 species of big game trophies and by the fact that (unlike in the rest of Africa where hunting is seasonal), hunting takes place all year round.[27] Hunting is extremely profitable but (with the exception of the Campfire programme in Zimbabwe) mainly benefits the white safari operators who dominate the industry.

Mercenaries

Another category of non-state actors involved in the demand for light weapons are mercenaries. According to one source in South Africa there are several mercenary operations which are highly organised with extensive sub-contracting to smaller companies involved in a range of activities concerning drugs, car thefts, ivory, rhino horn, and illicit diamond buying.

There are at least two large private firms of mercenaries operating from South Africa—Security Options and Executive Outcomes (EO). EO has apparently provided armed personnel to assist both UNITA and government forces in Angola; it is reported to have stationed a 2,000 strong force, including some 300 former South African soldiers, in Saurimo, near the northern border of Angola since 1993.[28] Sources have told Human Rights Watch that EO has assisted the Angolan government in weapons procurement. According to one informant EO is highly internationalised; it operates in Turkey and seven African countries including Angola and Sierra Leone, has offices in Europe and is active in a number of other sectors, such as the construction industry. The personnel of EO are reported to be veterans of conflict in Namibia, Angola and Mozambique.

Private Security Firms

The number of private security firms providing armed guards to companies and residences has increased dramatically in recent years. Security is the fastest growing industry in South Africa after tourism, and the number of private security guards —estimated at 180,000—now outstrips the size of the police force. In 1994 there were some 130,000 registered security guards employed in 2,700 companies in South Africa, around 40,000 of which were armed.[29]

Johannesburg alone has 120 security companies. Some of these companies operate throughout the Southern African region; for example Gray Security Services, the second-largest security company in South Africa, also operates in Lesotho and Namibia. This privatisation of security is also illustrated by the number of citizens acquiring firearms.

Licensed Firearm Holders

White South Africans are rated amongst the most heavily armed groups in the world. There are 3.8 million licensed firearms in South Africa owned by 1.8 million licensed gun owners. A dramatic increase in firearm sales dates from 1976 and mirrors increasing black resistance to apartheid. In 1985 there were 135,382 applications to possess a firearm licence which increased to 256,989 applications in 1993 and 248,976 licences issued.[30]

Licences are fairly easily available and enforcement is minimal. The vast majority of licensed gun owners in South Africa are white. Whites were granted firearm licences more easily than blacks. It was customary during the apartheid era to demand that blacks, coloureds and Indians had training before they were granted a firearm licence, although whites were not required to undergo such training.[31] According to one informant there is a massive amount of forgery of firearm licence. Many young white South African men are involved in a 'gun culture' and militaristic social practices such as participation in war games, membership of rifle clubs, frequenting of shooting ranges, and readership of gun magazines.[32]

Most licensed firearm owners acquire their weapons from dealers who are supplied both by local manufacturers (see below) and importers. In 1993 640 licences to deal in arms and ammunition were issued.[33] According to one source, gun dealers import a good deal from countries such as Brazil, Spain, the USA, Germany, and Israel. These are said to be cheaper and of superior quality to locally manufactured handguns.[34] There have also been reports of dealers' involvement in the illegal arms trade. For example in 1993, the owner of an arms and ammunition shop in Witbank was found to be illegally in possession of arms and ammunition worth more than R100,000.[35]

The Security Forces

The largest category of people who possess light weapons are the security forces in the region. The new Angolan army will have force levels of 70,000, the Namibian National Defence force numbers 7,000, the Mozambican army 12,000 (considerably less than the 30,000 planned), and Zimbabwe is currently reducing force levels from 51,000 to 40,000. The integration process which created the new South African National Defence Force (SANDF) was aimed at hugely inflated, overblown force levels of 130,000 before 'rationalisation' and demobilisation began. This structure inherited the weaponry of the SADF—the most powerful army in sub-Saharan Africa. Considerable amounts of weaponry were issued to security force personnel in Kwazulu-Natal, the Transkei and Lebowa before the 1994 elections. It is estimated that some 3,000 G3 rifles were issued by the Kwazulu police to civilians such as 'headmen and self protection units' at this time. The government is currently attempting to repossess these arms.[36] However the IFP has said it would resist moves by central government to disarm traditional chiefs of Kwa-Zulu issued firearms such as shotguns and G3s.

Arms were also issued to commando units of the SADF's Area Defence System in rural areas. According to Colonel Williams of the SANDF there was poor weapons control, and 'it is doubtful whether the SANDF can provide an audit of the weapons it has provided the commandos in the past 20 years'. On the assumption of seven weapons to each security force member, Mills estimated that there could be 4.9 million small arms in the South African security forces (including government issue to the police and the army and confiscated arms); 1.1 million in the Angolan army, 600,000 in the Zimbabwe army and 700,000 in Mozambique, 'making a total for the security forces of the region of around 8.7 million'.[37]

The Supply of Light Weapons

Demand from the social categories listed above means that there is a resilient market in both legal and illegal arms. Arms smugglers operate in secrecy but with relative ease. The market involves an expansive social network and incorporates diverse social groups. Money is not the only means of exchange since ivory, rhino horn, diamonds, drugs and even second-hand clothing may be tended in exchange for weapons. This suggests that light weaponry is a widespread source of currency in the region. Much of the available supply dates back to the period of armed conflict in the region.

Past Sources of Supply

During armed conflict in the Southern African region from 1975 to the present, there were three main sources of light weaponry:

- Former Warsaw Pact countries, as well as Cuba and China, which supplied arms to the MPLA in Angola, PLAN (the People's Liberation Army) in Namibia, MK (Umkhonto we Sizwe) in South Africa, the liberation movement in Zimbabwe, and FRELIMO in Mozambique. These included rifles, carbines, AK-47s, landmines, limpet mines, mortars, hand grenades, pistols and ammunition. Control over this material was uneven.[38] From 1987-1991 the Angolan government imported $4.6 billion in arms, 90 per cent of them from the former Soviet Union.[39] Russia remains a major supplier since the conflict was resumed in 1992. A South African police source estimated that the former Soviet Union had dumped an estimated 300,000 AK-47s in Mozambique during the mid-eighties.[40]
- Western countries including the USA, West Germany, France, Great Britain and Israel. All these countries provided the apartheid state with military hardware. Various western arms manufacturers sent clandestine military aid to South Africa in defiance of the UN arms embargoes. For example during the 1970s, two US gun manufacturers shipped thousands of firearms and millions of rounds of ammunition to South Africa through front companies.[41] Both apartheid South Africa and the US were major sources of weaponry in Angola. According to Klare, 'in 1975-76 the CIA provided anti-communist insurgents in Angola with 622 crew-served mortars, 42,100 antitank rockets, and 20,900 rifles, and millions of rounds of ammunition. ... So abundant was this assistance that ... UNITA in Angola have been able to keep fighting for years after the cessation of US aid with arms stockpiled during the Reagan period'.[42]
- During 1976-1990 the ideology of 'total onslaught' provided the ideological underpinning for the militarisation of South African society as the apartheid state mobilised resources for war on political, ideological and economic levels.[43] This process was spearheaded by the SADF. The SADF was at the centre of an undeclared war of destabilisation that was directed first against neighbouring states creating what has been described as a 'holocaust',[44] and later against the ANC inside South Africa. As part of

> this process the apartheid state supplied weapons to the SADF, SAP and various 'homeland' armies and surrogate forces inside the country, as well as to UNITA in Angola, RENAMO in Mozambique and other rebel movements in the Southern African region. This was done via the former SADF Directorate of Special Tasks (operating under Military Intelligence). According to Roland Hunter's court evidence, at least during 1982/3, four such projects existed: OP Disa (support of UNITA in Angola), Op Drama (support of Zimbabwe dissidents), Op Latsa (support of Lesotho Liberation Army in Lesotho) and Op Mila (support of Mozambican RENAMO dissidents). Weapons for these projects were procured either via the South African arms procurement agency, ARMSCOR, or were captured by the SADF during their direct military action in Angola and Namibia. Many of these arms were of Soviet and Eastern bloc origin and included AK-47s, LMGs, RPG7s, hand grenades, mortar bombs and mines. Almost 40,000 AK-47s were purchased from Poland, Romania, Bulgaria, Yugoslavia, Hungary and China between 1976 and 1986 specifically to be given to UNITA.[45] AK-47s from Hungary and Bulgaria obtained through ARMSCOR were also supplied to RENAMO.[46] Overall the South African government amassed a large stockpile of captured light weapons.

One of the most deadly light weapons produced and supplied by the SADF was anti-personnel landmines. It is estimated that 10-20 million landmines currently lie undetected in Angola, Mozambique, Zimbabwe and Namibia, although most of these are not of South African origin. This was part of the apartheid state's destabilisation strategy; the SADF delivered anti-personnel landmines as well as other weapons, ammunition and 'propaganda material' including maize seed, sugar and tobacco to RENAMO. According to an informant who was involved in Op Mila the material supplied was fairly constant from month to month and in August 1983 involved 500 AK rifles as well as various other types of weapons and large quantities of ammunition.[47] There are many reports of how this South African assistance was paid for with ivory and rhino horn.[48]

After 1990 the destabilisation strategy of the apartheid regime was turned inward to weaken the ANC and block the democratisation process. A crucial element in this strategy was the training and arming of a surrogate force in the form of Inkatha vigilantes who operated largely under the direction and control of what came to be known as a 'third force'. This 'third force' was made up of elements of the army and police, and there is now evidence that much of the township violence between 1990 and 1994 was organised by them. For example there is now clear evidence of SADF training of Inkatha agents as hit squads which were deployed against the ANC; the SADF supplied these agents with arms as well as training.

Deaths from violent conflict involving light weapons between supporters of the ANC and the IFP peaked between 1990 and 1993 when almost 10,000 people were killed. The apartheid regime was not the only source of weaponry. Several informants maintained that IFP members had been involved in buying arms directly from RENAMO. In 1991 an extensive and sophisticated arms network supplying members of Inkatha in the Johannesburg area with AK-47s, shotguns, Makarov pistols and Scorpion sub-machine guns was exposed. The source of weapons was cited as ex-Mozambican soldiers and distribution was coordinated by an Inkatha supporter, originally from Natal, with strong links to hostel residents.[49] Hostels housing mainly Zulu, Inkatha supporting migrants from Natal were crucial elements in the political violence on the Reef which took various forms including terrorist attacks on train and taxi commuters, and ethnic cleansing of hostels as non-Zulu migrants were driven out. The hostels were used as launching pads to attack surrounding township residents and ANC supporters. These antagonisms were rooted in the social construction of different political, ethnic and class identities.

In this 'low-intensity conflict' many migrant workers defined the conflict as a 'war' and many hostels on the Reef became armouries. In a recent study of the relation between hostels and political violence on the Reef, all 31 residents of Meadowlands hostel interviewed mentioned one or more of the following weapons as frequently used by hostel residents against township inhabitants: AK-47s, R5, R4 and R1 rifles, pistols,shotguns, knives, axes, spears, knobkierries, sharpened iron poles, stocks, tomahawks, pangas and machetes. In the same study a third of the residents interviewed from Merafe hostel maintained that many of the weapons used in the political violence were manufactured in the hostel by inmates themselves. These handmade guns fired various objects such as nails as well as conventional ammunition.[50] Thus hostels became not only armouries where weapons are stored but factories where they are manufactured.

While the apartheid regime, the USA and the Eastern bloc countries plus China and Cuba were the major sources of supply of light weapons throughout the region during the period of armed conflicts, the lack of effective disarmament in the settlement of these conflicts is behind much of the current proliferation of weaponry.

Ineffective Disarmament in Post-conflict Peace Building

The assembly, audit, control and disposal of weapons was an important feature of most of the comprehensive peace settlements in the region. While the United Nations played an important role in most of these settlements, disarmament has not been totally effective. Throughout the region,in Mozambique, Namibia, Zimbabwe and South Africa, the cessation of armed conflict involved the creation of new national defence forces which integrated previously antagonistic guerilla and conventional armed formations. The process of integration theoretically involved the disarming of rival armies and collection of stocks of weapons and ammunition.

In South Africa this was particularly complicated as it involved the integration of seven different armed formations into a single, legitimate and representative defence force. The most significant of these armed formations were Umkhonto we Sizwe (MK, the armed wing of the ANC), the SADF and the four homeland armies. During the process there was meant to be a full disclosure of arms caches established in South Africa by MK. However a 'leaking' of weapons from MK as well as homeland military arsenals has occurred since 1990, and has undoubtedly contributed to criminal activity.

MK arms caches were only cleared by the new defence force in 1994. This was because in South Africa, as in the course of peace negotiations in various countries, weapons and equipment have been held back for a variety of both individual and political purposes including the desire for an insurance policy if peace negotiations were to fail, or to maintain a material base for future political bargaining.

In several countries of the region there was weak control over the former guerrilla armies and their weaponry in the run-up to the integration process: 'Many armouries and caches established prior to independence were not claimed during the post-election period and these either lay dormant (and were incrementally reclaimed for various uses) or "leaked" into civil society for use in a range of criminal and political activities'.[51] Williams cites the following examples:

> • The weapons depots in central and southern Mozambique established by the Zimbabwe African National Liberation Army (ZANLA) during the liberation struggle in Zimbabwe. In 1980 with the advent of independence in Zimbabwe many of these armouries and caches were left in the rear bases as ZANLA combatants returned home to be integrated into the new Zimbabwe National Defence Force. These caches were to be used, variously, by FRELIMO, RENAMO and commercial arms smugglers depending on access and identification during the 1980s and the early 1990s.[52]
>
> • The arms caches established within South Africa by MK which included AK-47s, pistols, landmines, hand grenades and limpet mines. Williams gives particular weight to the weaponry smuggled in during Operation Vula; this was an ANC initiative carried out between 1988 and 1990 to establish MK operatives with access to weaponry inside the country to promote the armed struggle against the apartheid regime. Williams estimates this weaponry to be in the region of 20 tons, and this estimate was confirmed by another source from the state intelligence service. Williams maintains that 'the mass repatriation of guerrillas during the 1990-1995 period, the inadequate accounting of MK inventories within the country after 1990, and the use of weapons by besieged ANC communities during the political violence of the 1991-1994 period, saw the gradual, and uncontrolled, decimation of these caches inside South Africa'.[53]

In the last three years there have been frequent press reports of arms caches discovered near the Swaziland, Lesotho and Mozambican borders. During the course of 1992 25 arms caches were uncovered by the police.[54] In 1993 a cache of about 10,000 AK-47 rounds of ammunition was discovered near the Lesotho border. A police source said they suspected the ammunition was hidden years ago by the Lesotho liberation Army.[55] Arms continued to be smuggled into South Africa after the cessation of hostilities by MK. In January 1993 police discovered arms,ammunition and explosives hidden in the false bottom of a car allegedly belonging to a member of the ANC on the Transvaal/Swaziland border. Five alleged members of MK were arrested in the same month in connection with arms smuggling.[56]

A SAP source estimated that there were some 1.5 million AK-47s in existence in Mozambique in 1993, remnants of the war.[57] According to a number of informants the integration and demobilisation process in Mozambique involved substantial leakage of weaponry. Hidden arms caches were of major concern to the Ceasefire Commission as Mozambique prepared for national elections. According to one source in Mozambique many weapons were stored in the assembly areas and were not secure. (This is in contrast to Namibia where, according to Bachelor, weapons were moved from the assembly areas to a central state armoury and subject to very strict verification and control procedures). A total of 186,000 weapons were collected by the UN, registered and handed over to the Mozambican government. The serial numbers of the weapons collected was supplied to the South African government. However 'many weapons were kept in unguarded buildings', and there was no independent verification of the storage. According to one source the UN later located some 200 undeclared arms caches. A source pointed out that 186,000 weapons is considerably more than is required by the new national defence force which has force levels of 12,000.

Inadequate Control Over New Armed Formations

Leakages from various official armouries not only occurred during the demobilisation process, but continued after the formation of new national armies. The new Mozambican army is not strong or cohesive. 'Low military salaries, inadequate discipline, low levels of morale, and a ready market for the weapons in South Africa, has led to senior members of the Mozambican armed forces being implicated in illegal arms deals ... the Mozambican armed forces have in the past, according to one source, "leaked like sieves". South African members of the joint task force ... estimate that the rate of recovery of weapons is fractional and isolate Mozambique as the major and unaudited ongoing source of arms transactions in the region'.[58]

The Failure of Demobilisation Policies

Lack of control over new armed formations is related to the failure of demobilisation policies in Zimbabwe, Mozambique and Namibia particularly. Demobilisation has rarely involved effective social integration in the sense of restoring ex-combatants to their communities with access to employment, supportive social networks and a culture of peace and respect for human rights. Instead many ex-combatants throughout the region have reported a sense of marginalisation and social dislocation.[59]

In Mozambique the UN set up some 49 assembly points where RENAMO and FRELIMO soldiers were demobilised and disarmed. Some 90,000 soldiers have been demobilised and supplied with transport to the district of their choice as well as eighteen months salary 'as a personal incentive to actively reintegrate into economic and social life'.[60] However this integration has been problematic given the general lack of economic opportunity in Mozambique. Several informants reported that demobilised soldiers had sold their weapons to support their families. As Rana observes, 'the sale of weapon spells cash to buy transportation, food, shelter and medical equipment for those who have left war behind'.[61]

The SANDF has begun the process of reducing its present inflated force levels of 130,000 to 75,000. This is planned to occur over the next four years and will involve cash payments based on years of military service, as well as low level skills training in the Service Corps. The inadequacy of these measures to provide for effective social integration is obvious. Angola has begun the integration of the 150,000 strong government army and UNITA's 90,000 strong rebel army under UN supervision. It is planned that the new Angolan army will have force levels of 70,000 leaving 170,000 soldiers to be demobilised; each is scheduled to receive $2,000 per year for two years.

There is a clear need throughout the region, not only for effective disarmament, but also for demobilisation policies which provide for the effective social integration of ex-combatants. Such social integration involves a complicated process of re-socialisation and re-casting of social relations—a process which is far more complex than one-off cash payments.

In summary, the tragic case of Angola described by Mathiak[62] illustrates the social processes outlined above. Armed conflict in the region, ineffective disarmament in the negotiations ending these conflicts, inadequate control over the new armed forces and ineffective demobilisation policies all provide important sources of supply for the diverse social categories mentioned in the first section of this paper which represent markets for light weapons.

In South Africa, as elsewhere, the arms market contains both 'deep black' and shades of grey; both dead-of-night smuggling of undocumented weapons and covert shipment of arms licensed under false pretenses. While it seems unlikely that the illegal arms market in Southern Africa is controlled by some coordinated cabal of 'deep black' operators, both the scale on which it occurs and the linkages between illegal arms and a diverse range of economic activities connected to the trades in ivory, diamonds and rhino horn to second-hand clothing, are striking.

The Illegal Arms Market

No one has any idea how many illegal firearms are in circulation. According to a 1993 report 'whites are at the head of many of the illegal arms smuggling rackets in Southern Africa ...'.[63] The state is presently using a combination of amnesty, reward and heavy penalties to deal with the proliferation of illegal firearms. The South African police seized a total of 70,925 illegal weapons between March and July 1995.[64] At present there are three main sources of supply of illegal arms:

- Cross Border Smuggling: Smuggling of light weapons across the porous borders of Swaziland, Namibia and Mozambique into South Africa is common. According to the SAPS Centre for the Analysis and Interpretation of Crime Information and numerous informants the main source of illegal weapons is Mozambique. Such arms are often swapped for basic commodities or carried across the border by illegal aliens and then sold. According to a number of informants a major source is ex-Mozambican soldiers. There are also reports of young women exchanging AK-47s for second-hand clothes on the Namibian border with Angola.[65] The exchange of guns for food by Angolans and Mozambicans is also said to be contributing to the dramatic increase in armed criminal violence in Zambia.[66] Weapons are smuggled into the country by air, rail road and foot. According to one source smugglers use many ingenious methods, including hiding weapons in specially adapted fuel tanks. According to another source smuggling into KwaZulu-Natal is organised as a large scale commercial operation and involves ski boats and sugar cane trucks as well as private aircraft. This source also reported unloading of weapons off the coast from Czech arms factories. In 1992 the police established a special task force to deal with cross-border arms trade, and in January 1995 President Mandela and President Joaquim Chissano of Mozambique signed an agreement for cross border police co-operation to find illegal weaponry. 'Operation Rachel' was launched in June 1995, and within the first three months traced 1,164 weapons, 685 of them AK-47s.[67]
- Illegal Imports: Illegal exports from various countries including the USA to South Africa in defiance of US law and the 1977-1994 United Nations arms embargo against the apartheid regime are another important line of supply. There have been media reports of an illegal trade in weapons from the United States to South Africa, including shotguns made by US companies which have been used in township political violence. In May 1992 a sergeant in the KwaZulu police was arrested in connection with an arms cache which included shotguns made by a US gun manufacturer, Mossberg and Sons of Connecticut.[68] According to the Africa Fund, hundreds of semi-automatic pistols, revolvers, rifles, magazines and hundreds of thousands of rounds of ammunition, worth millions of dollars,

left the US but never arrived at their stated destination of Harare, Zimbabwe. In June 1995 a former US gun dealer, Robert Mahler was sentenced to 18 months in jail for illegally shipping more than 200 guns from Oregon to South Africa. South African Police reports said that Mahler belonged to the right wing Afrikaans extremist group, the AWB. In October 1993 South African authorities seized a container on a plot near Pretoria belonging to Mahler that held more than 220 rifles, pistols and shotguns and 46,983 rounds of ammunition.[69]

• Leaks From State Armouries and Security Force Personnel: There is weak control over weapons issued to the SANDF and inadequate control over state armouries. According to one informant, attacks on members of the security forces are much more common than is publicly admitted. Several informants maintained that security force personnel were themselves involved in the illegal arms trade largely for profit. There are also reports of sales of R4s and R5s by 'high ranking former SADF officers', who had obtained them when the SADF left Namibia and Angola. Several sources maintained that poorly paid black policemen frequently sold their semi-automatic rifles (R5s), shotguns and handguns on the black market to the highest bidder. There are also reports of Mozambican policemen selling their weapons.[70] In 1993 two policemen were arrested in connection with a large illegal arms network.[71] In 1995 five policemen were arrested in connection with the theft of weapons from the police training college at Koeberg on the Cape West coast in July 1995. Thirty eight firearms, 203 magazines and more than 2,000 rounds of ammunition were taken in the theft. A police spokesman said he believed the theft had been 'for financial gain and not for any political reasons'.[72] In 1993 it was reported that a Ciskei state armoury had been broken into and R-4 rifles stolen.[73] Several informants maintained that large numbers of G3s and ammunition issued to the KwaZulu police had made their way onto the black market. In 1994 an official investigation found that only 3,514 of the 5,634 firearms issued to police stations in the former homeland of Transkei could be accounted for. The missing 2,120 firearms included R4 rifles and various handguns.[74] Many of these light weapons are locally produced. A range of domestically manufactured small arms are available commercially and include the production of semi-automatic rifles modelled on the R4 in standard use within the South African army, and small handguns manufactured by Lyttleton Engineering. They are an important part of South Africa's indigenous arms industry, which is the other crucial source of supply.

Legal Arms Marketing and Manufacture

South Africa's armaments industry was ranked as the 10th large arms industry in the world in the mid 1980s, and one of the leading Third World arms producers.

This was largely due to the state production and procurement organisation ARMSCOR (formerly the Armaments and Development and Production Corporation). ARMSCOR developed into one of the largest industrial organisations in the country, and its importance to the national economy was demonstrated by ARMSCOR's export performance—arms became 'the country's principal manufactured export, and the third largest export after gold and coal'.[75]

In 1992 there was a reorganisation and 'commercialisation' of ARMSCOR into two parts: Denel (production) and ARMSCOR (procurement). Overall ARMSCOR, Denel and the 700 private companies comprising the local arms industry contributed nearly 1 per cent of GDP in 1994 according to Willet and Batchelor.[76] According to Krish Naidoo of ARMSCOR there are a total of six major companies involved in the production of light weapons: Pretoria Metal Pressings, Musgrave and LIW from the Denel group, and three independent companies, Republic Arms in Pretoria, Tressitu Ammunition and Aserma (part of the Reutech group). The total number of people employed in South Africa's arms industry is of the order of 50,000; this figure reflects a decline since 1989 when military spending reached R20 billion and employment in the defence industry was 160,000).

South Africa is the largest but not the only source of arms production in the region. Other sources are:

- Namibia: Namib Arms and Ammunition at Keetsmanshoop is Namibia's first arms factory. It was claimed that this company will supply weapons for the Namibian Defence Force and be able to produce 30,000 rounds of ammunition a day.[77]
- Zimbabwe: In Harare a small arms factory employing 300 people is producing up to five million bullets a month and is exporting small arms ammunition and explosives to at least six African countries.[78] A new landmines factory has been established.

South African Arms Exports

South Africa has become a key player in the world's small arms export market with $187 million worth of arms exports in 1993 to over 50 countries. During the apartheid era, legislation regulating arms exports was weak, susceptible to duplicity, and void of any ethical considerations. Arms sales were sanctioned to repressive governments as well as to countries involved in civil war. South Africa provided arms to both sides in the Iran-Iraq war, the Pinochet regime in Chile, the Khmer Rouge in Cambodia, as well as Israel, Taiwan, UNITA and RENAMO. The bulk of weapons have been going to the Middle East but there is evidence that South Africa supplied arms to Rwanda, as well as Croatia in defiance of the United Nations arms embargoes. Despite the transition from apartheid to democracy.

Until 1995 ARMSCOR operated officially in terms of a world-wide country and weapons categorisation which was instituted in 1983 in order to regulate the marketing and sale of arms. The Defence Foreign Policy Committee was responsible for the list of countries which was subject to Cabinet approval and based largely on Cold War thinking and attitudes to the apartheid regime. This included a category of countries to which only 'non-sensitive' armaments could be exported.

South African arms trade policy is currently being revised and new policy guidelines and legislation are being determined. The crucial event leading to the current situation was the discovery in September 1994 that two consignments of surplus SANDF weapons—8,500 AK-47s, 15,665 G3 rifles and 14 million rounds of ammunition—supposedly destined for Lebanon, had apparently been sold to Yemen, a prohibited destination for South African arms. This was followed by the appointment of a judicial commission by President Mandela—the Cameron Commission—and early in 1995, a Cabinet Committee to recommend a responsible arms trade policy.

The Cameron Commission recommended that the arms trade should be guided by new social values, specifically 'to promote democracy, human rights and international peace and security'. The Commission pointed out that ARMSCOR was a product of the apartheid era and 'has not been subject to a transparent process of transformation in keeping with our new democracy'.[79] It recommended that government should play a more active role, at ministerial level, in considering and approving applications to market or sell South African arms abroad.

The restructuring of ARMSCOR, and creation of a new arms control body was largely the result of the Cameron Commission report. A new control body created in August 1995, the National Conventional Arms Control Commission (NCACC), includes several members of the Cabinet Committee appointed early in 1995. It is a four-tier organisation headed by the Defence Secretary and accountable to the Cabinet.

The NCACC is responsible for decisions on arms sales which are made on a case by case basis and not on country classifications. However transfers and trade are to be avoided which is likely to be used for the violation or suppression of human rights and fundamental freedoms, to contravene South Africa's international commitments ... to endanger peace by introducing destabilising military capabilities into a region ... or to have a negative impact on South Africa's diplomatic and trade relations with other countries, to support or encourage terrorism, or to be used for purposes other than the legitimate defence and security needs of the recipient countries and contribute to the escalation of regional conflicts.[80] Each weapons sale is made subject to an export permit issued by the NCACC and an independent inspectorate has been established. It has been suggested that a research capacity should be attached to this inspectorate to conduct social impact assessments on weapon sales. The NCACC is required to report to Parliament's joint standing committee on defence. One informant claimed that this is 'one of the tightest and most comprehensive frameworks anywhere in the world'.

Solutions to the Problem of Light Weapon Proliferation

The proliferation of light weapons in the region is now being challenged by an embryonic demilitarisation movement, though this is at present extremely small, fragmented, and in South Africa, mainly white and middle-class in its social composition. This movement is demanding a shift of power and resources away from the military and is challenging militarist values and social practices. The leadership of this embryonic movement involves significant numbers of women; in other countries in the region women's groupings such as the 'Roots of Peace' organisation in Angola have been established.

One source of this challenge is a focus on micro-disarmament by 'Gun-Free South Africa'. Their campaign was launched in September 1994 and focused on encouraging people to hand in their guns on 16 December 1994 in return for food vouchers, lottery tickets and a certificate of thanks from President Mandela. Only 270 firearms—mainly white owned and licensed—were handed in, but according to the coordinator of Gun-Free South Africa the campaign 'raised public awareness about the proliferation of firearms in our society and made it an issue for public debate. It also placed the issue on the political agenda; the ANC December national conference adopted a resolution supporting Gun-Free'. The campaign continues with imaginative strategies such as the melting down of collected firearms into window frames.

The second significant grouping in South Africa's embryonic demilitarisation movement is Ceasefire. This group is now involved in a national campaign against landmines, the objectives of which were endorsed at a meeting of NGOs in Johannesburg in June 1995. They include: promotion of the international ban on landmines; stopping the production and distribution of landmines in South and Southern Africa; the destruction of all existing landmine stockpiles in South Africa; demining, particularly in Southern African countries affected; contributions from South Africa to an international fund for demining; financial compensation and provision of rehabilitation services to landmine victims in South and Southern Africa.

These two social movements are focused on the two most lethal and plentiful categories of light weapons dispersed throughout the region at present: anti-personnel landmines and firearms. The two have opposing social meanings; landmines are increasingly stigmatised but firearms (particularly the ubiquitous AK-47) is still a legendary weapon linked to romantic images of revolutionary struggle and national liberation.

It is increasingly clear that the proliferation of light weapons is a destabilising force throughout the world. However establishing controls will be difficult since both the legal and illegal arms trade are embedded in intricate social relations, institutions and material interests. On the supply side governments, manufacturers, and individual dealers will want to continue making the enormous profits involved. On the demand side this paper has shown that there are strong economic interests, cultural meanings and social practices attached to the possession of light weapons. Thus meaningful arms control must be part of a broad process that emphasises demilitarisation and a shift in social values towards peace, and human rights, as well as economic development and political legitimacy. In short, arms control has to be understood as part of the transformation of social relations in post-apartheid South Africa. The culture of violence and secrecy created by apartheid has to be replaced by a respect for human rights and the transformation of our key institutions—parliament, as well as ARMSCOR—into accountable, transparent structures.

It is also crucial to establish the legitimacy of these structures. As has been stressed, 'politically, the critical issue in dealing with the use of small arms in intra-state conflicts is to bring small arms back under the authority of the State functioning through a democratic government which enjoys broad public support'.[81] This has particular pertinence given that one of the strategies of resistance to apartheid was a level of lawlessness to make the country 'ungovernable'; consequently one of the legacies of the apartheid regime is a distrust of authority and minimal public respect for the law.

There are grounds for optimism given that the latest Draft White paper on National Defence states that South Africa is committed to the international cause of arms control and disarmament. It shall participate in, and seek to strengthen, international and regional efforts to contain the proliferation of small arms, conventional armaments and weapons of mass destruction. Clearly, as Goldring has argued generally, South Africa needs 'an integrated policy of transparency, oversight and control'.[82] But we also need sustainable development; as Naylor points out, 'probably the single most important factor stoking the demand for arms is the prevailing gross disparity in income, wealth, and natural resource capital'. With an unemployment rate of 34 per cent and one of the most unequal distributions of income in the world, South Africa illustrates this factor, but there are high levels of poverty and unemployment throughout the region.

Conclusion

The processes of peace and democratisation in Southern Africa are extremely fragile. There are many threats to our future security in addition to the proliferation of light weapons. One such threat is environmental deterioration: the degradation of the natural resource base on which all economic activity depends. Now that we have secured a pluralist political system and universal franchise in all the states of the region, the consolidation of peace and democracy depends on the transformation of economic and social relations. A privatised militarisation which takes the form of the proliferation of light weapons in the region threatens the establishment of regional security on which such transformation depends. Clearly action is required at a number of levels, but in the final analysis the source and solutions to the problem of this privatised militarisation in the Southern African region are essentially social.

This paper has attempted to map the different social categories of both state and non-state actors that are involved with light weapons. Dealing with the proliferation of light weapons in the region is presently focused on controlling the *supply* through legal and technical measures such as more effective border patrols or arms transfer monitoring mechanisms. However it has been argued here that these are necessary but not sufficient measures. We need to address the underlying social factors which create the *demand* for these weapons. Once demand declines it may be possible to dismantle the social organisation involved in weapons production and distribution. In Saul Mendlovitz's powerful metaphor comparing the arms trade to the slave trade, the challenge is to mobilise a social movement to restructure social and economic relations so that we can, as we did with slavery—despite the massive interests and social organisation embedded in it—achieve a different social order. This is the challenge of demilitarisation.

Notes

1. Klare, Michael: 'Light Weapons Arms Trafficking and the World Security Environment of the 1990's' (Paper for the UNIDIR Conference, Berlin 1995), p. A1.
2. Møller, Bjørn: 'The Concept of Non-Offensive Defence. Implications for Developing Countries with Specific Reference to Southern Africa', *Working Papers*, no. 10 (Copenhagen: Centre for Peace and Conflict Research, 1994), p. 34.
3. Cock, Jacklyn & Laurie Nathan (eds.): *Society at War. The Militarisation of South Africa* (New York: St. Martins Press, 1989).
4. Klare: *loc. cit.* 1995.
5. Siko, Mohlolo & Gavin Cawthra: 'South Africa: Prospects for Non-Offensive Defence in the Context of Collective Regional Security', in *NOD & Conversion,* no. 33 (1995), pp. 16-22.
6. Cock, Jacklyn: *Women and War in South Africa* (Ohio: Pilgrim Press, 1991).
7. *Weekly Mail*, 30 May 1991.
8. *Dawn*, Souvenir Issue.
9. Cited by Roth, M.: '"If You Give Us Rights We Will Fight": Black Involvement in the Second World War', *South African Historical Journal*, vol. 15 (November 1983), pp. 85-103, quote from p. 101.
10. Hellman, E.: 'Non-Europeans in the Army', *Race Relations*, vol. 10, no. 2 (1943), pp. 45-53.
11. Mann, M.: 'The Roots and Contradictions of Modern Militarism', *New Left Review*, no. 162, 1987, p. 71.
12. Ezell: Foreword J. Ellis: *The Social History of the Machine Gun* (Baltimore: John Hopkins University Press, 1975), p. 2.

13. *The Citizen*, 25 April 1990, cited by Lessick, R.: 'The Gun Culture in South Africa'. Unpublished BA Honours Dissertation (Braamfontein: University of the Witwatersrand, 1990), p. 12.
14. *The Star*, 17 June 1995.
15. Human Rights Committee: *Human Rights Report: June 1995* (Johannesburg: Human Rights Committee, 1995), p. 2.
16. *Weekend Star*, 6 August 1994.
17. *The Star*, 21 June 1995.
18. Cochrane, T.: 'A Hole in Our Heads', *The Weekend Star*, 6 August 1994, p. 11.
19. Personal communication, Captain Botha of the SAP, September 1995.
20. Cochrane: *loc. cit.*
21. Quoted in *The Star*, 26 June 1995.
22. Xeketwane, B.: 'The Relation Between Hostels and the Political Violence on the Reef from 1990-1993: a Case Study of Merafe and Meadowlands Hostels in Soweto', Unpublished M.A. dissertation (University of the Witwatersrand, Johannesburg, 1995); Rosenthal, J.: 'Self Defence Units and their Relations to the Communities in which They Are Found', Sociology 111 research project (University of the Witwatersrand, 1994).
23. Rosenthal: *loc. cit.*
24. Personal communication Mike Murphy, August 1995.
25. SADRC (South African Research and Documentation Centre): *State of the Environment in Southern Africa* (Harare: SARDC, 1994), pp. 258-260.
26. *The Sunday Times*, 28 July 1991.
27. Mike Cameron, cited in *The Star*, 21 May 1988.
28. *Sunday Times*, 23 July 1995.
29. Mills, Greg: 'Small Arms Control—Some Early Thoughts', *African Defence Review*, no. 15 (1994), p. 44.
30. SAP: *loc. cit.*, p. 119.
31. *Saturday Star*, 12 May 1990.
32. Lessick: *op. cit.*
33. SAP: *loc. cit.*, p. 119.
34. Lessick: *op. cit.*
35. *The Star*, 30 September 1993.
36. *The Sunday Times*, 20 August 1995.
37. Mills: *loc. cit.*, p. 45.
38. Williams, Rocklyn: 'Small Arms Proliferation in Southern Africa: Problems and Prospects'. Paper delivered at the conference on *The Proliferation of Light Weapons in the Post-Cold War World: a Global Problem* (UNIDIR, Berlin, May 1995), p. 2.
39. Morrison, D.: 'Small Arms, Big Trouble', *National Journal*, 18 March 1995, p. 712.
40. *The Citizen*, 1 September 1993.

41. Klare, Michael: 'The Thriving Black Market for Weapons', *Bulletin of the Atomic Scientists*, April 1988, p. 23.
42. Klare: *loc. cit.* 1995, p. 15.
43. Cock & Nathan: *op. cit.*
44. Johnson, P. & D. Martin: *Apartheid Terrorism. The Destabilisation Report* (London: James Currey, 1989), p. 11.
45. Cameron Commission of Inquiry into Alleged Arms Transactions between Armscor and one Eli Wazan and other Related Matters: *First Report* (Johannesburg: 15 June, 1995).
46. Personal communication, Hunter 1995.
47. Same source.
48. SARDC: *loc. cit.*
49. *Weekly Mail*, vol. 7, no. 15 (1991).
50. Xeketewane: *loc. cit.*
51. Williams: *loc. cit.*, p. 2.
52. *ibid.*
53. *ibid.*, p. 3.
54. SAIRR (South African Institute of Race Relations): *Race Relations Survey*, 1993/4 (Johannesburg: SAIRR, 1994), p. 301.
55. *The Citizen*, 17 June 1993.
56. SAIRR: *loc. cit.*, p. 300.
57. *The Citizen*, 16 July 1993.
58. Williams: *loc. cit.*, p. 5.
59. Cock, Jacklyn: 'Towards a Common Society: the Integration of Soldiers and Armies in a Future South Africa' (Unpublished Human Sciences Research Council Report, 1993); Tapscott, C. & B. Mulongeni: *An Evaluation of the Welfare and Future Prospects of Repatriated Namibians in Northern Namibia* (Windhoek: NISER, 1990).
60. Republic of Mozambique: 'A Demobilization and Reintegration Programme for Mozambican Military Personnel. First phase 1991-1992' (Maputo: Government of Mozambique, 25 May 1992), p. 4.
61. Rana, S.: 'Small Arms and Intra-State Conflicts'. Paper presented at the conference on *The proliferation of light weapons in the Post-Cold War World: a Global Problem* (UNIDIR, Berlin, May 1995), p. 14.
62. Mathiak, L.: 'Light Weapons and Internal Conflict in Angola', in J. Boutwell, M. Klare and L. Reed (eds): *Lethal Commerce. The Global Trade in Small Arms and Light Weapons* (Cambridge: American Academy of Arts and Sciences, 1994), pp. 81-97.
63. *The Citizen*, 21 April 1993.
64. *The Argus*, 22 August 1995.
65. *TASS*, 9 November 1993. Information supplied by Karen Hansen.
66. *The Sunday Mail* (Zambia), 20 August 1995.
67. *The Argus*, 22 August 1995.

68. *Weekly Mail*, 18 September 1992.
69. *The Star*, 15 June 1995.
70. *The Sunday Times*, 27 August 1995.
71. *The Star*, 30 September 1993.
72. *The Star*, 20 July 1995.
73. *Business Day*, 13 October 1993.
74. *The Sunday Times*, 10 September 1995.
75. Batchelor, Peter: 'South Africa's Armaments Industry', paper prepared for Economic Trends Research Group meeting (University of Cape Town, November 1992), p. 22.
76. Willett, Susan & Peter Batchelor: 'To Trade or Not to Trade? The Costs and Benefits of South Africa's Arms Trade' (Johannesburg: Military Research Group, 1994).
77. *Engineering News*, 20 September 1991.
78. *The Star*, 17 February 1995.
79. *ibid.*, p. 3.
80. *Press Release*, 4 September 1995.
81. Rana: *loc. cit.*, p. 18.
82. Goldring, Nataly: 'Towards Restraint: Controlling the International Arms Trade', *Harvard International Review*, vol. 17, no. 1 (Winter 1994-5), p. 34.

10 Prospects for Common Security in Southern Africa

GAVIN CAWTHRA

The destinies of Southern African countries are intertwined, and much will depend on the way the Southern African Development Community (SADC) evolves. SADC now includes all the states of Southern Africa—Angola, Botswana, Lesotho, Swaziland, Malawi, Mozambique, Namibia, South Africa, Tanzania, Zambia and Zimbabwe. The Indian Ocean island of Mauritius was admitted to membership in 1995; twelve states in all, including some of the poorest countries in the world but also sub-Saharan Africa's richest and most powerful state.

While primarily concerned with economic integration, SADC is increasingly committed to political and security cooperation symbolised by the establishment during the course of 1996 of the Organ for Politics, Defence and Security. The framework it has adopted is essentially one of 'common security' in which an holistic approach to security, resting primarily on conflict resolution strategies, is adopted.

SADC will be able to build on the admittedly limited achievements of its predecessor, the Southern African Development Coordination Conference (SADCC), formed mainly to reduce the region's economic dependence on South Africa and to coordinate investment and aid. SADCC was deliberately termed a 'Conference' rather than an organisation and its functions were limited: a small secretariat was established in Botswana and its coordinating tasks, broken into sectors, were each allocated to member states.

SADCC did not take on any security functions, which were the responsibility of the informal Frontline States (FLS) grouping. Formed in 1970 specifically to assist the struggle for the liberation of the white-ruled countries of Southern Africa, the FLS initially consisted of Zambia, Tanzania and Botswana; Mozambique, Angola, Zimbabwe and then Namibia joined as they gained their independence. Lesotho and Swaziland stayed out on the grounds that their security would have been too compromised; Malawi had fairly close links with Pretoria and while it was prepared to join SADC would not support liberation movements.

The FLS operated very informally, and largely on a heads of state level: most of the FLS leaders knew each other personally and agreements were struck with little recourse to the niceties of diplomacy or bureaucratic process. The presidents of the South West African People's Organisation (SWAPO of Namibia) and the African National Congress (ANC) sat in on FLS meetings. The FLS included a military coordinating structure, now known as the Inter-State Defence and Security Committee (ISDSC), the functions of which expanded over time to include coordination of training and intelligence, but not joint control of operations.

Formation of SADC and Its Security Organ

After the independence of Namibia, it was decided to formalise the SADCC structure and extend its mandate—this process was given even greater impetus after February 1990, when negotiations began between the ANC and the apartheid regime and it became evident that South Africa would soon be democratised. These developments came at a time of a sea-change in African politics, precipitated largely by the end of the Cold War, in which a 'second wave' of democratisation came about.

The SADC Declaration and Treaty, signed in Windhoek in 1992 (South Africa acceded in 1994) commit member states to a set of principles including 'sovereign equality ... solidarity, peace and security; human rights, democracy and the rule of law; [and] peaceful settlement of disputes' and sets out objectives which include economic integration and the promotion of peace and security.[1] The associated Declaration further calls for the establishment of 'a framework and mechanisms to strengthen regional solidarity, and provide for mutual peace and security'.[2]

A subsequent agreement, the 1993 SADC Framework and Strategy for Building the Community argued for the adoption of a 'new approach to security' broadly reflecting integrated, multi-faceted approaches adopted internationally through the Conference on Security and Cooperation in Europe (CSCE) which in turn were reflected at the 1991 OAU meeting in Kampala which declared that 'there is a link between security, stability, development and cooperation in Africa'.[3] The SADC framework emphasised the non-military dimensions of security, linked democratisation and development to security, and called for a reduction in military expenditure and force levels and the adoption of non-offensive defence doctrines.[4]

These themes prevailed at a seminar hosted by the UN in Windhoek, Namibia in February 1993 on confidence- and security-building measures (CSBMs) in Southern Africa. While the seminar was characterised by disputes over whether South Africa's military capacity represented a threat to the region or not, it concluded that most of the major threats in the region were internal and had been generated by political and economic problems. It argued that 'there is ... a rich history of CSBMs in the military sphere, especially among Frontline States ... with the exception of South Africa' and that these needed to be strengthened.[5]

A ministerial workshop held in Windhoek in July 1994 at which many of the SADC ministers responsible for foreign affairs, defence, security and policing were present took this forward by formulating proposals on a wide range of security-related issues including human rights, arms control and disarmament, civil-military relations and conflict resolution. It called for the establishment of a Human

Rights commission, a Conflict Resolution Forum comprised of foreign ministers, a Security and Defence Forum involving ministers responsible for defence, policing and intelligence, and a SADC Sector on Defence and Security. It also provided for a Non-Aggression and Mutual Defence Pact and for the 'coordination of military and security policies and doctrines'.[6]

These proposals for structures to manage a comprehensive common security regime were in retrospect premature and too ambitious. They were also regarded by many governments as too complex and bureaucratic. Some governments preferred the old FLS approach where security issues were resolved in a non-bureaucratic manner by heads of state and military liaison took place on a technical level; there was also some debate over whether political and security functions should be combined with the economic tasks of SADC. The South African government feared a proliferation of structures and argued for a flexible approach; some commentators pointed out, however, that the conditions which made the FLS effective (a common threat, mutual friendship between presidents) had disappeared and that more formal structures were needed to hold countries to account and to protect weaker states.

The desire for flexibility led to a proposal which was adopted at the SADC foreign ministers meeting in March 1995 to establish an Association of Southern African States (ASAS) which would function independently of the SADC Secretariat. It would carry out political and security functions and report directly to the SADC heads of state Summit. Separate committees on defence and security and on political matters were envisaged. However, little progress was made amidst evident disagreements, and the communique which followed the SADC Summit in August 1995 made no mention of ASAS.[7]

In the meantime the Inter-State Defence and Security Committee (IDSSC) had been expanded to include the remaining SADC states which were not members of the Frontline States, as well as South Africa. Through a proliferating network of committees and sub-committees it efficiently carried out an expanding array of security cooperation tasks including policing, intelligence, border security, military exchanges, training and professional liaison.[8]

At the June 1996 SADC heads of state Summit endorsement was finally given for the establishment of the SADC Organ on Politics, Security and Defence, which would incorporate the ISDSC and adopt key features (informality, direct access to heads of state) of the ill-fated ASAS. Its mandate included a long list of principles and tasks, including:

- Preventive diplomacy
- Conflict mediation
- Develop 'a common foreign policy in areas of mutual concern and interest'
- Develop a 'Protocol on Peace, Security and Conflict Resolution' to provide *inter alia* for 'punitive measures' to be taken against states once

diplomatic means have been exhausted to resolve conflicts
- 'Promote and enhance the development of democratic institutions and practices within member states' and encourage the observance of human rights
- 'Promote peace-making and peacekeeping'
- 'Promote the political, economic, social and environmental dimensions of security'
- 'Develop a collective security capacity and conclude a Mutual Defence Pact for responding to external threats'
- Develop close co-operation between police and security services
- Encourage the ratification of international treaties and conventions on arms control and disarmament, human rights and peaceful relations between states
- Coordinate the participation of member states in international and regional peacekeeping operations
- 'Address extra-regional conflicts which impact on peace and security in Southern Africa'.[9]

President Mugabe of Zimbabwe was appointed the first chair—thereafter a 'troika' system would operate (the chair-elect, the outgoing chair and the incumbent), rotating on an annual basis.[10] It was agreed that the organ would operate on a Summit (heads of state or government) level, independent of other SADC structures, as well as at ministerial and 'technical levels' and that the ISDSC would be one of the institutions of the Organ. While the organ is thus a SADC structure, it is essentially based on the model of the FLS. A small secretariat is likely to be appointed to service the chair, but bureaucratic functions will be kept to a minimum: the aim will be to coordinate existing government structures rather than replicate them on a multilateral basis.

Inter-State Defence and Security Committee

The ISDSC will become the backbone of the Organ. It is structured on three main levels, with a plethora of sub-committees and sub-sub committees which meet as required or agreed, usually in the country chairing the committee concerned.[11]. It operates fairly informally, with no permanent secretariat—limited secretarial support is provided by the country chairing the ISDSC on an annual basis. In 1995-96 the ISDSC was chaired by South Africa's Minister of Defence, Joe Modise, with support provided by the South African National Defence Force (SANDF) - the chair passed to Malawi in October 1996 and had been previously held by Tanzania. It is as yet unclear what effect the likely integration of the ISDSC into the SADC Organ will have on these arrangements.

The ISDSC Ministerial Committee involves ministers responsible for defence, home affairs, policing and intelligence. It meets only occasionally, on a fairly formal basis—most of the work is carried out by three subcommittees:

Defence, Public Security (policing) and State Security (intelligence). While the focus of the ISDSC's work appears increasingly to revolve around policing and intelligence functions, the defence committee remains the most highly evolved. It consists of three sub-sub committees, the Functional Committee (divided into the usual staff functions of operations, intelligence, personnel and logistics), the Professional Committee (responsible for cooperation between military lawyers, medics and chaplains) and the Standing Committee, consisting of the Aviation and Maritime Committees.

The Public Security Committee has a range of coordination functions, mostly related to cross-border crime and including vehicle theft, drug trafficking, smuggling of light weapons, forged travel documents, counterfeit money and illegal immigration. It is supported by a Southern African Regional Police Chiefs Organisation. At a full meeting of the ISDSC (i.e. sub-committees followed by a ministerial meeting) in September 1995 in Cape Town an ambitious agenda was drawn up, much of which will overlap with the proposed functions of the SADC Organ. These tasks included:

- combating cross-border crime
- stopping the illegal flow of light weapons
- undertaking joint intelligence exercises and developing 'a regional threat analysis'
- training and logistic preparations for peace operations
- further development of confidence- and security-building measures
- assistance in 'building civil-military relations consistent with democracy'
- promoting naval cooperation
- preparing to assist in peace support operations in Angola.[12]

During the course of 1996 considerable although uneven progress was made in developing cooperation around many of these issues, especially in the coordination of training, and additional issues were added to the agenda, such as military cooperation for disaster relief. As is the case with SADC as a whole, multilateral coordination within the ISDSC does not exclude or restrict bilateral or other multilateral defence and security cooperation.

It is clear from these developments that SADC's cooperative framework for coordination of defence and security is already quite well established. However, many issues are unclear: in the remainder of this chapter I will highlight some of the key challenges in the security field.

The Southern African Security Complex

A security complex such as Southern Africa may be conceived of as lying along a continuum of insecurity-security which may evolve in one direction or the other. At one end of the continuum, where there is a high degree of conflict, rivalry and polarisation, a 'conflict formation' may be identified. This was characteristic of the apartheid era (although the conflict was almost entirely with South Africa and not between other states of the region). When this conflict becomes mediated through 'principles, rules and norms that permit nations to be restrained in the belief that others will reciprocate', a 'security regime' in the sense used by Jervis may be identified. This may be formally constructed or emerge on the basis of tacit understandings.[13]

Further evolution of the security regime might lead to a condition of regional 'common security'. In this states would adopt cooperative or collaborative approaches to security on the basis of the development of reciprocal restraint mechanisms. This could entail, amongst other things, the institutionalisation of a range of confidence- and security-building measures, defensive restructuring along non-offensive lines, harmonisation of some aspects of foreign policy, and moves towards economic integration.[14] The term 'cooperative security' (implying perhaps a greater degree of formal agreement) may also be applied to this condition. SADC is clearly embarking on this route.

SADC as a Sub-regional Organisation

Although usually referred to in Southern Africa as a regional body, within the international system SADC is better conceived of as a sub-region of Africa - the Organisation of African Unity (OAU) being generally recognised as a regional organisation within the meaning of the UN Charter.

The security functions of regional organisations (and by extension sub-regional organisations) are legitimised in the international system through the UN Charter. Article 51 recognises the 'inherent right of individual and collective self-defence' for states in the case of an armed attack; Article 53 provides for the UN to recommend action to prevent war by regional organisations as well as individual states; and Article 52(1) provides that regional organisations may deal 'with such matters relating to the maintenance of international peace and security as are appropriate for regional action', provided that this action is consistent with the purposes and principles of the UN. Article 53 states that 'no enforcement action shall be taken under regional arrangements or by regional agencies without the authorization of the Security Council'.[15] The Security Council is also required to be kept informed of activities undertaken or contemplated by regional agencies for the maintenance of peace and security.

The track record of regional and sub-regional organisations is mixed at best. Regional and sub-regional cooperation on security issues seems to be most effective when the governments (or regimes) involved share similar threat perceptions (both internal and external) and seek a similar approach to external powers as a result. In the developing world, internal threats appear to be more important than external ones. Although regime security and stability can be enhanced through security cooperation this does not necessarily entail the enhancement of human security or the consolidation of democracy. Indeed (sub-)regional security arrangements may help to keep undemocratic regimes in power and to protect weak regimes that might otherwise have collapsed. More recently, however, there has been a tendency for (sub-)regional organisations to entrench human security and democratic processes. This necessarily entails a revision of principles of non-interference in internal affairs of member states.

(Sub-)regional security cooperation is less likely to succeed when conflict is endemic within the region and regional hegemony is contested (South Asia, North-East Asia, the Middle East) or when member states are too heterogeneous (Arab League)[16] or too weak (sub-Saharan Africa). It is also unlikely to succeed when ancient conflicts which have been 'overlaid' by the Cold War have re-emerged, as in the Caucasus and the Balkans: here conflict formations are likely to remain for some time until ethnic balances of power can be settled.

Many factors determine why and how countries are willing to enter into regional cooperation agreements. Most regional organisations appear to evolve within security complexes and by increments: they wax or wane according to political and economic circumstances and the level of commitment by individual countries is driven by perceptions of national self-interest. There is thus no guarantee that SADC will prosper or even survive—it will always be a hostage to political fortune, and many obstacles can be identified as it seeks to develop a common security regime in Southern Africa. One of the most important decisions SADC will have to take is on the nature and extent of its security functions - in particular, whether it will restrict itself to common security or will also attempt to develop a collective defence capacity.

Collective Security or Collective Defence?

An important distinction needs to be made between collective security (essentially, where member states seek to prevent conflict between each other) and collective defence or alliance (where states ally with each other and put in place arrangements for joint defence against external threat).

Initially, most discussion within SADC took place around collective security principles, based on CSBMs such as those developed in common security initiatives such as the CSCE/OSCE process in Europe; these formed the basis of the proposals adopted at the 1994 Windhoek workshop. Most of the provisions of the communique of 28 June 1996 which set up the SADC Organ are essentially those of collective security, but it also lists the objective of developing 'a Mutual Defence Pact for responding to external threats'.[17] This would imply an organisation - to use a European analogy again - more along the lines of NATO than the OSCE.

Common security provisions can be, and often are, combined with commitments to collective defence. However, the implications of collective defence are enormous. To be effective, this would require common military doctrine, joint training, some harmonisation of equipment and some formula for sharing command

and control (or handing it over to one country). It would also require considerable harmonisation of foreign policy, at least as regards potential external threats.

Furthermore, it would be impossible to build up any credible force without consideration of contingencies and likely threats—and at present it is difficult to see what these might be. What is the alliance to prepare itself against? Are the threats from within Africa or from without? If the latter, then this would imply a degree of military preparedness and coordination that could lead to arms-racing in the Indian or Atlantic Ocean areas. If the former, then South Africa's overwhelming superiority comes into play: essentially, it would be incumbent on South Africa to 'defend' all the countries of the region. In order so to do it would need to build up a force-projection capacity that would almost certainly be viewed with alarm by other African states not in SADC.

There is no evidence that South Africa is preparing to build capacity for collective defence. Despite agreeing to the SADC commitment, South African policy documents make no mention of collective defence and during the 1996 Defence Review process which laid the basis for future force design the issue was not even discussed. The debate in South Africa revolves around whether the country should bother to retain a conventional defence capability to guard against external defence, or reconfigure its forces to deal with internal security challenges and border protection: no one is even considering the prospect of defending the entire SADC region. Why then did the South African government agree to collective defence?

In discussions with senior South African officials, the standard response to questioning around the implications of the Communique is to the effect that it provides a broad mandate which ought not to be interpreted too literally: it is merely a framework, an agenda. This may be the case. But such ambiguity, while it might be useful in the short term, could have very negative effects over the longer term, especially if smaller or weaker states are reading the text differently and seeing in it guarantees. Furthermore, if it is a framework, there is a lack of clarity. SADC will have to set itself on quite different courses for common security and collective defence. Clarification will no doubt ensue with the expected development of a non-aggression pact—which is something quite different to a mutual defence pact.

Collective defence raises many difficulties and sits uneasily alongside common security: in essence collective defence constitutes a balance-of-power and bloc-building approach to international security which was a characteristic of the Cold War era. One alliance and one bloc will almost inevitably lead to another, thus potentially creating a new 'security dilemma' on an inter-regional or inter-sub-regional basis. Common security represents a more holistic approach, and provides opportunities for (sub-)regional security organisations to contribute to the universalisation of security. South African defence policy, and that of an increasing number of SADC states acknowledges that non-military and sub-state threats to security are paramount: these can best be addressed by common security rather than collective defence.

The advantages of collective defence in the Southern African context appear to be few and the dangers and difficulties great. There is not the capacity for it, nor is there is any apparent need, and the consequences will almost certainly be negative beyond Southern Africa and probably within SADC as well.

Peace Support Operations[18]

Whether it likes it or not, SADC will have to develop a capacity to carry out UN peacekeeping operations. UN peacekeeping operations have expanded exponentially during the 1990s and have increasingly come to involve complex multi-task operations in the context of intra-state conflicts. There is a growing belief that peacekeeping operations can best (or most easily and cheaply) be devolved to contingents drawn from states within the affected region, and delegated to regional powers or regional organisations. The US in particular is exerting none too subtle pressure on Third World countries, particularly in Africa, to undertake their 'own' peacekeeping - hence the offer of Secretary of State Warren Christopher in October 1996 to fund a Southern African peacekeeping force under South African leadership.

There are many dangers in this approach. Most obviously, regional powers might seek to use peacekeeping operations to advance their own strategic interests. Essentially this could undermine one of the basic principles of UN peacekeeping: impartiality. Another potential problem is that this could lead to a 'two tier' approach to peacekeeping whereby the developed world would carry out expensive, well-equipped operations in areas of strategic concern but leave (sub-)regional security organisations to take care of most Third World conflicts as best they can. President Mandela shrugged off Christopher's proposal: no doubt he was influenced by the financial and political implications.

Despite these drawbacks, the principle of 'in-area' peacekeeping by (sub-) regional organisations is becoming rapidly established.[19] The deployment of NATO in the IFOR operation in former Yugoslavia marks a qualitative departure, but the 1990s have also witnessed ECOMOG, the involvement of the Commonwealth of Independent States (CIS) in UN sanctioned and monitored operations in Georgia, and the involvement of the Organisation of American States (OAS) in the UN operation in Haiti.[20] The CSCE-supervised elections in Bosnia in September 1996 marked a further development of this trend.

In Africa, the international community has increasingly expected the OAU to take the lead since the Somalia debacle. African countries have been earmarked for possible operations in Burundi, while in Southern Africa Zimbabwean and Zambian troops are deployed with UNAVEM III in Angola. While not a UN operation, nor strictly speaking a peacekeeping one, Zimbabwean and Tanzanian troops were deployed in Mozambique before the end of the civil war there to protect the Beira corridor. There is thus already some experience within SADC states of in-area peacekeeping, as well as with wider peacekeeping.

South Africa, under pressure not only from the Western countries but also from its SADC partners to take a lead on peacekeeping within Sub-Saharan Africa, has adopted a cautious policy, as Mills has discussed elsewhere in this book. While South Africa and most other SADC states accept that national defence forces are likely to be involved in peacekeeping within or on the periphery of the SADC region, there is no commitment to developing a standing peacekeeping force (even with American money), although logistical and operational support centres are likely to emerge, probably under SADC/ISDSC auspices.[21]

In his 1995 *Supplement to an Agenda for Peace*, UN Secretary-General Boutros-Ghali identified five ways in which regional organisations could assist the UN in peace support activities:

- Consultations and exchanges of views
- Diplomatic support for peacemaking
- Operational support for UN diplomatic initiatives (NATO air support for UNPROFOR)
- Co-deployment of forces in which the regional organisation bears the brunt but a UN mission ensures compliance with Security Council resolutions (UN support to ECOMOG and CIS forces in Georgia)
- Joint operations, in which costs, staffing and direction are shared (OAS-UN in Haiti).[22]

SADC would find it relatively easy to participate in negotiations and possibly to carry out limited operational support. However large-scale deployment of forces will be very difficult without a far greater degree of standardisation of doctrine and equipment and the development of joint command and control systems. Capacity within the region is limited as a result of defence cutbacks, political transitions and internal weaknesses. While some countries have acquitted themselves well in UN operations (Zimbabwe, Tanzania, Namibia, Botswana) the difficulty of maintaining impartiality in complex situations with relatively poorly-trained and poorly-equipped military forces which may have ethnic, cultural or other links in the target country should not be underestimated.[23] As Rupiya has argued in this book, capacity for peacekeeping in the region is not as great as might first be imagined, and the strongest power, South Africa, is in the throes of transition. Any effective peacekeeping in Southern Africa on a significant scale would probably need to rely on UN-coordinated multilateral support from outside the region.

Democracy and Internal Security

Democracy in Southern Africa is fragile. Tanzania, Malawi and Zambia have only recently made the transition to multi-party elections, and political tensions are high in all three countries—to make matters even more volatile, many political conflicts take on ethnic dimensions. In Swaziland democratisation has yet to take place, while Angola and Mozambique have only very recently emerged from horrific civil wars. Zimbabwe, although stable, is virtually a one-party state by virtue of the grip on power of the ruling ZANU party. South Africa's 'miracle' of transition to democracy is belied by the civil war in KwaZulu-Natal, which has taken more than 15,000 lives: a sharp reminder of how badly things can go wrong if ethnicity is not dealt with effectively.

The SADC Communique establishing the Organ on Defence, Politics and Security includes clauses which commits it to assist in promoting 'the development of democratic institutions and practices within member states and to encourage the observance of universal human rights'. It is not clear how SADC will do this: no institutional mechanisms have been set up, although earlier proposals (the 1994 Windhoek Workshop) provided for this. The Communique was criticised by a number of South African NGOs on the grounds that it gave insufficient weight to human rights issues and did not provide any resources for human rights work.

At the SADC Summit which set up the Organ, human rights and internal political and security issues in Swaziland, Lesotho, Zambia, South Africa and Tanzania were discussed, and these deliberations were reflected for the first time in the public communique issued after the Summit. The recommendations are bland—'noting with appreciation' and 'expressing satisfaction with' the actions of governments,[24] but an important principle of multilateral discussion of internal affairs was established (and the Communique might not reflect the intensity of discussion).

Internal Military Deployment

Military forces in various SADC states have been and continue to be deployed in internal security tasks—in South Africa for example, at least 5,000 troops are deployed on a daily basis in this way. A particularly acute problem for the SADC Organ would be the possible deployment of national military forces in the suppression of human rights or democratic freedoms. This would be a challenge for collective security particularly if forces strengthened through collective defence or peacekeeping tasks were utilised for internal security operations. Member states might also request assistance from other SADC states to combat internal dissent. Where would SADC stand? The OAU has neatly avoided such issues through the principle of 'non-interference' but this expedient stance is no longer possible. At the very least, SADC will have to develop a set of principles and probably mechanisms for monitoring of such issues, which have implications for sovereignty.

The OSCE has adopted a clause in its Code of Conduct on Political-Military Aspects of Security which states:

> Each participating State will ensure that any decision to assign its armed forces to internal security missions is arrived at in conformity with

> constitutional procedures. Such decisions will prescribe the armed forces's missions, ensuring that they will be performed under the effective control of constitutionally established authorities and subject to the rule of law. If recourse to force cannot be avoided in performing internal security missions, each participating State will ensure that its use must be commensurate with the needs for enforcement. The armed forces will take due care to avoid injury to civilians or their property.[25]

These are sound principles, but the difficulty is enforcement—while the OSCE can exert moral and political pressures, it has been unable, for example, to prevent Russian military abuses in Chechnya. Nevertheless, given the history of military deployment in internal security tasks in Africa, SADC would be well advised to consider attempting to entrench such principles to cover this eventuality.

Combating Coups

Throughout Africa (although less so in Southern Africa than in most other regions of the continent), defence forces have proven a threat to democracy. The danger of institution building in the defence sector without concomitant strengthening of democratic institutions, and in particular consolidating democratic control over defence, is that militaries will utilise their institutional strength and their ability to wield force to take over government at times of crisis.

SADC has already had experience in managing such a threat, in Lesotho in August 1994, when the military (instigated by the monarchy) intervened to overthrow a recently-elected civilian government. The crisis was handled by the presidents of South Africa, Botswana and Zimbabwe, meeting under the auspices of the Frontline States. It was easy to bring pressure to bear on Lesotho, entirely surrounded as it is by South Africa and vulnerable to border closure, and democratic rule was rapidly restored (a 'coincidental' South African military manoeuvre near the border may have helped concentrate minds in Maseru).[26] Coups in any other Southern African country will be far more difficult to deal with, but the credibility of the SADC Organ will be severely undermined if it fails to deal effectively with such eventualities (and will it expel from SADC any state which falls to military rule?).

Coups can be inhibited by the entrenchment of democratic controls through building healthy civil-military relations and a democratic ethos within the defence forces. The OSCE has clear guidelines in this regard: member states are committed to establishing 'democratic political control of military, para-military and internal security forces as well as of intelligence services', ensuring that 'its armed forces as such are politically neutral', providing for 'transparency and public access to information related to the armed forces' and so on.[27] (Sub-)regional organisations can also put into place mechanisms to automatically take previously agreed multinational steps in cases where coups are threatened or take place. These could include sanctions, border closures and diplomatic isolation and could be a powerful disincentive for coup plotters. The Organisation of American States, for example, has committed itself to the maintenance of democracy through the 1991 Declaration of Santiago and subsequent agreements, which provide for rapid regional action to restore democracy in the event of military intervention.

Defence and Development

SADC is committed to disarmament, and simultaneously to improving capacity for peacekeeping and collective defence. The question must be asked whether it is possible to combine economic growth with defence modernisation.

Economists now tend to agree that, on balance, high or increasing levels of military spending usually detract from economic growth in developing countries, especially over the long term. There may, however, be particular circumstances where increased investment in the military and defence industries helps to kick-start an industrialisation process: the pattern is uneven and complex and the interpretation of the data is contested.

The UN Development Programme (UNDP) has argued strongly that Third World countries need to move away from spending on defence for the state (more often the regime in power rather than the people) towards spending for human security. Poor countries spend US$130 billion a year on armaments alone—while this is a fraction of what the developed countries allocate, channelling it towards human security would make a huge difference.[28] In part, this is happening. Third World security spending peaked at the end of the 1980s and has been declining since then. This, however, is not necessarily a result of political elites coming to their senses: the causes include chronic debt (preventing the import of arms), donor pressures, the end of military clientship arrangements with the superpowers and the implosion of states.

The dilemma is that for development to occur there needs to be at least a degree of stability and law-and-order; and the state needs to be able to carry out at least some ordering and delivery functions. But if this is achieved though militarism or authoritarianism the long term consequences are unpredictable and instability may result. Successful sub-regional development will depend on the evolution of strong civil societies and a democratic system in which human security is achieved. This could entail programmes to strengthen parliamentary democracies (SADC has already established a parliamentary forum), the development of NGO networks and a focus on primary health care, education and job-creation programmes.

South African Hegemony

Potential South African hegemony within SADC is undisputed, even if the post-apartheid South African government is reluctant to assert it. South Africa spends more on defence and its GDP is greater than the rest of SADC combined. Its military and economic superiority is undisputed and it alone has the capacity to underpin joint peacekeeping operations or collective defence.

Post-apartheid South Africa has been reluctant to take too strong a leadership role in the region, given its recent history of aggression, and has been careful not to dominate the process leading to the emergence of the SADC Organ. Nevertheless (albeit after some debate) the new South Africa is committed to development on a regional, not just a national, basis, in the recognition that uneven development in the region will foment insecurity.

In the context of a policy orientation of pursuing peaceful relations with other Southern African states and seeking 'a high level of political, economic and military cooperation' South Africa has also made firm commitments to common security and multilateralism.[29] There is little reason why any of the weaker SADC states should resist this—they have far more to gain than to lose. While SADC will provide South Africa with opportunities to consolidate its regional influence, just as ASEAN has done for Indonesia, this will be achieved in a climate of restraint in which smaller nations have implicit or explicit security guarantees and stand to benefit within cooperative arrangements.

At the same time South Africa has concluded a number of bilateral agreements with its neighbours, particularly in relation to border security. Both bilateral and multilateral arrangements can have the effect of 'reining in' hegemonic states, just as powerful states may employ both to secure their preeminence. South Africa's potential hegemony within SADC will have important impacts as the organisation evolves: domestic events in South Africa often affect the entire region and many countries will seek to emulate successful South African policies.

Expansion and Periphery

SADC will have to develop strategies to deal with peripheral states, and decide whether it can be enlarged or not. With the exception of Madagascar and other Indian Ocean islands, SADC would appear to have reached, if not gone beyond, the boundaries of 'Southern Africa'. That, of course, would not prevent its being expanded further into Africa or the incorporation of some more Indian Ocean island states. Zaire has requested membership of SADC, which has been refused, and criteria for membership have now been drawn up which would effectively allow SADC to exclude any African state it wanted to.

An alternative to piecemeal incorporation of peripheral states could be a cooperation agreement or even a merger with, say, the Commonwealth of East and Southern African States (COMESA) or perhaps with one of the other sub-regional organisations in Africa at some later date. This would effectively create an East, Central and Southern African organisation. Such developments, however, are a long way off, although it is worth noting that it has long been a pan-African ambition to establish a coherent system of sub-regional organisations within the framework of the OAU. Indeed, the OAU's 1991 commitment to the creation of an African Economic Community by the year 2025 rests on a first stage of consolidating sub-regional bodies.[30] The prospects for success in this endeavour are not good, however, given the history of failures in African integration efforts and the internal weaknesses of the large countries which could drive sub-regional consolidation (Nigeria, Zaire, Kenya and Egypt).[31] In sub-Saharan Africa, only SADC appears to offer much chance of success.

Defence Restructuring and Non-Offensive Defence

The issue of defence restructuring and the prospects for institutionalising non-offensive defence (NOD) have been the subject of this book. It is worth repeating that the benefits of this are obvious but the onus must be on South Africa, with its massive superiority and its historic orientation towards an offensive posture and 'forward defence' which led to the destabilisation of neighbouring countries. The ANC made an early call for the South African defence force to be restructured along non-offensive lines, a position which gave rise to government policy commitments in this regard.

As a result the 1996 White Paper on Defence (and the Interim Constitution, although not the final version adopted in 1996) provides that the SANDF should be 'primarily defensive'. During the 1996 Defence Review process which followed the ratification by parliament of the White Paper, consideration was given to what this might mean in practice. As Williams has pointed out in his chapter, the Defence Review Working Group which met during 1996 considered various options, noting that a defensive posture was 'a reality at the political and national strategic level' but arguing that this did not preclude 'an operationally offensive orientation and/or the absence of offensive capabilities at the operational or tactical levels'. It called for the elimination of strategic offensive capability, the scrapping of 'manifestly offensive weapon systems', a reduction in force levels and pre-emptive strike capability, limitations on the reach of military forces and the strengthening of defensive capabilities.

At the same time, the Working Group noted that low force-to-space ratios in the region, coupled with the need for South Africa to play a role in regional defence cooperation and peace operations, as well as budgetary restraints, prevented the SANDF from adopting a fully defensive posture at an operational level.[32] In my view these assumptions could be questioned. Strategic reach (probably needed for peace operations) is not necessarily the same as strike capability, for example. It might also be possible to configure forces in such a way that while they were capable of being deployed in multilateral actions they would lack a key component which would need to be drawn from a neighbouring country, for example airlift (see Møller's chapter). The latter scenario, would, however, depend on a much greater degree of regional integration and sophistication.

The stabilising effects of a non-offensive posture would, of course, be multiplied if all countries of the region adopted this approach. In practice, most countries have been disarming and reducing force levels, with the exception of foreign-exchange rich Botswana, which (as Honwana has noted) has recently embarked on a defence modernisation and expansion drive during the 1990s, including the acquisition of Leopard tanks and CF-5 jet aircraft.[33] This has alarmed some neighbouring states, especially Namibia, but given the financial pressures on Southern African governments rearmament seems an unlikely scenario. In South Africa, the defence budget has been cut by just over fifty per cent since 1989, and now accounts for less than six per cent of government expenditure (down from almost a quarter at the end of the 1980s). There are also plans to cut the size of the defence from over 100,000 to around 75,000. Similar cuts are taking place in Zimbabwe, Mozambique, Angola, Tanzania, Zambia and Malawi and overall defence spending in the region has declined significantly (see Rupiya).

Conclusion

Sub-regional organisations in the Third World which have experimented with collective defence have not generally been successful. Common security has a slightly better track record in contributing to stability between and within states and in helping to create conditions for economic growth. At the same time, however, without commitments to processes of democratisation and human rights, any form of sub-regional security organisation can enhance regime security at the expense of human security.

Socio-economic development and security are complexly intertwined: one cannot take place without the other. SADC has adopted an integrated programme within a unified but largely informal political structure—the trick will be to simultaneously achieve the consolidation of democracy, economic growth and stability. Factors which will contribute to success will include the strengthening of civil society; the institutionalisation of democratic civil-military relations; the restraining of possible hegemonic ambitions by South Africa; the development of peacekeeping capacities without inducing unnecessary rearmament; the extension of confidence-building on the periphery of the region rather than bloc-building; responsible demobilisation and disarmament; and successful defensive restructuring of the armed forces of Southern African countries.

Notes

1. Heads of State or Government of Southern African States: 'Declaration, Treaty and Protocol of the Southern African Development Community' (Windhoek, 17 August 1992).
2. *ibid.*
3. Organisation of African Unity: 'Kampala Document for a Proposed Conference on Security, Stability, Development and Cooperation in Africa' (Kampala, 23 May 1991).

4. Nathan, Laurie & Joao Honwana: 'The Establishment of SADC Forums for Conflict Resolution and Security and Defence' (Cape Town: Centre for Conflict Resolution, 1994).
5. United Nations: 'International Seminar on Confidence- and Security-Building Measures in Southern Africa, Windhoek, Namibia, 24-26 February 1993 (Windhoek: United Nations, 1993), p. 14; see also United Nations: 'Confidence- and Security-Building Measures in Southern Africa', *Disarmament: Topical Papers*, no. 14 (New York: United Nations, 1993).
6. 'Workshop on Democracy, Peace and Security: Workshop Resolutions' (Windhoek: 11-16 July 1994); 'Workshop on Democracy, Peace and Security: Report of the Officials' (Windhoek: 11-16 July 1994).
7. 'SADC Summit Communique' (Johannesburg, 28 August 1995).
8. Hamman, D.: 'ISDSC: Defence Sub-Committee', paper presented to the Institute for Defence Policy 'Seminar on South Africa and Global Peace Support Operations' (Cape Town, 17-18 May 1995).
9. 'SADC Heads of States or Government Summit Communique' (Gaborone, 28 June 1996).
10. Discussions with senior South African Department of Foreign Affairs officials.
11. Information on the ISDSC is based on the author's discussions with ISDSC participants and material drawn from Cilliers, Jakkie: 'Towards Collaborative and Cooperative Security in Southern Africa: The OAU and SADC', in idem & Markus Reichardt: *About Turn: The Transformation of the South African Military and Intelligence* (Halfway House: Institute for Defence Policy, 1995).
12. 'SANDF Communication Bulletin', 12 September 1995.
13. Jervis, Robert: 'Security Regimes', *International Organization*, vol. 36, no. 2 (Spring 1982), pp. 357-378.
14. Palme Commission: *Common Security: A Blueprint for Survival* (New York: Simon & Schuster, 1982).
15. Farer, Tom J.: 'The Role of Regional Collective Security Arrangements', in Thomas G. Weiss (ed.): *Collective Security in a Changing World* (Boulder: Lynne Rienner, 1993), p. 161.
16. ASEAN has succeeded in conditions of great heterogeneity, but on the basis of shared regime values and threat perceptions.
17. SADC: 'Communique Heads of State or Governments of the Southern African Development Community' (Gaberone, 28 June 1996).
18. The term is used to include preventive diplomacy, peacemaking (mediation etc), peacekeeping (military or para-military operations undertaken with the consent of the disputant authorities), peace enforcement (military force authorised by the Security Council), humanitarian and relief activities and post-conflict peace-building. This section focuses on peacekeeping and other UN-authorised operations requiring deployment of force.

19. Ratner, Steven R.: *The New UN Peacekeeping: Building Peace in Lands of Conflict After the Cold War* (New York: St Martin's Press, 1995), p. 83.
20. Goodby, James (ed.): *Regional Conflicts: The Challenge to US-Russian Collaboration* (Oxford: Oxford University Press, 1995).
21. Institute for a Democratic South Africa: 'Training for Peacekeeping in Southern Africa: Report of the Study Team' (Johannesburg: IDASA, 1996).
22. United Nations Security Council: 'Supplement to an Agenda for Peace: Position Paper of the Secretary-General' (New York: United Nations, 1995), p. 20.
23. See Cilliers, Jakkie & Mark Malan: 'A Regional Peacekeeping Role for South Africa: Pressures, Problems and Prognosis', *African Security Review*, vol. 5, no 6 (1996).
24. SADC: 'Communique', 28 June 1996, section 5.
25. Conference on Security and Cooperation in Europe: 'Budapest Declaration V: Code of Conduct of Politico-Military Aspects of Security' (Budapest, 6 December 1994).
26. Sejanamane, M.: 'Peace and Security in Southern Africa: The Lesotho Crisis and Regional Intervention', monograph, 1995.
27. Conference on Security and Cooperation in Europe: 'Budapest Decision V: Code of Conduct on Politico-Military Aspects of Security' (Budapest, 6 December 1994), Section VII.
28. Ul Haq, M.: 'New Imperatives of Human Security', *Towards Human Security*, no. 4 (New York: UN Development Programme, 1995).
29. *White Paper on Defence*, 1996, Section 11.3.
30. Adeniji, Oluyemi: 'Regionalism in Africa', *Security Dialogue*, vol. 24, no. 2 (1993), pp. 211-220.
31. See Lancaster, C.: 'The Lagos Three: Economic Regionalism in Sub-Saharan Africa', in J.W. Harbeson & D. Rothchild (eds.): *Africa in World Politics* (Boulder: Westview, 1995).
32. Defence Review Working Group: 'Position Paper on SA Defence Posture First Draft', July 1996.
33. 'Khama hits out at Mail and Guardian', *Botswana Guardian*, 19 April 1996.

Appendices

Constitution of Republic of South Africa 1996

As adopted by the Constitutional Assembly on 8 May 1996 and as amended on 11 October 1996.

Chapter 11: Security Services

198. The following principles govern national security in the Republic:
(a) National security must reflect the resolve of South Africans, as individuals and as a nation, to live as equals, to live in peace and harmony, to be free from fear and want and to seek a better life.
(b) The resolve to live in peace and harmony precludes any South African citizen from participating in armed conflict, nationally or internationally, except as provided for in terms of the Constitution or national legislation.
(c) National security must be pursued in compliance with the law, including international law.
(d) National security is subject to the authority of Parliament and the national executive.

199. Establishment, structuring and conduct of security services
(1) The security services of the Republic consist of a single defence force, a single police service and any intelligence services established in terms of the Constitution.
(2) The defence force is the only lawful military force in the Republic.
(3) Other than the security services established in terms of the Constitution, armed organisations or services may be established only in terms of national legislation.
(4) The security services must be structured and regulated by national legislation.
(5) The security services must act, and must teach and require their members to act, in accordance with the Constitution and the law, including customary international law and international agreements binding on the Republic.
(6) No member of any security service may obey a manifestly illegal order.
(7) Neither the security services, nor any of their members, may, in the performance of their functions –
(a) prejudice a political party interest that is legitimate in terms of the Constitution; or

(b) further, in a partisan manner, any interest of a political party.

(8) To give effect to the principles of transparency and accountability, multi-party parliamentary committees must have oversight of all security services in a manner determined by national legislation or the rules and orders of Parliament.

200. Defence force

(1) The defence force must be structured and managed as a disciplined military force.

(2) The primary object of the defence force is to defend and protect the Republic, its territorial integrity and its people in accordance with the Constitution and the principles of international law regulating the use of force.

Summit of Heads of State or Governments of the Southern African Development Community (SADC)
(Extract of Communique)

1. The Summit of Heads of State or Government of Southern African Development Community (SADC) met in Gaborone, the Republic of Botswana, on 28th June 1996 under the Chairmanship of His Excellency, Sir Ketumile Masire, President of the Republic of Botswana, to launch the SADC Organ on Politics, Defence, and Security.

4. The Summit reaffirmed that the SADC Organ constituted an appropriate institutional framework by which SADC countries would coordinate their policies in the areas of politics, defence and security. The Summit, therefore, agreed as follows:

4.1 Principles

As, inter alia, set out in Article 4 of the SADC Treaty, the following shall be the guiding principles for the SADC Organ on Politics, Defence and Security:
a) sovereign equality of all member states;
b) respect for the sovereignty and territorial integrity of each State and for its inalienable right to independent existence;
c) achievement of solidarity, peace and security in the region;
d) observance of human rights, democracy and the rule of law;
e) promotion of economic development in the SADC region in order to achieve for all member states, equity, balance and mutual benefit;
f) peaceful settlement of disputes by negotiation, mediation and arbitration;
g) military intervention of whatever nature shall be decided upon only after all possible political remedies have been exhausted in accordance with the Charter of the OAU and the United Nations.

4.2 The Objectives of the organ

4.2.1 The SADC Organ on Politics, Defence and Security shall work to the following objective, namely to:
a) protect the people and safeguard the development of the region, against instability arising from the breakdown of law and order, inter-state conflict and external aggression;
b) promote political co-operation among member States and the evolution of common political value systems and institutions;
c) develop a common foreign policy in areas of mutual concern and interest,

and to lobby as a region, on issues of common interest at international fora;
d) cooperate fully in regional security and defence through conflict prevention management and resolution;
e) mediate in inter-state and intra-state disputes and conflicts;
f) use preventative diplomacy to pre-empt conflict in the region, both within and between states through an early warning system;
g) where conflict does occur, to seek and to end this as quickly as possible through diplomatic means. Only where such means fail would the Organ recommend that the Summit should consider punitive measures. These responses would be agreed in a Protocol on Peace, Security and Conflict Resolution;
h) promote and enhance the development of democratic institutions and practices within member states, and to encourage the observance of universal human rights as provided for in the Charters and Conventions of the OAU and the United Nations;
i) promote peace-making and peace-keeping in order to achieve sustainable peace and security;
j) give political support to the organs and institutions of SADC;
k) promote the political, economic, social, and environmental dimensions of security;
l) develop a collective security capacity and conclude a Mutual Defence Pact for responding to external threats and a regional peacekeeping capacity within national armies that could be called upon within the region, or elsewhere on the Continent;
m) develop close cooperation between the police and security services of the region, with a view to addressing cross border crime, as well as promoting a community-based approach on matters of security;
n) encourage and monitor the ratification of United Nations, Organisations of African Unity, and other international conventions and treaties on arms control and disarmament, human rights and peaceful relations between states;
o) coordinate the participation of member states in international and regional peacekeeping operations; and
p) address extra-regional conflicts which impact on peace and security in Southern Africa.

4.3 Institutional Framework

4.3.1 The SADC Organ on Politics, Defence and Security shall operate at the Summit level, and shall function independently of other SADC structures. The Organ shall also operate at Ministerial and technical levels. The Chairmanship of the Organ shall rotate on an annual and on a Troika basis.

4.3.2 The Summit elected His Excellency, President Mugabe as Chairman of the Organ.(...)
4.3.3 The Summit also agreed that the Inter-State Defence and Security Committee shall be one of the institutions of the Organ. The Organ may establish other structures as the need arises.

Defence in Democracy. White Paper on National Defence for the Republic of South Africa
as approved by Parliament on 14 May 1996 (Extract).

Chapter 2: The Challenge of Transformation

National security policy and the RDP

1. In the new South Africa national security is no longer viewed as a predominantly military and police problem. It has been broadened to incorporate political, economic, social and environmental matters. At the heart of this new approach is a paramount concern with the security of people.
2. Security is an all-encompassing condition in which individual citizens live in freedom, peace and safety; participate fully in the process of governance; enjoy the protection of fundamental rights; have access to resources and the basic necessities of life; and inhabit an environment which is not detrimental to their health and well-being.
3. At national level the objectives of security policy therefore encompass the consolidation of democracy; the achievement of social justice, economic development and a safe environment, and a substantial reduction in the level of crime, violence and political instability. Stability and development are regarded as inextricably linked and mutually reinforcing.
4. At international level the objectives of security policy include the defence of sovereignty, territorial integrity and political independence of the South African state, and the promotion of regional security in Southern Africa.
5. The Government of National Unity recognises that the greatest threats to the South African people are socio-economic problems such as poverty, unemployment, poor education, the lack of housing and the absence of adequate social services, as well as the high level of crime and violence.
6. Accordingly, one of the government's policy priorities is the Reconstruction and Development Programme. The RDP is the principal long-term means of promoting the well-being and security of citizens and, thereby, the stability of the country.
7. There is consequently a compelling need to reallocate state resources to the RDP. The challenge is to rationalise the SANDF and contain military spending without undermining the country's core defence capability in the short or long-term. As a matter of sound organisational practice, any cuts to the defence budget should be rational and well planned.
8. The new approach to security does not imply an expanded role for the armed forces. The SANDF may be employed in a range of secondary roles as prescribed by law, but its primary and essential function is service in

defence of South Africa for the protection of its sovereignty and territorial integrity.

9. The SANDF therefore remains an important security instrument of last resort but it is no longer the dominant security institution. The responsibility for ensuring the security of South Africa's people is now shared by many government departments and ultimately vests in Parliament.

Defence in a democracy

10. The theme of this White Paper is the formulation of a new defence policy and the transformation of the Department of Defence. Transformation is essential in the light of three sets of factors: the history of armed forces in our country; the new strategic environment at international, regional and domestic levels; and, most importantly, the advent of democracy in South Africa.

11. The process of transformation will he guided by the following principles of defence in a democracy. These principles derive from the Constitution and government policy:

11.1 National security shall be sought primarily through efforts to meet the political, economic, social and cultural rights and needs of South Africa's people, and through efforts to promote and maintain regional security.

11.2 South Africa shall pursue peaceful relations with other states. It will seek a high level of political, economic and military co-operation with Southern African states in particular.

11.3 South Africa shall adhere to international laws on armed conflict and to all international treaties to which it is parties.

11.4 The SANDF shall have a primarily defensive orientation and posture.

11.5 South Africa is committed to the international goals of arms control and disarmament. It shall participate in, and seek to strengthen international and regional efforts to contain and prevent the proliferation of small arms, conventional armaments and weapons of mass destruction.

11.6 South Africa's force levels, armaments and military expenditure shall be determined by defence policy which derives from an analysis of the external and internal security environment, which takes account of the social and economic imperatives of the RDP, and which is approved by Parliament.

11.7 The SANDF shall be a balanced, modern, affordable and technologically advanced military force, capable of executing its tasks effectively and efficiently.

11.8 The functions and responsibilities of the SANDF shall be determined by the Constitution and the Defence Act.

11.9 The primary role of the SANDF shall be to defend South Africa against external military aggression. Deployment in an internal policing

capacity shall be limited to exceptional circumstances and subject to parliamentary approval and safeguards.
11.10 The SANDF shall be subordinate to and fully accountable to Parliament and the Executive.
11.11 The SANDF shall operate strictly within the parameters of the Constitution, domestic legislation and international humanitarian law. It shall respect human rights and the democratic political process.
11.12 Defence policy and military activities shall be sufficiently transparent to ensure meaningful parliamentary scrutiny and debate, insofar as this does not endanger the lives of military personnel or jeopardize the success of military operations.
11.13 The SANDF shall not further or prejudice party-political interests.
11.14 The SANDF shall develop a non-racial, non-sexist and non-discriminatory institutional culture as required by the Constitution.
11.15 The composition of the SANDF shall broadly reflect the composition of South Africa. To this end, affirmative action and equal opportunity programmes will be introduced.
11.16 The SANDF shall respect the rights and dignity of its members within the normal constraints of military discipline and training.

The regional context

7. The most significant strategic development over the past few years is South Africa's new status in Southern Africa, previously an arena of intense conflict. With the election of the Government of National Unity, relations with neighbouring states have changed from suspicion and animosity to friendship and cooperation.

8. The region as a whole has undergone substantial change since the end of the Cold War. Considerable progress has been made towards the resolution of internal conflicts, the establishment of democratic political systems, and demilitarisation and disarmament. The prospects for regional peace and stability are greater today than at any other time in recent decades.

9. Nevertheless, much of the subcontinent is stricken by chronic underdevelopment and the attendant problems of poverty, illiteracy and unemployment. There are large numbers of refugees and displaced people; an acute debt crisis; widespread disease and environmental degradation; and a proliferation of small arms. Certain states remain politically volatile. The worst-case scenario, as was experienced most intensely in Angola and Mozambique, is civil war.

10. These phenomena are not confined to national borders. They impact negatively on neighbouring states in the form of a range of nonmilitary threats: environmental destruction, the spread of disease, the burden of refugees, and cross-border trafficking in drugs, stolen goods and small arms.

11. Regional instability and underdevelopment can be addressed meaningfully, only through political reform, socioeconomic development and inter-state cooperation in these spheres. Similarly, the prevention and management of inter and intra-state conflict is primarily a political and not a military matter.
12. Following trends in other parts of the world, South Africa will encourage the development of a multi-lateral 'common security' approach in Southern Africa. In essence, the SADC states should shape their political, security and defence policies in co-operation with each other. This does not preclude the conclusion of bilateral and trilateral security agreements.
13. A common approach to security in Southern Africa is necessary for a number of reasons. Firstly, many of the domestic threats to individual states are shared problems and impact negatively on the stability of neighbouring countries.
14. Secondly, it is possible that inter-state disputes could emerge in relation to refugees, trade, foreign investment, natural resources and previously suppressed territorial claims.
15. Thirdly, since the subcontinent is politically volatile and its national and regional institutions are relatively weak, internal conflicts could give rise to cross-border tensions and hostilities. This volatility and weakness also makes the region vulnerable to foreign interference and intervention from land, sea and air.
16. Common security arrangements would have many advantages in this context. They would facilitate the sharing of information, intelligence and resources; the early warning of potential crises; joint problem-solving; implementing confidence and security-building measures (CSBMs); negotiating security agreements and treaties; and resolving inter-state conflict through peaceful means.
17. Certain of these endeavours are the responsibility of the Department of Foreign Affairs. Chief amongst them is the settlement of conflict through preventive diplomacy, mediation or arbitration.
18. Other types of activity, some of which are under discussion in the newly formed security and defence forums of the SADC, will be undertaken by the DOD.
19. Firstly, regional defence cooperation could be promoted in the fields of training and education; intelligence; combined exercises; secondment of personnel; and the development of common doctrines and operational procedures.
20. Secondly, the government might be called upon by neighbouring countries to play a number of supportive roles. For example, the SANDF could provide assistance with respect to disaster relief; controlling cross-border trafficking in small arms; clearing minefields: military training; and maintaining and upgrading weaponry and equipment.
21. Thirdly, the DOD is keen to pursue the implementation of CSBMs. These

are measures which provide for greater transparency in military matters in order to alleviate possible mistrust, prevent misunderstandings from developing into crises and thereby promote collective confidence and stability.

22. Appropriate CSBMs might include the following:

22.1 Annual consultation and exchange of information on defence budgets, force structure, modernisation plans and troop deployment.

22.2 Consideration of national threat perceptions which influence force structure and modernisation plans.

22.3 The establishment of a regional arms register which records information on imports, exports, production and holdings of conventional arms and light weaponry.

22.4 Notification and on-site observation of military exercises and other specified activities.

22.5 Verification procedures in respect of the above.

22.6 A communications network and a 'crisis hotline'.

22.7 Procedures for dealing with unusual or unscheduled military incidents.

23. Situations may arise in Southern Africa where inter or intra-state conflict poses a threat to peace and stability in the region as a whole. If political efforts to resolve the conflict are unsuccessful, it may become necessary to deploy the SANDF in multinational peace support operations.

24. South Africa shares the view of many of its neighbours that the creation of a standing peacekeeping force in the region is neither desirable nor practically feasible. It is far more likely that the SADC countries will engage in ad-hoc peace support operations if the need arises.

25. Nevertheless, the SADC states are committed to regional cooperation in preparing for peace support operations. It may therefore be worthwhile to establish a small peace support operations centre, under the auspices of regional defence structures, to develop and coordinate planning, training, logistics, communication and field liaison teams for multi-national forces.

26. South Africa will support the conclusion of multi-lateral treaties on disarmament, conventional arms control, the prohibition of weapons of mass destruction, and foreign military involvement in the region. The most important agreement would be a non-aggression pact which endorses the international prohibition on the threat or use of force.

27. Given South Africa's relative military strength on the sub-continent, the adoption of a defensive and non-threatening posture would contribute to confidence and positive relationships.

28. Further, reductions in South Africa's force levels and weapons holdings might stimulate a broader process of disarmament in Southern Africa. This would release resources for development and thereby promote stability. However, force reductions should be kept within reasonable proportions if South Africa is to play an active supportive role in the region.

29. Finally, South Africa has a common destiny with Southern Africa. Domestic peace and stability will not be achieved in a context of regional instability and poverty. It is therefore in South Africa's long-term security interests to pursue mutually beneficial relations with other SADC states and to promote reconstruction and development throughout the region.

Bibliography

Common Security and NOD

Bahr, Egon & Dieter S. Lutz (eds.): *Gemeinsame Sicherheit. Konventionelle Stabilität. Bd. 3: Zu den militärischen Aspekten Struktureller Nichtangriffsfähigkeit im Rahmen Gemeinsamer Sicherheit* (Baden-Baden: Nomos Verlagsgesellschaft, 1988).

Booth, Ken & John Baylis: *Britain, NATO and Nuclear Weapons. Alternative Defence versus Alliance Reform* (London: Macmillan, 1988).

Borg, Marlies ter & Wim Smit (eds.): *Non-provocative Defence as a Principle of Arms Control and its Implications for Assessing Defence Technologies* (Amsterdam: Free University Press, 1989).

Boserup, Anders & Robert Neild (eds.): *The Foundations of Defensive Defence* (London: Macmillan, 1990).

Brauch, Hans Günter & Robert Kennedy (eds.): *Alternative Conventional Defence Postures for the European Theatre. Vol. 1: The Military Balance and Domestic Constraint* (New York: Taylor & Francis, 1990).

Brauch, Hans Günter & Robert Kennedy (eds.): *Alternative Conventional Defense Postures in the European Theatre. Vol. 2: The Impact of Political Change on Strategy, Technology, and Arms Control* (New York: Taylor & Francis, 1992).

Caceres, Gustavo & Thomas Scheetz (eds.): *Defensa no Provocativa. Una propuesta de reforma militar para la Argentina* (Buenos Aires: Editora Buenos Aires, 1995).

Dean, Jonathan: *Watershed in Europe. Dismantling the East-West Military Confrontation* (Lexington: Lexington Books, 1987).

Gates, David: *Non-Offensive Defence. An Alternative Strategy for NATO?* (London: Macmillan, 1991).

Møller, Bjørn: *Resolving the Security Dilemma in Europe. The German Debate on Non-Offensive Defence* (London: Brassey's, 1991).

Møller, Bjørn: *Common Security and Nonoffensive Defense. A Neorealist Perspective* (Boulder, Col.: Lynne Rienner and London: UCL Press, 1992).

Møller, Bjørn: *Dictionary of Alternative Defense* (Boulder, Col.: Lynne Rienner, 1995).

Møller, Bjørn & Håkan Wiberg (eds.): *Non-Offensive Defence for the Twenty-First Century* (Boulder: Westview Press, 1994).

Neild, Robert: *An Essay on Strategy as it Affects the Achievement of Peace in a Nuclear Setting* (London: Macmillan, 1990).

Nolan, Janne E. (ed.): *Global Engagement. Cooperation and Security in the 21st Century* (Washington, D.C.: The Brookings Institution, 1994).

Palme Commission (Independent Commission on Disarmament and Security

Issues): *Common Security. A Blueprint for Survival. With a Prologue by Cyrus Vance* (New York: Simon & Schuster, 1982).

SAS (eds.): *Vertrauensbildende Verteidigung. Reform deutscher Sicherheitspolitik* (Gerlingen: Bleicher Verlag, 1989).

Singh, Jasjit & Vatroslav Vekaric (eds.): *Non-Provocative Defence. The Search for Equal Security* (New Delhi: Lancer, 1989).

UNIDIR (ed.): *Nonoffensive Defense. A Global Perspective* (New York: Taylor & Francis, 1990).

Southern Africa

Cawthra, Gavin: *Brutal Force. The Apartheid War Machine* (London: International Defence & Aid Fund for Southern Africa, 1986).

Cawthra, Gavin: *Policing South Africa. The SAP and the Transition from Apartheid* (London: Zed Books, 1993/Claremont, South Africa: David Philips Publishers, 1994).

Cawthra, Gavin: *Securing South Africa's Democracy: Defence, Development and Security in Transition* (London: Macmillan, 1997).

Cilliers, Jakkie & Greg Mills (eds.): *Peacekeeping in Africa*, vols. 1-2 (Braamfontein: South African Institute of International Affairs/Halfway House: Institute for Defence Policy, 1996).

Cilliers, Jakkie & Markus Reichardt (eds.): *About Turn: The Transformation of the South African Military and Intelligence* (Halfway House: Institute for Defence Policy, 1996).

Deng, Francis M., Sadikiel Kimaro, Terrence Lyons, Donald Rothchild & I. William Zartman: *Sovereignty as Responsibility. Conflict Management in Africa* (Washington, D.C.: The Brookings Institution, 1996).

Du Toit, Pierre: *State Building and Democracy in Southern Africa. Botswana, Zimbabwe, and South Africa* (Washington, D.C.: United States Institute for Peace Press, 1995).

Edmonds, Martin & Greg Mills: *Uncharted Waters. A Review of South Africa's Naval Options* (Braamfontein: South African Institute of International Affairs/Lancaster: Centre for Defence and International Security Studies, 1996).

El-Ayoutu, Yassin (ed.): *The Organization of African Unity After Thirty Years* (Westport, Connecticut: Praeger Press, 1994).

Gastrow, Peter: *Bargaining for Peace. South Africa and the National Peace Accord* (Washington, D.C.: United States Institute for Peace, 1995).

Gutteridge, William (ed.): *South Africa's Defence and Security into the 21st Century* (Aldershot: Dartmouth, 1996).

Gutteridge, William (ed.): *South Africa. From Apartheid to National Unity, 1981-1994* (Aldershot: Dartmouth, 1995).

Keller, Edmond J. & Donald Rothchild (eds.): *Africa in the New World Order*

(Boulder: Lynne Rienner Publishers, 1996).

Mills, Greg (ed.): *From Pariah to Participant. South Africa's Evolving Foreign Relations, 1990-1994* (Johannesburg: The South African Institute of International Affairs, 1994).

Mills, Greg (ed.): *Maritime Policy for Developing Nations* (Braamfontein: South African Institute of International Affairs, 1995).

Moorcraft, Paul L.: *African Nemesis. War and Revolution in Southern Africa 1945-2010* (London: Brassey's, UK, 1994).

Nathan, Laurie: *The Changing of the Guard. Armed Forces and Defence Policy in a Democratic South Africa* (Pretoria: Human Sciences Research Council Publications, 1994).

Ohlson, Thomas & Stephen John Stedman, with Robert Davies: *The New Is Not Yet Born. Conflict Resolution in Southern Africa* (Washington, D.C.: The Brookings Institution, 1994).

Oosthuysen, Glenn: *Small Arms Proliferation and Control in Southern Africa* (Braamfontein: South African Institute of International Affairs, 1996).

Ottaway, Marina: *South Africa. The Struggle for a New Order* (Washington, D.C.: The Brookings Institution, 1993).

Smock, David R. & Chester A. Crocker (eds.): *African Conflict Resolution. The U.S. Role in Peacemaking* (Washington, D.C.: United States Institute for Peace Press, 1995).

Smock, David R.: *Making War and Waging Peace. Foreign Intervention in Africa* (Washington, DC: United States Institute for Peace, 1993).

Spanger, Hans-Joachim & Peter Vale (eds.): *Bridges to the Future. Prospects for Peace and Security in Southern Africa* (Boulder: Westview Press, 1995).

List of Contributors

Barry Buzan is professor in International Relations at the School of Social and Policy Sciences, University of Westminster and project director at the Copenhagen Peace Research Institute (COPRI). He is the author of, inter alia, *People, States and Fear. An Agenda for International Security Studies in the Post-Cold War Era* (1983 and 1991).

Gavin Cawthra, Ph.D., is Senior Lecturer at the Graduate School of Public and Development Management, University of the Witwatersrand, Johannesburg. He directs the Defence Management Programme at the School, which runs educational courses in civil-military relations for senior military officers and defence officials from all twelve countries of the Southern African Development Community. He is the author of *Policing South Africa: The SAP and the Transition from Apartheid* (1993) and *Securing South Africa's Democracy: Defence, Development and Security in Transition* (1997). He has been extensively involved in the South African liberation struggle and spent many years in exile. He holds a Ph.D. in War Studies from the University of London.

Jacklyn Cock is professor of Sociology at the University of the Witwatersrand, Johannesburg. She is active in organisations involved with peace, environmental and feminist issues and has published widely in these areas.

Carl Conetta and **Charles Knight** are co-directors of the Project on Defense Alternatives (PDA) at the Commonwealth Institute, Cambridge, Massachusetts, USA. Prior to founding PDA in 1991 they were research fellows at the Institute for Defense and Disarmament Studies in Boston.

Robert W. Higgs is the Director of Naval Strategy at South African Naval Headquarters. He is a graduate of the United States Naval War College's Naval Command College and holds a BSc degree from the South African Military Academy and an MA degree in international relations from Salve Regina University, Newport, Rhode Island in the United States.

Joao Bernardo Honwana, Colonel (retired), was the Commander of the Mozambique Air Force from 1987 to 1992, when he retired to take on a Senior Researcher position at the Centre for Conflict Resolution, University of Cape Town. Since then, Joao has conducted and published academic and policy-oriented research on Southern African defence and security issues. His areas of interest include regional security, civil- military relations, peacekeeping operations, post-conflict demilitarisation and peacebuilding.

Greg Mills, Ph.D., is National Director, The South African Institute of International Affairs, University of the Witwatersrand, Johannesburg.

Bjørn Møller, Ph.D. and MA, is senior research fellow at the Copenhagen Peace Research Institute (COPRI) and editor of the international research newsletter *NOD & Conversion*. He is the author of the following books: *Resolving the Security Dilemma in Europe. The German Debate on Non-Offensive Defence* (1991); *Common Security and Nonoffensive Defense. A Neorealist Perspective* (1992) and *Dictionary of Alternative Defense* (1995). From 1997, he is Secretary General of the International Peace Research Association (IPRA).

Martin Rupiya is retired Lt.Colonel from the Zimbabwe Defence Force and since 1990 Lecturer in War & Strategic Studies, University of Zimbabwe, Department of History, Harare. He is presently finishing his Ph.D. on 'The Development of the Southern Rhodesian (now Zimbabwe) Defence System from 1926 to 1963'.

Lutz Unterseher, Dr. is the Chairman of the Study Group Alternative Security Policy (SAS) and has lectured at military academies around the world as well as served as a consultant for governments and political parties in several countries.

Rocklyn Williams, Ph.D, is Director Policy at the South African Defence Secretariat, but writes in his personal capacity. Formerly a commander in the ANC's armed wing, Umkhonto we Sizwe, he was a colonel in the South African National Defence Force before taking up his current post, where he has been responsible for overseeing the Defence Review process. He has published extensively on defence and security issues in South Africa and internationally and holds a Ph.D. in military sociology from the University of Essex.

Index